U0868423

英语文化选读

刘育文 主 编

Selected Readings On English Culture

ZHEJIANG UNIVERSITY PRESS
浙江大学出版社

图书在版编目(CIP)数据

英语文化选读 / 刘育文主编；—杭州：浙江大学出版社，2012.12（2020.6 重印）
ISBN 978-7-308-10639-9

I. ①英… II. ①刘… III. ①英语—阅读教学—自学参考资料 IV. ①H319.4

中国版本图书馆 CIP 数据核字(2012)第 225710 号

英语文化选读
主 编 刘育文

责任编辑 陈丽勋
封面设计 春天书装
出版发行 浙江大学出版社
(杭州市天目山路 148 号 邮政编码 310007)
(网址：http://www.zjupress.com)
排 版 杭州中大图文设计有限公司
印 刷 杭州杭新印务有限公司
开 本 787mm×1092mm 1/16
印 张 18.75
字 数 563 千
版 印 次 2012 年 12 月第 1 版 2020 年 6 月第 3 次印刷
书 号 ISBN 978-7-308-10639-9
定 价 49.00 元

版权所有 翻印必究 印装差错 负责调换
浙江大学出版社市场运营中心联系方式：0571-88925591；http://zjdxcbs.tmall.com

前言

英语专业本科教育的目的就是培养高等英语应用人才，这就要求英语教育必须以社会需求为目标，以应用能力的培养为主线设计学生的知识、能力、素质结构和培养方案，以应用为主旨和特征构建课程体系和教学内容体系。《英语文化阅读》就是以“提高学生素质，服务专业学习”为指导思想，根据《高等学校英语专业英语教学大纲》精心设计的教材。

英语专业基础阶段阅读教材的一个重要目标就在于培养学生的阅读技能。因此本教材将注重系统训练学生掌握词、句、段、篇的阅读技巧和略读、寻读、细读等阅读方法，并将技巧讲解和专题训练有机地结合起来，通过大量的练习，让学生将所学到的阅读技能运用到实践中去。

拓展学生知识面，提高其人文素质也是编写本教材的一个重要指导思想。因此，本教材根据主题编排中西文化差异，选材突出文化特征，既有理性的西方文化知识介绍，又有鲜活的感性领悟，做到知识性与趣味性相结合，有助于学生从西方传统文化和现当代文化中汲取精华部分，了解其独特的精神内涵。目的在于培养学生对文化差异的敏感性、宽容性以及处理文化差异的灵活性，以丰富学生文化知识，提高其跨文化交际能力；同时引导学生去解读、思考、分析、批判，以提高学生的思辨能力和判断能力。

此外，本教材的编写以满足学生需求、适应市场需要为出发点。针对目前日益高涨的考研热、出国热，本教材练习的编排尽量与国内研究生入学考试、国外的托福、雅思、GRE 或 GMAT 等重大考试接轨，以激发学生强烈的阅读热情。阅读在各类考试中所占比重都较大，通过对学生进行系统的阅读测试训练，可以帮助他们全面提高阅读水平和阅读能力，从而获得进一步深造的机会。

总之，这本教材与当下教育发展趋势接轨、切合学生实际需求，融知识性、趣味性于一体，做到技能与应试并举，有利于学生阅读技能和跨文化交际能力的提高。

教材共分为 15 个单元。每个单元围绕同一主题展开，包括四个部分。第一部分为阅读技能介绍，并配相应习题；第二部分是与主题有关的习语、谚语或格言；第三部分提供与主题密切相关的阅读文章两篇，其中说明性或议论性文章及记叙性文章各 1 篇,后面附相应练习；第四部分为阅读测试，每个测试由 4~5 篇长短不一的文章构成。本书第 1、4、7、10、11 单元由刘育文负责编写，龚昭编写了第 2 和第 3 单元，黄庆欢编写了第 5 和第 6 单元，杨丽斌编写了第 8 和第 9 单元，兰晓茹编写了第 12 和第 14 单元，第 13 和第 15 单元由查叶娟编写。在本书的编写过程中，作者引用了国内外书籍、报刊以及网络上的文章作为阅读理解的素材，在此一并致谢。由于编者水平有限，书中难免会存在错误和缺陷，敬请广大读者和同行专家学者批评指正。

编　者

浙江大学城市学院

2012 年 10 月

目 录

Contents

Unit 1

Cultural Differences

Part 1 Reading Skills

Good reading requires both speed and comprehension. If you read fast enough but get little of the writer's message or even misunderstand the message, you're not an effective reader. Likewise, if you are too slow to finish a certain passage within the time limit, even if you have a perfect comprehension of a part of it, you are not an efficient reader.

Effective and efficient reading means understanding information from what you read without spending too much time in the process. To be an effective and efficient reader, you need to grasp some reading skills. One of the most important reading skills you should develop is to use the context clues as well as word formation to guess unknown words. Besides, to have a good understanding of complicated sentences is also a premise for good reading as there are more often than not long and complicated sentences in English. What's more, some knowledge about topic, main idea and patterns of details to support the main idea is also necessary to better understand what you read. Finally, reading skills like skimming, scanning and detailed reading will help to read effectively and efficiently.

The reading skills will be systematically introduced in each unit in this book. However, as the saying goes, practice makes perfect, so if you want to read both effectively and efficiently you have to practice more with the help of the reading skills.

Section A Guessing Unknown Words from the Context I

Readers will inevitably come across words that they don't know when they are reading. They don't need to consult a dictionary each time they meet a new word. Instead, they can guess the meaning of unfamiliar words in several ways.

One of the most important reading skills is to make use of the context, that is, words or phrases or even sentences that come before or after a certain word, to figure out its meaning.

Usually authors intend to use many different types of context clues to help their readers understand the meaning of a new or difficult word. Generally there are seven types of context clues: 1. Definition/Explanation Clues, 2. Example Clues, 3. Class Relationship, 4. Synonym and Antonym Clues, 5. Comparison and Contrast Clues, 6. Cause and Effect Relationship, 7. Common Knowledge.

Once a reader grasps these skills, he can easily guess the meaning of the unknown words. In the first three units, these skills will be introduced one by one.

1. Definition / Explanation Clues

A definition is to define or explain the meaning of a word, or a phrase or a type of thing. Definition clues join the unknown word with the word(s) that rename it or tell its meaning.

There are clues for us to judge a definition or explanation. They may be verbs or verbal phrases like *be*(*is*, *was*, *are*), *mean*, *i.e.*, *involve*, *be called*, *be defined as*, *be known as*, *that is*, *refer to*, *represent*, *signify*, *deal with* etc. They can also be indicated by punctuation marks such as commas, parentheses, brackets, or dashes. For example,

1) Pedagogy *is defined as* the art, science, or profession of teaching.

2) Syntax, the study of sentences, is a branch of linguistics.

3) A piranha—a carnivorous freshwater fish that inhabits South American rivers—is known for its sharp teeth and a voracious appetite for meat.

In Sentence 1) the word "pedagogy" is explained immediately following its use. From the definition we know "pedagogy" is related to education and can refer to an art or science or profession. In Sentence 2) the words between the commas—the study of sentences—define the word "syntax". A "piranha" in Sentence 3) is a kind of freshwater fish that likes to eat meat.

2. Example Clues

Example clues can help you guess the meaning of an unknown word from the example or by determining what the examples have in common. By using examples or illustrations, an author tries to show what a word may refer to. Example clues are usually introduced by the following words and phrases: *including, such as, for example, for instance,* and *like*. Colons and dashes can also signal examples. Here are two examples:

1) The historian wrote many books about potentates in England, *for example*, Queen Elizabeth I, King Henry VIII and King George VI etc.

2) The late billionaire left a large sum of money to his only son who was still a child. So before his death, he chose fiduciaries, including 2 lawyers and 5 bankers, to help manage his money.

In Sentence 1), we know Elizabeth I, Henry VIII, James XI are queen and kings in Britain, so we can derive from the examples that "potentates" most probably refer to rulers. Likewise, from examples "lawyers" and "bankers", we can infer that "fiduciaries" may refer to persons who hold assets in trust for a beneficiary.

3. Class Relationship

In English, some words are higher in rank or order than other words which are more specific. The former is called superordinate which is a general term that includes various different words representing narrower categories, that is, hyponyms or subordinates. For example, fruit is a superordinate which includes apples, pears, melons, and so on and so forth. From the association between a superordinate and subordinates, we can get a general, but maybe not specific meaning of an unknown word. For example,

1) Oranges, grapefruits, lemons, limes are all varieties of citrus fruits which originate in Southeast Asia and have been cultivated in an ever-widening area since ancient times.

2) The old lady grows many kinds of flowers in her garden, roses, tulips, sunflowers, lilies, orchids, carnations, hibiscus, just to name a few.

It's easy for us to get an idea of the word "citrus" in Sentence 1) as we know the characteristics of the four fruits listed. However it's hard for us to figure out the specific meaning of "hibiscus" in Sentence 2), but we know it's a kind of flower.

Section B Practice

Directions: Choose the word that is closest in meaning to the underlined word according to the context.

1. Myopia—shortsightedness—can cause a person to fail the vision test required to obtain a driver's license.
   A. blindfold B. vision test C. color blindness D. nearsightedness
2. After a day's hard work, Bob is always ravenous. Yesterday, for example, he ate salad, a large chicken, a large chocolate cake and two bowels of soup before he was finally satisfied.

A. unsatisfied B. very angry C. exhausted D. very hungry

3. Carbon monoxide (CO) is a noxious gas which can cause death.

A. smelly B. poisonous C. terrible D. fragrant

4. He had such a wan, or colorless look, that we thought he was ill.

A. furious B. sad C. pale D. strange

5. The criminal used different aliases in each state. For example, in New York, he called himself Tom; in Boston, he said he was Robert.

A. real name B. false name C. surname D. given name

6. Precipitation is a measure of the quantity of water in the form of either rain, hail or snow which reaches the ground.

A. water B. rainfall C. hail D. snow

7. The plane is scheduled to leave for Shanghai at 9:00 a.m., but it is said to be retarded for two hours. That is to say, it will leave at 11:00 a.m. instead.

A. postponed B. stopped C. canceled D. extended

8. The compactor is an appliance that crashes bones, bottles, cans, and cardboard, paper, all kinds of garbage, compacts it and puts it into one disposable bag.

A. clothing B. a place where automobiles are kept
C. a rope D. any kind of waste matter

9. She is studying glaucoma and other diseases of the eye.

A. scalp ringworm on the skin B. freckle on the face
C. disease related to the eyeball D. eczema on the skin

10. Snakes and crocodiles are both reptiles.

A. animals which live on meat B. animals that feed on grass
C. animals that creep and crawl D. animals that live in water

Part 2 Idioms, Proverbs and Sayings

Directions: Idioms, proverbs can show great differences between different cultures. Read the following English idioms and choose what you think is correct and try to find the Chinese equivalents.

1. to spend money like ________

A. land B. soil C. sand D. water

2. to look for a needle in the ________

A. sea B. ocean C. sand D. haystack

3. to spring up like ________

A. mushrooms B. cabbages C. bamboo shoots D. cucumbers

4. as strong as a(n) ________

A. ox B. horse C. elephant D. cow

5. as stupid as a ________

A. hen B. pig C. goose D. cow

6. to kill the ________ that lays the golden eggs

A. goose B. peahen C. hen D. pigeon

7. Better be the head of a dog than the tail of a ________.

A. tiger B. bear C. lion D. crocodile

8. A ________ lie refers to a minor or unimportant lie, especially one uttered in the interests of tact or politeness.

A. black B. green C. red D. white

9. A pot calls the kettle ________.

A. green B. black C. dark D. purple

10. ________ refers to a state of confusion or disorder.

A. At seven and eight B. At sevens and eights

C. At six and seven D. At sixes and sevens

Part 3 Reading Passages

Section A American Values and Assumptions

By Gary Althen

People who grow up in a particular culture share certain values and assumptions. That doesn't mean they all share exactly the same values to exactly the same extent; it does mean that most of them, most of the time, mostly agree with each other's ideas about what is right and wrong, desirable and undesirable, and so on. They also agree, mostly, with each other's assumptions about human nature, social relationships, and so on.

One of the most important things to understand about Americans is probably their devotion to "individualism". They are trained since very early in their lives to consider themselves as separate individuals who are responsible for their own situations in life and their own destinies.

They are not trained to see themselves as members of a close-knit, tightly interdependent family, religious group, tribe or any other collectivity.

You can see it in the way Americans treat their children. One day I was at a local shopping mall, waiting in line to buy an Orange Julius. Behind me in the line was a woman with two children, a boy who was about three years old and a girl who was about five. The boy had his hand in the pocket of his blue jeans, and I could hear that he had some coins in there.

The boy asked his mother, "Can I get an Orange Julius?"

"No," she said to him. "You don't have enough money left for an Orange Julius. Remember you bought that cookie a while ago. You do have enough money for a hot dog. So you could get a hot dog now if you want to. Or, you could save your money, and sometime later when you have enough money, we could come back here and you could get an Orange Julius."

Here is a young child whose own mother is forcing him to make a decision that affects not just his situation at the moment, but that will affect him at some unspecified time in the future, when he will have more money. Through this process, Americans come to see themselves as separate human beings who have their own opinions and who are responsible for their own decisions.

Indeed, American child-rearing manuals state that the parents' objective is for the child to move out of the parents' house and make his or her own way in life. Americans take this advice very seriously, so much so that someone who remains dependent on their parents longer than the norm may be thought to be "immature", "tied to the mother's apron strings," or otherwise unable to lead a normal independent life.

It isn't unusual for Americans who are beyond the age of about 22 and are still living with their parents to pay their parents for room and board. Elderly parents living with their grown children may do likewise. Paying for room and board is a way of showing independence, self-reliance, and responsibility for oneself.

Many Americans do not display the degree of respect for their parents that people in more traditional or family-oriented societies commonly display. They have the conception that it was a sort of historical or biological accident that put them in the hands of particular parents, that the parents fulfilled their responsibilities to the children while the children were young, and now that the children have reached "the age of independence" the close child-parent tie is loosened, if not broken.

The American version of the "ideal individual" prefers an atmosphere of freedom, where neither the government nor any other external force or agency dictates what the individual does. For Americans, the idea of individual freedom is strongly positive. By contrast, people from many other cultures regard some of the behavior Americans justify as "individual freedom" to be self-centered and lacking in consideration for others.

Closely associated with the value they place on individualism is the importance Americans assign to privacy. Americans assume that people "need some time to themselves" or "some time alone" to think about things or recover their spent psychological energy. Americans have great difficulty understanding someone who always wants to be with another person, who dislikes being alone.

Americans assume that people have their "private thoughts" that might never be shared with anyone. Doctors, lawyers, psychiatrists, and others have rules governing "confidentiality" that are intended to prevent information about their clients' personal situations from becoming known to others. Americans' attitudes about privacy can be difficult for foreigners to understand. Americans' houses, yards, and even their offices can seem open and inviting, yet, in the Americans' minds, there are boundaries that other people are simply not supposed to cross. When the boundaries are crossed, Americans will visibly stiffen and their manner will become cool.

Americans are also distinctive in the degree to which they believe in the ideal, as stated in their Declaration of Independence, that "all men are created equal." Although they sometimes violate the ideal in their daily lives, particularly in matters of interracial relationships and sometimes relationships among people from different social classes, Americans have a deep faith that in some fundamental way all people (at least all American people) are of equal value, that no one is born superior to anyone else. "One person, one vote," they say, conveying the idea that any person's opinion is as valid and worthy of attention as any other person's opinion.

Americans are generally quite uncomfortable when someone treats them with obvious deference. They dislike being the subjects of open displays of respect—being bowed to, being deferred to, being treated as though they could do no wrong or make no unreasonable requests.

Their notions of equality lead Americans to be quite informal in their general behavior and in their relationships with other people. Store clerks and table servers, for example, may introduce themselves by their first names and treat customers in a casual, friendly manner. American clerks, like other Americans, have been trained to believe that they are as valuable as any other people, even if they happen to be engaged at a given time in an occupation that others might consider lowly. This informal behavior can outrage foreign visitors who hold high stations in countries where it is not assumed that "all men are created equal."...

People from societies where general behavior is more formal than it is in America are struck by the informality of American speech, dress, and body language. Idiomatic speech and slang are liberally used on most occasions, with formal speech reserved for public events and fairly formal situations. People of almost any station in life can be seen in public wearing jeans, sandals, or other informal attire. People slouch down in chairs or lean on walls or furniture when they talk, rather than maintaining an erect bearing.

Americans are generally less concerned about history and traditions than are people from older societies. "History doesn't matter," many of them will say. "It's the future that counts." They look ahead. They have the idea that what happens in the future is within their control, or at least subject to their influence. The mature, sensible person, they think, sets goals for the future and works systematically toward them.

Americans believe that people, as individuals or working cooperatively together, can change most aspects of the physical and social environment if they decide to do so, then make appropriate plans and get to work. Changes will presumably produce improvements. New things are better than old things.

Closely associated with their assumption that they can bring about desirable changes in the future is the Americans' assumption that their physical and social environments are subject to human domination or control. Early Americans cleared forests, drained swamps, and altered the course of rivers in order to "build" the country. Contemporary Americans have gone to the moon in part just to prove they could do so! "If you want to be an American," says cross-cultural trainer L. Robert Kohls, "you have to believe you can fix it." ...

This fundamental American belief in progress and a better future contrasts sharply with the fatalistic (Americans are likely to use that term with a negative or critical connotation) attitude that characterizes people from many other cultures, notably Latin American, Asian, and Arab, where there is a pronounced reverence for the past. In those cultures the future is often considered to be in the hands of fate, God, or at least the few powerful people or families that dominate the society.

The idea that they could somehow shape their own futures seems naive, arrogant, or even sacrilegious. Americans are generally impatient with people they see as passively accepting conditions that are less than desirable. "Why don't they do something about it?" Americans will ask. Americans don't realize that a large portion of the world's population sees the world around them not as something they can change, but rather as something to which they must submit, or at least something with which they must seek to live in harmony....

(1,493 words, based on a chapter in *American Ways: A Guide for Foreigners in the United States*, 2003)

I. Reading Comprehension

Directions: Choose the best answer to finish the incomplete statements according to the above passage.

1. The author discusses the American values and assumptions in the order of ________.
   A. informality, individualism, equality, privacy, attitudes toward past and future
   B. individualism, privacy, equality, informality, attitudes toward past and future
   C. individualism, equality, informality, privacy, attitudes toward past and future
   D. equality, informality, individualism, privacy, attitudes toward past and future
2. "Individualism" is a word with ________ connotations to Americans.
   A. negative B. positive C. neutral D. critical
3. Americans' assumption that they see themselves as separate individuals ________.
   A. comes from their cultural training B. is an ideal they are born with
   C. is their religious belief D. comes from their responsibility

4. It's ________ for an American beyond 22 to live with his parents without paying for his accommodation.
   A. acceptable B. appreciated C. advocated D. shameful
5. If you display your respect to an American by addressing his honor title, ________.
   A. he likes it very much B. he thinks that you're very polite
   C. he doesn't like it. D. he thinks you are well-educated
6. Store clerks and table servers are used as examples to show that ________.
   A. Americans are friendly people B. good service is provided in U.S.
   C. Americans think they're superior D. nobody is inferior to anybody else
7. According to the passage, we can infer that all of the following people tend to believe in fate EXCEPT ________.
   A. Koreans B. Arabians C. Italians D. Brazilians
8. The word "objective" in Paragraph 7 most probably means ________.
   A. goal B. unbiased C. business D. concrete
9. In Paragraph 9 the word "tie" is closest in meaning to ________.
   A. neckwear B. string C. attach D. relationship
10. From the context, we can infer the word "attire" in Paragraph 16 most probably refers to ________.
   A. clothing B. shoes C. shorts D. hats

II. Vocabulary

Directions: Choose the word that best fits the blank.

1. Thousands of black children in America like to play basketball because they believe that it may change their ________ just like Michael Jordan.
   A. informality B. destiny C. inequality D. collectivity
2. Twin blasts were reported in a northern province in Syria on 30 April, leaving an ________ number of victims.
   A. unspecified B. immature C. unreasonable D. impatient
3. To maintain the social stability is the primary ________ of the present government.
   A. manual B. norm C. objective D. version
4. The saleswoman was very successful because she was good at establishing an emotional ________ with her customers.
   A. interdependence B. ideal C. independence D. tie
5. The Olympic champion says after the match that what ________ in her success is that she believes in herself and plays her own game.
   A. fulfills B. stiffens C. alters D. counts
6. Scientific development, as a ________ theme for contemporary China, has shown its enormous power in directing China toward development and progress.
   A. valid B. distinctive C. casual D. external

7. Chinese badminton team swept all the gold medals at the Beijing Olympics and continues its ________ of the sport.
   A. domination B. devotion C. conception D. occupation
8. The ________ between the manufacture and service industries is becoming increasingly vague, as more and more manufacturers tend to combine more services with their products.
   A. deference B. harmony C. boundary D. reverence
9. The Iranian leader attacked U.S and Europe as being greedy, ________ and too ready to use military force.
   A. desirable B. sensible C. naive D. arrogant
10. A large number of American universities ask overseas applicants to ________ their applications by the end of November if they want to study there.
   A. justify B. submit C. reserve D. dominate

III. Discussion

Directions: Read the following joke and try to conclude the characteristics shown for each nation in the joke.

A group of sociologists and anthropologists would like to know the characteristics of some nationalities, including the English, the French, the Russian and the Spanish. So they decide to send three people, two men and one woman from each nation to live on four different isolated islands where they have built a house. Each of them is given some seeds to grow there.

Half a year later, the sociologists and anthropologists visit each island. First they go to the island where the three English live. They find that the two men and the woman are working hard in the fields, but silently and separately. So they ask, "Why don't you work together and talk with each other?" "Because you haven't introduced us to each other," they answer in chorus.

Then they visit the island where the three Russians stay. They see the woman working in the field. So they ask, "Where are the two men?" "They haven't reached an agreement as to what to grow in the field and are still quarrelling in the house."

Next they go to visit the French. To their surprise they find only one man is working in the field but he is humming a tune merrily. "Where are the other man and the woman?" "Since we come to this island we reach an agreement to take turns to live with the woman in the house. You see last month it's my turn to live with the woman and so this month it's that guy's turn."

Finally they land the island where the Spaniards live. The woman is growing plants there. "Where are the two men?"

"When we just arrived at this island, the two men fought for me. One was killed on the spot and the other was seriously injured and died soon."

Section B Is This Chinese Candor or a Cultural Handicap?

By Vida Zhang Fargis

Directions: Read the following text and mark

Y (for Yes) if the statement agrees with the information given in the text;

N (for No) if the statement contradicts the information given in the text;

NG (for Not Given) if the information is not given in the text.

Pam, a good friend of mine recently came back to the Bay Area from Taiwan with her family. She told me that her daughter had a tough time in Taiwan.

"How come?" I asked.

"People are too direct. In Taiwan they tell her right in front of her face that she's fat and needs to lose weight," Pam said.

"Oh no. Don't say that…" I said, shaking head with desperation. Regrettably, I know just what she means.

"My family said this to her. My friends used this language too. People I didn't even know on the street told her she was fat. It's so terrible, rude and cruel to use such language to a nine year-old girl. Why do they do that? I hate it, hate it, hate it!" Pam said with anger and desperation.

I TOTALLY understand you Pam. I share your pain as a mother. I too struggle as someone who lives between two cultures.

In my own life I've experienced similar rudeness with my older five-year old daughter after we moved to Hong Kong from San Francisco.

Story one:

A few days in a row, my daughter came home saying the Chinese words for "big fat" (Da Pang Zi). I asked her where she learned these words.

"People on the playground said I am a Da Pang Zi," she told me.

Story two:

My babysitter told me that some people had said that my younger daughter is prettier than my older one on the playground right in front of my older daughter.

"Mom, do you think Siena (my younger daughter) is really prettier than me?" My older daughter asked me with a sad tone.

Needless to say, I am mad and angry with these oafs who choose their words so carelessly. Sometimes I do feel hopeless, trying to protect my children from this sort of Chinese bluntness in the vast world of Greater China.

"My mom said people do this out of good will. They hope you will look better. They mean nothing harmful," my friend Pam said.

As a matter of fact, these people have hurt Pam, me and our daughters with something they are not even aware of. They may not know any better, but they are abusive, nonetheless.

"It seems people there (Taiwan) have less tolerance of other people's differences. I feel like we have a different sense of what is right and what is wrong," Pam said.

I think that's absolutely true. My perceptions of what is acceptable have been fundamentally altered by my time outside of Greater China. With regards to my daughter's case it is simply ridiculous for anyone to use the word "fat". She's tall for her age and looks as if she's seven when she is in fact only five. She seems big, particularly compared to most of the Chinese kids who are relatively smaller physically. Needless to say she is gorgeous in her own way, just as my younger daughter is. Each has their own unique beautiful features and comparing on relative beauty is a waste of oxygen.

I am speaking for myself and for my friend Pam. We were hurt in a manner, which is nearly impossible to describe as a mother. Accordingly, I'd like to call for a cultural moratorium on adults using derogatory language when they speak to children. It's not only Chinese who do this of course. But we can collectively ask ourselves for a higher standard of mutual support and discretion.

I would like to see all the relevant media organs: TV, radio, magazines, newspapers, web ports, etc., in Greater China to ask for a higher standard from our civilization. The message should be:

"No one has the right to put a child down. Stop using such language!"

People like Pam and myself grew up within a culture where we hear people said things like this all the time, but somehow, we learned how to deal with it as adults. We're familiar with it and we can filter out such put-down. We have our own immunization system to protect us from idiotic words like this. But how can you expect a young child of five or nine to protect herself from it?

(702 words)

1. Pam's daughter had a good time in Taiwan. ________
2. From the passage we can infer that the writer has lived in different regions of China and America. ________
3. The babysitter said that the writer's younger daughter is prettier than her older daughter. ________
4. Both Pam and the writer are Chinese descendents. ________
5. It is very impolite and even rude to tell an American that he or she is fat. ________

Part 4 Reading Comprehension Test

Passage 1

Directions: Read the following passage. Choose the best answer to each question.

The English, as a race, have the reputation of being very different from all other nationalities, including their closest neighbours, the French, Belgians and Dutch. It is claimed that living on an island separated from the rest of Europe has much to do with it. Whatever the reasons, it may be fairly stated that the Englishman has developed many attitudes and habits which distinguish him from other nationalities.

Broadly speaking, the Englishman is a quiet, shy, reserved person who is fully relaxed only among people he knows well. In the presence of strangers or foreigners he often seems inhibited, even embarrassed. You have only to witness a commuter train any morning or evening to see the truth of this. Serious-looking businessmen and women sit reading their newspapers or dozing in a corner; no one speaks. In fact, to do so would seem most unusual.

It is a well-known fact that the English have an obsession with their weather and that, given half a chance, they will talk about it at length. Some people argue that it is because English weather defies forecast and hence is a source of interest and speculation to everyone. This may be so. Certainly Englishmen cannot have much faith in the meteorological experts—the weathermen—who, after promising fine, sunny weather for the following day, are often proved wrong when an anti-cyclone over the Atlantic brings rainy weather to all districts. The man in the street seems to be as accurate—or as inaccurate—as the weathermen in his predictions. This helps to explain the seemingly odd sight of an Englishman leaving home on a bright, sunny, summer morning with a raincoat slung over his arm and an umbrella in his hand. So variable is the weather that by lunchtime it could be pouring.

The overseas visitors may be excused for showing surprise at the number of references to weather that the English make to each other in the course of a single day. Very often conventional greetings are replaced by comments on the weather. "Nice day, isn't it?" "Beautiful!" may well be heard instead of "Good morning, how are you?" Although the foreigner may consider this exaggerated and comic, it is worthwhile pointing out that it could be used to his advantage. If he wants to start a conversation with an Englishman or woman but is at a loss to know where to begin, he could do well to mention the state of the weather. It is a safe subject which will provoke an answer from even the most reserved of Englishmen.

In many parts of the world it's quite normal to show openly extremes of enthusiasm, emotion, passion etc., often accompanied by appropriate gestures. The Englishman is somewhat different. Of course, an Englishman feels no less deeply than any other nationality, but he tends to display his feelings far less. This is reflected in his use of language. For example an Englishman will flatly comment in the great beauty of a young girl "Um, she's all right". The overseas visitor must not be disappointed by this apparent lack of interest and involvement; he must realize that for English, words like "all right", "no bad", and "nice" are very often used as superlatives with the sense of "first-class", "excellent", "beautiful". This special use of language is known as understatement.

(554 words)

1. Which of the following would be the most probable reason for the unique character of the Englishman?
   A. The geographic isolation
   B. The lack of enthusiasm
   C. The superiority of the language
   D. The uniqueness of the weather
2. According to the passage, among whom will the Englishman feel easy?
   A. strangers
   B. foreigners
   C. nodding acquaintances
   D. close friends
3. Why do the English have such an interest in and speculation on the weather?
   A. Because they live on an isolated island.
   B. Because they are skeptical about the official weather reports.
   C. Because they'd like to express their disappointment at the weather reports.
   D. Because they would show their accuracy in forecasting the weather.
4. Which of the following words can best convey English's comments on others?
   A. extremely emotional
   B. openly moderate
   C. most reserved
   D. most suspicious
5. What's the topic of the passage?
   A. the characteristics of the English
   B. the changeable weather in Britain
   C. English—the universal language
   D. the understated English

Passage 2

Directions: Read the following passage. Choose the best answer to complete each statement.

Identities and roles refer to conceptions of the self. Am I an individual unit, autonomous, a free agent, ultimately responsible for myself? Or am I first and foremost a member of a group, weighing choices and actions by how the group will perceive them and be affected by them? Those who see themselves as separate individuals likely come from societies anthropologists call individualist. Those for whom group allegiance is primary usually come from settings anthropologists call collectivist, or communitarian.

In collectivist settings, the following values tend to be privileged: cooperation, filial piety (respect for and deference toward elders), participation in shared progress, reputation of the group and interdependence.

In individualist settings, the following values tend to be privileged: competition, independence, individual achievement, personal growth and fulfillment and self-reliance.

When individualist and communitarian starting points influence those on either side of a conflict, escalation may result. Individualists may see no problem with "no holds barred" confrontation, while communitarian counterparts shrink from bringing dishonor or face-loss to their group by behaving in unseemly ways. Individualists may expect to make agreements with communitarians, and may feel betrayed when the latter indicate that they have to take their understandings back to a larger public or group before they can come to closure. In the end, one should remember that, as with other patterns described, most people are not purely individualist or communitarian. Rather, people tend to have individualist or communitarian starting points, depending on one's upbringing, experience, and the context of the situation.

(249 words)

6. The last sentence in Paragraph 1 can be best paraphrased as ________.
   A. group-centered people usually come from what anthropologists call collectivist societies
   B. anthropologists think collectivists come from group allegiance
   C. anthropologists think group allegiance is important for collectivist settings
   D. a member's choices and actions are primarily decided by a group of people
7. Collectivism-centered people advocate all of the following values except ________.
   A. cooperation　　B. respect for elders
   C. independence　　D. collective honor
8. Whether one tends to be an individualist or a collectivist depends on ________.
   A. his or her family background　　B. his or her experience
   C. his or her social background　　D. all of the above
9. The main purpose of this passage is to ________.
   A. analyze the advantages of individualism and collectivism
   B. analyze the disadvantages of individualism and collectivism
   C. compare the similarities between individualism and collectivism
   D. contrast the differences between individualism and collectivism
10. According to the passage the writer's attitude toward collectivism is ________.
   A. positive　　B. neutral　　C. negative　　D. biased

Passage 3

Directions: Fill in each blank with the most suitable word from the passage.

In fact, in order to understand the real Chinaman and the Chinese civilisation, a man must be deep, broad and simple, for the three characteristics of the Chinese character and the Chinese civilisation are: depth, broadness and simplicity.

The American people, I may be permitted to say here, find it difficult to understand the real Chinaman and the Chinese civilisation, because the American people, as a rule, are broad, simple, but not deep. The English cannot understand the real Chinaman and Chinese civilisation because the English, as a rule, are deep, simple, but not broad. The Germans again cannot understand the real Chinaman and the Chinese civilisation because the Germans, especially the educated Germans, as a rule, are deep, broad, but not simple. The French, —well the French are the people, it seems to me, who can understand and has understood the real Chinaman and the Chinese civilisation best. The French, it is true, have not the depth of nature of the Germans nor the broadness of mind of the Americans nor the simplicity of mind of the English, —but the French, the French people have to a preeminent degree a quality of mind such as all the people I have mentioned above as a rule, have not, —a quality of mind which, above all things, is necessary in order to understand the real Chinaman and the Chinese civilisation; a quality of mind viz: *delicacy*. For, in addition to the three characteristics of the real Chinaman and Chinese civilisation which I have already mentioned, I must here add one more, and that the chief characteristic, namely delicacy; delicacy to a preeminent degree such as you will find nowhere else except perhaps among the ancient Greeks and their civilisation.

It will be seen from what I have said above that the American people if they will study the Chinese civilisation, will get depth; the English, broadness; and the Germans, simplicity; and all of them, Americans, English and Germans by the study of the Chinese civilisation, of Chinese books and literature, will get a quality of mind which, I take the liberty of saying here that it seems to me, they all of them, as a rule, have not to a preeminent degree, namely, *delicacy*. The French people finally, by the study of the Chinese civilisation, will get all, —depth, broadness, simplicity and a still finer delicacy than the delicacy which they now have. Thus the study of the Chinese civilisation, of Chinese books and literature will, I believe, be of benefit to all the people of Europe and America.

(428 words, by Ku Hung-ming, 1915)

According to the writer, it's difficult for westerners to understand Chinaman and Chinese civilisation in that they don't have the 11. __________ of Chinese except French. Besides, the Americans lack the 12. __________ of the Chinese while the English lack the 13. __________, and the German lack the 14. __________. Among the four characteristics of the Chinaman, 15. __________ is regarded as the most important one.

Passage 4

Directions: Read the following passage. Choose the best answer to each question or to complete each statement.

The Oxford Dictionary defines culture shock as *disorientation experienced when suddenly subjected to an unfamiliar culture or way of life.* Culture shock can be characterised by periods of frustration, adjustment, and even depression. Nearly everyone, regardless of maturity, disposition, previous experience abroad, or knowledge of the country in which they will be living, experiences some degree of culture shock when initially moving to a new country. Rather like the grieving process, there are stages that we go through.

Step 1: The Honeymoon Stage

When you first arrive in a new culture, differences are intriguing and you may feel excited, stimulated and curious. Like any new experience, there's a feeling of euphoria when you first arrive and you're in awe of the differences you see and experience. You feel excited, stimulated, enriched. During this stage, you still feel close to everything familiar back home.

Step 2: The Distress Stage

A little later, differences create an impact. Everything you're experiencing no longer feels new; in fact, it's starting to get you down. You feel confused, isolated or inadequate and realise that your familiar support systems (e.g. family and friends) are not easily accessible.

Step 3: Re-integration Stage

During this stage, you start winging about your new home. You dislike the culture, the language, the food. You reject it as inferior. You may even develop somc prejudices towards the new culture. You're angry, frustrated and even feel hostile to those around you. You wonder why you made the decision to change. You start to idealise life "back home" and compare your current culture to what is familiar. Don't worry. This is absolutely normal and a healthy reaction—it means you're adjusting. You are reconnecting with what you value about yourself and your own culture.

Step 4: Autonomy Stage

This is the first stage in acceptance. Sometimes called the *emergence* stage when you start to come out of the 'fog' and finally begin to feel like yourself again. You start to accept the differences and feel like you can begin to live with them. You feel more confident and better able to cope with any problems that may arise based on your growing experience. You no longer feel isolated and instead you're able to look at the world around you and appreciate where you are.

Step 5: Independence Stage

You are yourself again! You embrace the new culture and see everything in a new, yet realistic light. Things start to become enjoyable. You feel comfortable, confident, able to make decisions based on your own preferences and values. You no longer feel alone and isolated. You understand and appreciate both the differences and similarities of both your own and the new culture. You start to feel at home.

It is important to stress that culture shock is entirely normal, usually unavoidable and not a sign that you have made a mistake or that you won't manage. In fact there are very positive aspects of culture shock. The experience can be a significant learning experience, making you more aware of aspects of your own culture as well as the new culture you have entered. It will give you valuable skills that will serve you in many ways now and in the future.

(536 words, adapted from *Orientated for Success* by M. Barker, 1990)

16. According to the passage, during the culture shock period one may experience all of the following except ________.
    A. disappointment B. modification C. inferiority D. depression
17. The word "intriguing" in Line 9 most probably means ________.
    A. challenging B. disappointing C. saddening D. terrifying
18. During the ________ stage, you begin to adjust yourself to the new culture.
    A. first B. second C. third D. fourth
19. Which of the following statements is true according to the passage?
    A. At the honeymoon stage, one usually feels uneasy.
    B. At the distress stage, one feels everything around is fresh and stimulating.
    C. At the reintegration stage, one likes the new culture and dislikes his own.
    D. At the autonomy stage, one has begun to adapt to the new life.
20. What is discussed in this passage?
    A. The definition of culture shock B. The five stages of culture shock
    C. The positive aspects of culture shock D. All of the above

Unit 2

Education and Examinations

Part 1 Reading Skills

Section A Guessing Unknown Words from the Context II

4. Synonym and Antonym Clues

Synonyms are different words with almost identical or similar meanings. For example, the words "shut" and "close" are synonyms. Antonyms refer to words opposite in meaning, such as "ugly" and "beautiful", "evil" and "nice". Synonyms and antonyms are helpful to figure out unknown words from the context. Usually there are signal words helping us identify synonyms, such as "*and*", "*or*", "*that is*", sometimes even a comma. For antonyms, those signal words include "*or*" as well as "*not*". Here are some examples:

1) Jennifer's neighbors always try to avoid her because she is too loquacious, or talkative.

2) The little girl held fast her mother's sleeve. She clutched her so tightly that she couldn't leave home at once.

3) Recently a new kind of stationary or not mobile telephone was put on the market.

In the first sentence the word "talkative" and "loquacious" have the same meaning. In the second sentence the word "clutch" means "hold" and "fast" refers to "tightly". In the third one, the word "stationary" is opposite to "mobile".

5. Comparison and Contrast Clues

Comparison is the act of finding out the similarities between two or more persons or things. Comparison can easily be identified with the help of signal words such as *like*, *similarly*, *likewise* etc. For example:

1) Like his stubborn father, he is also very pigheaded."

2) Our offers were rejected. Likewise, all their attempts were spurned too.

In the first sentence, the word "like" indicates a comparison between the father and son. We can infer that the son is also stubborn just like his father. So "pigheaded" is close in meaning to "stubborn". In the second sentence, "likewise" is used to compare "rejected" to "spurned". Thus, the word "spurned" has the similar meaning to "rejected".

Contrast is just opposite to comparison in that it emphasizes the differences of two or more things or persons. A contrast is usually indicated by words such as *but*, *however*, *yet*, *on the other hand*, *while*, *although*, *instead of*, *rather than*, *contrary to*, *unlike* etc. For example:

1) Mary goes to the gym quite often. However, her roommate Erica only does exercises once in a blue moon.

2) He did not do his duty and he was not honest. We should censure him rather than praise him.

As we know, the word "however" is used to introduce contrasting ideas or words. So we can infer that "once in a blue moon" in the first sentence probably means "rarely", just opposite to "often". And "censure" in the second sentence is contrary to "praise", meaning "criticize".

Section B Practice

Directions: Choose the best word that is closest in meaning to the underlined word or phrase according to the context.

1. Online message boards were soon full of people both applauding and condemning Skenazy's decision to let her son go it alone.

   A. tolerating   B. blaming   C. polishing   D. investigating

2. The successful businessman shows contrast personalities. He is sometimes gregarious, however, at other times he prefers isolation.

   A. gorgeous   B. purified   C. independent   D. sociable

3. Their ideal was to combine individual liberty with material equality, a goal that has not yet been realized and that may be as chimerical as transmutation of lead into gold.

   A. unrealistic   B. indispensable   C. historical   D. inharmonious

4. Refuting the claim that the surest way to reduce anger is to express it, the author holds that venting anger can actually increase its intensity.
   A. denying B. understanding C. overcoming D. voicing
5. The European Central Bank prevented an immediate euro meltdown with its purchases of Spanish and Italian debt, but there's little to indicate that government leaders have the inclination or the stomach to use the time they've been handed to strengthen the currency union.
   A. thrill B. desire C. assurance D. resolution
6. It's hard to say whether ozone is good or bad. It can be beneficial or detrimental, depending on where it is located.
   A. helpful B. mutual C. harmful D. infinite
7. In America, the Dow dropped 5.55%, and the S&P tumbled a stunning 6.66%. Brazil's exchange was down just over 8%. Commodities sank. West Texas Intermediate oil fell 7% while copper was off 4.5%. However, gold rose over 4%, topping $1,721 an ounce. Within bond markets, anything resembling a safe haven saw rising prices and falling yields.
   A. soared B. decreased C. boosted D. fluctuated
8. There has been an upsurge of interest in chamber music. Likewise opera is receiving a boost from increased record sales.
   A. a drop B. a degrading C. an increase D. an anticipation
9. Contrary to the mayor's claims that her economic policies have solved the city's traditional crime problem, statistics suggest that these policies have in fact exacerbated it.
   A. resolved B. decreased C. worsened D. improved
10. "A father is like a general, and there are rules to abide by and punishment to shoulder if they are broken," said the 47-year-old. "Nowadays Chinese parents are too soft; they have abandoned the traditional Chinese way of good parenting."
   A. take B. shift C. avoid D. convey

Part 2 Idioms, Proverbs and Sayings

Directions: The following are idioms, proverbs or sayings by famous people about education. Choose what you think is correct and compare with the right ones.

1. Better be unborn than untaught, for ________ is the root of misfortune. (Plato)

A. knowledge B. wisdom C. ignorance D. pride

2. Education is a progressive ________ of our ignorance. (Will Durant)

A. discovery B. invention C. power D. strength

3. Education commences at the ________'s knee, and every word spoken within the hearsay of children tends towards the formation of character. (Hosea Ballou)

A. father B. mother C. grandmother D. grandfather

4. What sculpture is to a block of marble, education is to the human ________. (Joseph Addison)

A. brain B. hand C. soul D. nature

5. The fruit of liberal education is not learning, but the capacity and ________ to learn, not knowledge, but power. (Charles W. Eliot)

A. desire B. strength C. satisfaction D. content

6. Next in importance to freedom and justice is popular education, ________ which neither freedom nor justice can be maintained. (James A. Garfield)

A. with B. besides C. without D. for

7. Learning is like rowing upstream: not to ________ is to drop back. (Chinese Saying)

A. move B. advance C. go D. flow

8. Knowledge makes humble, ignorance makes ________. (Proverb)

A. proud B. modest C. honest D. mean

9. Instruction ends in the school-room, but education ends only with ________. (Frederick W. Robertson)

A. life B. college C. MBA D. PhD

10. Genius without education is like silver in the ________. (Benjamin Franklin)

A. factory B. water C. mine D. air

Part 3 Reading Passages

Section A TOEFL and IELTS

A. The **Test of English as a Foreign Language**, or **TOEFL**, evaluates the ability of an individual to use and understand English in an academic setting. It sometimes is an admission requirement for non-native English speakers at many English-speaking colleges and universities. Additionally, institutions such as government agencies, licensing bodies, businesses, or scholarship programs may require this test. A TOEFL score is valid for two years.

B. Since its introduction in late 2005, the Internet-based Test (iBT) has progressively replaced both the computer-based tests (CBT) and paper-based tests (PBT), although paper-based testing is still used in select areas.

C. The four-hour test consists of four sections, each measuring one of the basic language skills and all tasks focus on language used in an academic, higher-education environment. Note-taking is allowed during the iBT. The test cannot be taken more than once a week.

D. The Reading Section consists of 3–5 passages, each approximately 700 words in length and questions about the passages. The passages are on academic topics; they are the kind of material that might be found in an undergraduate university textbook. Passages require understanding of rhetorical functions such as cause-effect, compare-contrast and argumentation. Students answer questions about main ideas, details, inferences, essential information, sentence insertion, vocabulary, rhetorical purpose and overall ideas. New types of questions in the iBT require filling out tables or completing summaries.

E. The Listening Section consists of six passages 3–5 minutes in length and questions about the passages. These passages include two student conversations and four academic lectures or discussions. A conversation involves two speakers, a student and either a professor or a campus service provider. A lecture is a self-contained portion of an academic lecture, which may involve student participation and does not assume specialized background knowledge in the subject area. Each conversation and lecture stimulus is heard only once. Test-takers may take notes while they listen and they may refer to their notes when they answer the questions. Each conversation is associated with five questions and each lecture with six. The questions are meant to measure the ability to understand main ideas, important details, implications, relationships between ideas, organization of information, speaker purpose and speaker attitude.

F. The Speaking Section consists of six tasks: two independent tasks and four integrated tasks. In the two independent tasks, test-takers answer opinion questions on familiar topics. They are evaluated on their ability to speak spontaneously and convey their ideas clearly and coherently. In two of the integrated tasks, test-takers read a short passage, listen to an academic course lecture or a conversation about campus life and answer a question by combining appropriate information from the text and the talk. In the two remaining integrated tasks, test-takers listen to an academic course lecture or a conversation about campus life and then respond to a question about what they heard. In the integrated tasks, test-takers are evaluated on their ability to appropriately synthesize and effectively convey information from the reading and listening material. Test-takers may take notes as they read and listen and may use their notes to help prepare their responses. Test-takers are given a short preparation time before they have to begin speaking.

G. The Writing Section measures a test taker's ability to write in an academic setting and consists of two tasks: one integrated task and one independent task. In the integrated task, test-takers read a passage on an academic topic and then listen to a speaker discuss the same topic. The test-taker will then write a summary about the important points in the listening passage and explain how these relate to the key points of the reading passage. In the independent task, test-takers must write an essay that states, explains, and supports their opinion on an issue, supporting their opinions or choices, rather than simply listing personal preferences or choices.

H. The iBT version of the TOEFL test is scored on a scale of 0 to 120 points. Each of the four sections (Reading, Listening, Speaking, and Writing) receives a scaled score from 0 to 30. The scaled scores from the four sections are added together to determine the total score. Each speaking question is initially given a score of 0 to 4, and each writing question is initially given a score of 0 to 5. These scores are converted to scaled scores of 0 to 30.

I. **IELTS**, or **'International English Language Testing System'**, is an international standardised test of English language proficiency. It is jointly managed by University of Cambridge ESOL Examinations, the British Council and IDP Education Pty Ltd. IELTS is accepted by most Australian, British, Canadian, Irish, New Zealand and South African academic institutions, over 3,000 academic institutions in the United States, and various professional organisations. It is also a requirement for immigration to Australia, New Zealand and Canada.

J. No minimum score is required to pass the test. An IELTS result or Test Report Form is issued to all candidates with a score from 1 (no knowledge) to 9 (expert user) and each institution sets a different threshold. Institutions are advised not to consider valid a report older than two years, unless the user proves that he has worked to maintain his level.

K. The IELTS incorporates the following features:

- A variety of accents and writing styles have presented in text materials in order to minimize linguistic bias.
- IELTS tests the ability to listen, read, write and speak in English.
- Band scores used for each language sub-skill (Listening, Reading, Writing, and Speaking). The Band Scale ranges from 0 ("Did not attempt the test") to 9 ("Expert User").
- The speaking module—a key component of IELTS. This is conducted in the form of a one-to-one interview with an examiner. The examiner assesses the candidate as he or she is speaking, but the speaking session is also recorded for monitoring as well as re-marking in case of an appeal against the banding given.
- IELTS is developed with input from item writers from around the world.

L. All candidates must complete four Modules—Listening, Reading, Writing and Speaking—to obtain a band score, which is shown on the IELTS Test Report Form (TRF). **The listening module** comprises four sections. Each section begins with a short introduction telling the candidates about the situation and the speakers. They then have some time to look through the questions. The first three sections have a break in the middle allowing candidates to look at the remaining questions. Each section is heard only once. **The reading test** comprises three sections, with 3 texts normally followed by 13 or 14 questions for a total of 40 questions overall. The General test also has 3 sections. However the texts are shorter, so there can be up to 5 texts to read. **Writing** consists of two sections with the second section taking the form of an essay. **The speaking test** contains three sections. The first section takes the form of an interview during which candidates may be asked about their hobbies, interests, reasons for taking IELTS exam as well as other general topics such as clothing, free time, computers and the internet or family. In the second section candidates are given a topic card and then have one minute to prepare after which they must speak about the given topic. The third section involves a discussion between the examiner and the candidate, generally on questions relating to the theme which they have already spoken about in part 2.

M. IELTS is scored on a nine-band scale, with each band corresponding to a specified competence in English. Overall Band Scores are reported to the nearest half band. The following rounding convention applies: if the average across the four skills ends in .25, it is rounded up to the next half band, and if it ends in .75, it is rounded up to the next whole band.

N. Just over half (51%) of candidates take the test to enter higher education in a foreign country. The IELTS minimum scores required by academic institutions vary. As a general rule, institutions from English-speaking countries require a higher IELTS band. A number of Commonwealth countries use IELTS scores as a proof of prospective immigrants' competence in English.

(1,372 words, based on *http://en.wikipedia.org/wiki/TOEFL / IELTS*)

I. Reading Comprehension

Questions 1-6

Directions: The passage has 14 paragraphs A-N. Which paragraphs discuss the following points? Write the appropriate letters A-N on the left.

1. ________ The iBT score of TOEFL
2. ________ IELTS characteristics
3. ________ Banding of IELTS
4. ________ IELTS test structure
5. ________ Brief introduction to TOEFL
6. ________ The writing section of TOEFL

Questions 7-10

Directions: Do the following statements agree with the above passage? Mark

Y for Yes	if the statement agrees with the passage
N for No	if the statement does not agree with the passage
NG for NOT GIVEN	if it is impossible to know from the passage

7. ________ A TOEFL score is valid for three years.
8. ________ The reading of a TOEFL test consists of about 700 words altogether.
9. ________ IELTS is accepted by most colleges and universities in Japan.

10. ________ Nearly half of the candidates take IELTS not in order to enter higher education in a foreign country.

II. Vocabulary

Directions: Fill in each blank with an appropriate word from the box below. Each word can be used only once.

academic	participation	integrated	spontaneously	coherently	converted
proficiency	threshold	incorporate	comprise	prospective	bias

1. We reserve the right not to run all or part of the program if the number of successful applicants falls below a minimum __________.
2. The Institute of Higher Education of the Shanghai Jiao Tong University ranks universities by several indicators of __________ or research performance.
3. A recent research has shown that people who react __________ in any situation live longer than people who are slow in their reactions.
4. Gender __________ in education is not only a problem of inequality; better educated women, in fact, have lower fertility rates, have more healthy children and contribute to a more equal household's resources distribution.
5. Linguistic __________ is the ability of an individual to speak or perform in an acquired language.
6. As a rising global power, China should learn how to treat global issues and take firm steps on the peaceful road toward a harmonious world. That will require it to increase its __________ in international affairs.
7. "Some of China's brightest young minds come to our university for our programs," the president said. "Our programs are __________, so our students learn not only from the lecturers but from each other as well."
8. Both law and literature require the ability to express ideas __________ and logically—something that the Chinese education system should emphasize more.
9. Mr. Li and two other teachers live in a house __________ from a classroom which has been declared unsafe for living.
10. The management firmly believes that young Chinese parents should __________ broader values when educating their children. "As parents, they should be conscious on how to bring up their children."
11. A poll of 23-to 35-year-olds across China on their attitude to love and marriage found 8.5 percent of Beijingers believe an apartment and a car is a must-have for __________ partners, *Beijing Youth Daily* reported.
12. In some big and medium-sized cities, empty-nest homes __________ 70 percent of households.

III. Debate

Directions: Read the following short passage and have a debate over the topic "The Pen is mightier than the Sword."

"The Pen is mightier than the Sword." There have been many writers who wielded their pens to fight things that were wrong. Charles Dickens was one of them. Schoolboys should certainly be grateful to him. He did much to put out of existence such schools as those belonging to Mr. Squeers in *Nicholas Nickleby*. He did much to end the dreadful conditions in workhouses which he describes so vividly at the beginning of *Oliver Twist*.

Mrs. Harriet Beecher Stowe, who was born in 1811, was not a literary genius like Dickens. Yet one of her books not only made her famous, but has been described as one that stirred the world. This book that shook the world was called *Uncle Tom's Cabin*. There was a time when practically every English-speaking man, woman and child had read this novel that did so much to abolish slavery. Not many people read it today, but it is still very interesting, if only to show how an enthusiastic writer can arouse people's sympathies. The author herself had neither been to the Southern States nor seen a slave. The Southern Americans were very angry at the book, which they said did not at all represent the true state of affairs, but the Northern Americans were wildly excited over it, and were so inspired by it that they were ready even to go to war to set the slaves free.

(Based on "Books That Moved the World", *English Learning*, Vol. 2 1984)

Section B The Two Kinds (Excerpt)

by Amy Tan

Directions: Read this section and decide whether the statements that follow are true or false according to the passage. Write T for True and F for False.

My parents invited all the couples from their social club to witness my debut. Auntie Lindo and Uncle Tin were there. Waverly and her two older brothers had also come. The first two rows were filled with children either younger or older than I was. The littlest ones got to go first. They recited simple nursery rhymes, squawked out tunes on miniature violins, and twirled hula hoops in pink ballet tutus, and when they bowed or curtsied, the audience would sigh in unison, "Aw", and then clap enthusiastically.

When my turn came, I was very confident. I remember my childish excitement. It was as if I knew, without a doubt, that the prodigy side of me really did exist. I had no fear whatsoever, no nervousness. I remember thinking. This is it! This is it! I looked out over the audience, at my mother's blank face, my father's yawn, Auntie Lindo's stiff-lipped smile, Waverly's sulky expression. I had on a white dress, layered with sheets of lace, and a pink bow in my Peter Pan haircut. As I sat down, I envisioned people jumping to their feet and Ed Sullivan rushing up to introduce me to everyone on TV.

And I started to play. Everything was so beautiful. I was so caught up in how lovely I looked that I wasn't worried about how I would sound. So I was surprised when I hit the first wrong note. And then I hit another and another. A chill started at the top of my head and began to trickle down. Yet I couldn't stop playing, as though my hands were bewitched. I kept thinking my fingers would adjust themselves back, like a train switching to the right track. I played this strange jumble through to the end, the sour notes staying with me all the way.

When I stood up, I discovered my legs were shaking. Maybe I had just been nervous, and the audience, like Old Chong had seen me go through the right motions and had not heard anything wrong at all. I swept my right foot out, went down on my knee, looked up, and smiled. The room was quiet, except for Old Chong, who was beaming and shouting "Bravo! Bravo! Well done!" By then I saw my mother's face, her stricken face. The audience clapped weakly, and I walked back to my chair, with my whole face quivering as I tried not to cry, I heard a little boy whisper loudly to his mother. "That was awful," and mother whispered "Well, she certainly tried."

And now I realized how many people were in the audience—the whole world, it seemed. I was aware of eyes burning into my back. I felt the shame of my mother and father as they sat stiffly through the rest of the show.

We could have escaped during intermission. Pride and some strange sense of honor must have anchored my parents to their chairs. And so we watched it all. The eighteen-year-old boy with a fake moustache who did a magic show and juggled flaming hoops while riding a unicycle. The breasted girl with white make-up who sang an aria from *Madame Butterfly* and got an honorable mention. And the eleven-year-old boy who was first prize playing a tricky violin song that sounded like a busy bee.

After the show the Hsus, the Jongs, and the St. Clairs, from the Joy Luck Club, came up to my mother and father.

"Lots of talented kids," Auntie Lindo said vaguely, smiling broadly. "That was something else," my father said, and I wondered if he was referring to me in a humorous way, or whether he even remembered what I had done.

Waverly looked at me and shrugged her shoulders. "You aren't a genius like me," she said matter-of-factly. And if I hadn't felt so bad, I would have pulled her braids and punched her stomach.

But my mother's expression was what devastated me: a quiet, blank look that said she had lost everything. I felt the same way, and everybody seemed now to be coming up, like gawkers at the scene of an accident to see what parts were actually missing. When we got on the bus to go home, my father was humming the busy-bee tune and my mother kept silent. I kept thinking she wanted to wait until we got home before shouting at me. But when my father unlocked the door to our apartment, my mother walked in and went straight to the back, into the bedroom. No accusations, No blame. And in a way, I felt disappointed. I had been waiting for her to start shouting, so that I could shout back and cry and blame her for all my misery.

I had assumed that my talent-show fiasco meant that I would never have to play the piano again. But two days later, after school, my mother came out of the kitchen and saw me watching TV.

"Four clock," she reminded me, as if it were any other day. I was stunned, as though she were asking me to go through the talent-show torture again. I planted myself more squarely in front of the TV.

"Turn off TV," she called from the kitchen five minutes later. I didn't budge. And then I decided, I didn't have to do what mother said anymore. I wasn't her slave. This wasn't China. I had listened to her before, and look what happened she was the stupid one.

She came out of the kitchen and stood in the arched entryway of the living room. "Four clock," she said once again, louder.

"I'm not going to play anymore," I said nonchalantly. "Why should I? I'm not a genius."

She stood in front of the TV. I saw that her chest was heaving up and down in an angry way.

"No!" I said, and I now felt stronger, as if my true self had finally emerged. So this was what had been inside me all along.

"No! I won't!" I screamed. She snapped off the TV, yanked me by the arm and pulled me off the floor. She was frighteningly strong, half pulling, half carrying me towards the piano as I kicked the throw rugs under my feet. She lifted me up onto the hard bench. I was sobbing by now, looking at her bitterly. Her chest was heaving even more and her mouth was open, smiling crazily as if she were pleased that I was crying.

"You want me to be something that I'm not!" I sobbed. "I'll never be the kind of daughter you want me to be!"

"Only two kinds of daughters," she shouted in Chinese. "Those who are obedient and those who follow their own mind! Only one kind of daughter can live in this house. Obedient daughter!"

"Then I wish I weren't your daughter, I wish you weren't my mother," I shouted. As I said these things I got scared. It felt like worms and toads and slimy things crawling out of my chest, but it also felt good, that this awful side of me had surfaced, at last.

"Too late to change this," my mother said shrilly.

And I could sense her anger rising to its breaking point. I wanted see it spill over. And that's when I remembered the babies she had lost in China, the ones we never talked about. "Then I wish I'd never been born!" I shouted. "I wish I were dead! Like them."

It was as if I had said magic words. Alakazam!—her face went blank, her mouth closed, her arms went slack, and she backed out of the room, stunned, as if she were blowing away like a small brown leaf, thin, brittle, lifeless.

It was not the only disappointment my mother felt in me. In the years that followed, I failed her many times, each time asserting my will, my right to fall short of expectations. I didn't get straight A's. I didn't become class president. I didn't get into Stanford. I dropped out of college.

Unlike my mother, I did not believe I could be anything I wanted to be, I could only be me.

And for all those years we never talked about the disaster at the recital or my terrible declarations afterward at the piano bench. Neither of us talked about it again, as if it were a betrayal that was now unspeakable. So I never found a way to ask her why she had hoped for something so large that failure was inevitable.

And even worse, I never asked her about what frightened me the most: Why had she given up hope?

For after our struggle at the piano, she never mentioned my playing again. The lessons stopped. The lid to the piano was closed shutting out the dust, my misery, and her dreams.

(1,476 words, taken from *The Two Kinds* by Amy Tan)

1. My Debut turned out to be a disaster because I was over-concerned about my appearance. ________
2. The audience pretended that they had heard nothing wrong at all and shouted "Bravo! Bravo! Well done!" to encourage me. ________
3. Waverly was sympathetic to me about my screwing up the piano play in front of the audience. ________
4. By saying "This wasn't China." I meant I didn't want to be obedient to my mother any more like what a Chinese girl would do in China. ________
5. My mother didn't force me to play the piano again after the terrible struggle. ________

Part 4 Reading Comprehension Test

Section A

Directions: Read the following passages. Choose the best answer to each question.

Passage 1

As the twentieth century began, the importance of formal education in the United States increased. The frontier had mostly disappeared and by 1910 most Americans lived in towns and cities. Industrialization and the bureaucratization of economic line life combined with a new emphasis upon credentials and expertise to make schooling increasingly important for economic and social mobility. Increasingly, too, schools were viewed as the most important means of integrating immigrants into American society.

The arrival of a great wave of southern and eastern European immigrants at the turn of the century coincided with and contributed to an enormous expansion of formal schooling. By

1920 schooling to age fourteen or beyond was compulsory in most states, and the school year was greatly lengthened. Kindergartens, vacation schools, extracurricular activities, and vocational education and counseling extended the influence of public schools over the lives of students, many of whom in the larger industrial cities were the children of immigrants. Classes for adult immigrants were sponsored by public schools, corporations, unions, churches, settlement houses, and other agencies. Reformers early in the twentieth century suggested that education programs should suit the needs of specific populations. Immigrant women were one such population. Schools tried to educate young women so they could occupy productive places in the urban industrial economy, and one place many educators considered appropriate for women was the home.

Although looking after the house and family was familiar to immigrant women, American education gave homemaking a new definition. In preindustrial economies, homemaking had meant the production as well as the consumption of goods, and it commonly included income-producing activities both inside and outside the home, in the highly industrialized early-twentieth-century United States, however, overproduction rather than scarcity was becoming a problem. Thus, the ideal American homemaker was viewed as a consumer rather than a producer. Schools trained women to be consumer homemakers cooking, shopping, decorating, and caring for children "efficiently" in their own homes, or if economic necessity demanded, as employees in the homes of others. Subsequent reforms have made these notions seem quite out-of-date.

(341 words)

1. All of the following factors contributed to the growing importance of formal education in America in the twentieth century EXCEPT ________.
   A. industrialization and the bureaucratization of economic line life
   B. the decrease of social mobility
   C. a new emphasis upon credentials and expertise
   D. the disappearance of the frontier
2. The word "integrating" in Line 6 of Paragraph 1 is closest in meaning to ________.
   A. disposing B. intruding C. converting D. combining
3. The word "compulsory" in Line 3 of Paragraph 2 most probably means ________.
   A. obligatory B. optional C. alternative D. impulsive
4. Kindergartens and vacation schools played a role in ________.
   A. lengthening the school year of children
   B. helping spread the influence of public schools in the United States
   C. attracting more European immigrants to go to the United Stated
   D. helping women occupy productive places in the society
5. The word "it" in Line 3 of Paragraph 3 refers to ________.
   A. the consumption of goods B. preindustrial economies
   C. homemaking D. a new definition

Passage 2

Sending a child to school in England is a step which many parents do not find easy to take. In theory, at least, the problem is that there are very many choices to make. Let us try to list some of the alternatives between which parents are forced to decide. To begin with, they may ask themselves whether they would like their child to go to a single-sex school or a co-educational school. They may also consider whether he should go to a school which is connected to a particular church or religious group, or whether the school should have no such connections. Another decision is whether the school should be one of the vast majority financed by the state or one of the very small but influential minority of private schools, though this choice is, of course, only available to the small number of those who can pay. Also connected with the question of money is whether the child should go to a boarding school or live at home. Then there is the question of what the child should do at school. Should it be a school whose curriculum lays emphasis, for instance, on necessary skills, such as reading, writing and mathematics, or one which pays more attention to developing the child's personality, morally, emotionally and socially? Finally, with dissatisfaction with conventional education as great as it is in some circles in England and certainly in the USA, the question might even arise in the parents' minds as to whether the child should be compelled to go to school at all. Although in practice, some parents may not think twice about any of these choices and send their children to the only school available in the immediate neighborhood, any parent who is interested enough can insist that as many choices as possible be made open to him, and the system is theoretically supposed to provide them.

(317 words)

6. What makes the decision of English parents to send their children to school very difficult?
   A. Some parents are willing to educate their children by themselves.
   B. There are too many options for parents to choose from.
   C. English parents are overly indecisive.
   D. Schools available to their children are quite limited.
7. The word "co-educational" in Line 5 most probably means ________.
   A. boarding　　B. private　　C. instructional　　D. mixed-gender
8. The word "compelled" in Line 18 is closest in meaning to ________.
   A. convicted　　B. evoked　　C. forced　　D. motivated
9. Which of the following statements is true?
   A. Many state schools are exclusive to students who are from rich families.
   B. Britons are quite happy with the quality of traditional education.
   C. Most parents would choose schools in the neighborhood for their children after careful consideration.
   D. Most schools in England are sponsored by the State.

Section B

Directions: Decide whether the following statements are true or false according to the passage. Write T for True and F for False.

Passage 3 Review on "The Battle Hymn of the Tiger Mother"

The frenetic interest in Amy Chua's unexceptional memoir about her dedication to raising children who excel shows the ease with which our anxiety about being the best possible parent is aroused. *The Battle Hymn of the Tiger Mother* reveals a previously guessed-at but carefully closeted Chinese approach to child rearing. While western mothers praise a child for every squiggle drawn, Chua learned from her parents to accept nothing less than the best. "Chinese parents demand perfect grades because they believe that their child can get them. If their child does not get them, the Chinese parent assumes it's because the child didn't work hard enough."

This point in Chua's frequently repeated argument chimes with exciting new research emphasizing the importance of teaching children how their own efforts impact on their achievement. When children see that hard work results in achievement, they have far more real confidence than children who trust to their native-born wit. Is Amy Chua, herself a high achieving Yale professor, going to bring down the conventional wisdom about saturating a child with praise? But even before you have time to nod in agreement, you come up against the shock of "the solution to substandard performance is always to excoriate, punish and shame the child".

Chua is a lawyer, and her writing wields the magic of expert special pleading. The "Tiger Mother"—whom Chua sees as a type of Chinese parent—is cruel to be kind. The cruelty isn't fun, she insists, it is hard work. It doesn't tear a child down, it demonstrates a parent's respect for her child's toughness and potential. Anyway, the proof of the pudding is in the eating; her offspring come out ahead.

With a breezy style and slick logic, Chua draws cultural stereotypes that filter out one central fact: her approach to parenting is as mainstream in the west as it is in China. We all cherish our children's future. The shadow of downward mobility covers every inch of this small planet, and many parents in every country respond to this fear. Sometimes we respond by offering the best possible education; sometimes we respond by putting our child in a pressure cooker. The over-scheduled child, whose every waking moment is devoted to dance, music, art and maths, is a familiar sight in many western families. Few parents would allow a child to give up maths after one rough test, though Chua suggests this is a typical response. A meritocracy puts a great burden on parents as they compete with others who are also doing everything possible to ensure their child is high up in the meritocracy. Sometimes this race results in the "perfect madness" Judith Warner described five years ago, as she watched middle class New York mothers compete to be the best mother, who would of course have the best child.

Chua exercises the charm of apparent candor to minimize the dark side of her message. She summons up scenes that still smoke from the heat of the moment, wherein we sympathize with her plight even as she depicts herself as a manipulative bully. She threatens to take her daughter Sophia's doll's house to a charity shop if she does not master a difficult piano piece. She dismisses her daughter Lulu's longing for a pet by insisting the violin is her pet. Lulu's teenage rebelliousness is drawn with sympathetic clarity, and the teen's public outburst, "I hate you", pulses with comic desperation. Every parent of a teenager knows the sting of those words, so different when she is 13 from the petulant tantrums of a three-year-old. But once again the sense that Chua is offering insight and empathy is clouded over by smugness. ("I am right and she knows I am right.")

When Lulu begs to give up the violin, and Chua eventually "gives in", her daughter is confused and terrified by this uncharacteristic responsiveness. "I really do love the violin," she insists, "but couldn't things be a little less intense?" This achieves an uneasy truce, and Lulu knows she must find some other way to outshine everyone else.

There is unintentional poignancy in the daughter's impasse. The teen faces a profound dilemma: either excels at music and school and leaps over every hurdle I put in front of you, or I will excoriate, punish and shame you. As the memoir draws to a close, Lulu is a rising star in tennis. Her mother shouts instructions to her as she practises, secretly texts her coach, and basks in her conviction that her daughter knows her mother is right.

What inspires awe, however, is the sheer force of maternal control. The psychoanalyst Alice Miller coined the term "poisonous pedagogy" to describe some parents' conviction that cruelty and control are justified because it is in the child's best interests. They see the child's own will as something to be broken and reconfigured. Those who teach in (the best) universities have considerable experience with hothouse children, who come from Chinese and western backgrounds alike. What happens to these young people as they stand at the threshold of adulthood, no longer in pouncing distance of their tiger mother?

Many display bland compliance, tinged with deviousness—which may be essential to their personal survival. Obsessed with grades, they often lack interest in their subject. They relish all those frivolous distractions their tiger mother prohibited—television, all-night chats with friends—and some even sneak in pets. I wait, curious as a cat, to read their memoirs of being raised by tiger mothers.

(915 words, This passage is taken from *The Guardian*, by Terri Apter)

10. Amy Chua's child-teaching philosophy contradicts with the findings of a new research emphasizing the importance of teaching children how their own efforts influence their achievement. ______

11. The Tiger Mother believes her cruelty towards the children benefits them because it embodies her respect for her children's toughness and potential. ______

12. Amy Chua's book brings out a key fact that Chinese parents long for a good future for their children more than western parents. ________
13. Alice Miller coined the term "perfect madness" to describe middle class New York mothers who compete to be the best mother and have the best children. ________
14. The author of this passage expects to read the children's memoirs of being raised by their tiger mothers in the future. ________

Section C

Directions: Read the following passage and finish the exercises.

Passage 4

First read the question:

15. The passage introduces GRE in the order of ________.

A. its structure, purpose, use in admissions, difference between GRE and GMAT

B. its purpose, use in admissions, structure, difference between GRE and GMAT

C. its purpose, structure, use in admissions, difference between GRE and GMAT

D. the use in admissions, structure, purpose, difference between GRE and GMAT

Now go through the TEXT quickly to answer the question.

The Graduate Record Examination (GRE) is a standardized test intended to measure the abilities of all graduates in tasks of general academic nature, regardless of their fields of specialization and is an admission requirement for many graduate schools in the United States, in other English-speaking countries and for English-taught graduate and business programmes world-wide. The GRE is supposed to measure the extent to which undergraduate education has developed an individual's verbal and quantitative skills in abstract thinking. The GRE General Test is offered as a computer-based, computer adaptive exam administered by selected qualified testing centers; however, paper-based exams are offered in areas of the world where computer-based testing is not available. ETS erases all test records that are older than 5 years, although graduate program policies on the admittance of scores older than 5 years will vary.

The exam consists of four sections. The first section is a writing section, while the other three are multiple-choice style. One of the multiple choice style exams will test verbal skills, another will test quantitative skills and a third exam will be an experimental section that is not included in the reported score. The entire test procedure takes about 4 hours. **The verbal section** consists of analogies, completions, and reading comprehension passages. Multiple-choice response sections are graded on a scale of 200-800, in 10-point increments. This section primarily tests vocabulary. In a typical examination, this section may consist of 30 questions, and 30 minutes may be allotted for it. **The quantitative section** consists of problem solving and quantitative comparison questions that test high-school level mathematics. Multiple-choice response sections are graded on a scale of 200-800, in 10-point increments. In a typical examination, this section may consist of 28 questions, and test takers may be given 45 minutes to complete the section. This section typically includes 14 quantitative comparison questions, 10 discrete quantitative questions (multiple-choice) and 4 data interpretation questions. **The analytical writing section** consists of two different essays, an "issue task" and an "argument task". The writing section is graded on a scale of 0-6, in half-point increments. Each essay is scored by at least two readers on a six-point holistic scale. If the two scores are within one point, the average of the scores is taken. If the two scores differ by more than a point, a third reader examines the response. For **Issue task, t**he test taker will be able to choose between two topics upon which to write an essay. The time allowed for this essay is 45 minutes. For **Argument task**, the test taker will be given an "argument" and will be asked to write an essay that critiques the argument. Test takers are asked to consider the argument's logic and to make suggestions about how to improve the logic of the argument. The time allotted for this essay is 30 minutes. **The experimental section**, which can be either a verbal, quantitative, or analytical writing task, contains new questions that ETS is considering for future use. Although the experimental section does not count toward the test-taker's score, it is unidentified and appears identical to the real (scored) part of the test. As test takers have no clear way of knowing which section is experimental, they are forced to complete this section. This section does not appear on all GRE examinations. Furthermore, an identified and unscored section of such experimental questions, asked for research purposes, can appear at the end of the test.

The common (Verbal and Quantitative) multiple-choice portions of the exam currently use computer-adaptive testing (CAT) methods that automatically change the difficulty of questions as the test taker proceeds with the exam, depending on the number of correct or incorrect answers that are given. The test taker is not allowed to go back and change the answers to previous questions, and some type of answer must be given before the next question is presented. The first question that is given in a multiple-choice section is considered to be an "average level" question that half of the GRE test takers will answer correctly. If the question is answered correctly, then subsequent questions become more difficult. If the question is answered incorrectly, then subsequent questions become easier, until a question is answered correctly. This approach to administration yields scores that are of similar accuracy while using approximately half as many items.

Many graduate schools in English-speaking countries (especially in the United States) require GRE results as part of the admissions process. The use and weight of GRE scores vary considerably not only from school to school, but from department to department, and from program to program also. Programs in liberal arts topics may only consider the applicant's verbal score to be of interest, while mathematics and science programs may only consider quantitative ability; however, since most applicants to mathematics, science, or engineering graduate programs all have high quantitative scores, the verbal score can become a deciding factor even in these programs. Admission to graduate schools depends on a complex mix of several different factors. Schools see letters of recommendation, statement of purpose, GPA, GRE score etc. Some schools use the GRE in admissions decisions, but not in funding decisions; others use the GRE for the selection of scholarship and fellowship candidates, but not for admissions. In some cases, the GRE may be a general requirement for graduate admissions imposed by the university, while particular departments may not consider the scores at all. Graduate schools will typically provide information about how the GRE is considered in admissions and funding decisions, and the average scores of previously admitted students. The best way to find out how a particular school or program evaluates a GRE score in the admissions process is to contact the person in charge of graduate admissions for the specific program in question.

GRE is different from GMAT (The Graduate Management Admission Test) which is a computer adaptive standardized test in mathematics and the English language for measuring aptitude to succeed academically in graduate business studies. Business schools commonly use the GMAT as one of many selection criteria for admission into an MBA program. However, there are many business schools that also accept GRE scores.

(1,025 words, based on *http://en.wikipedia.org/wiki/Graduate_Record_Examinations*)

Read again and mark

Y (for Yes) if the statement agrees with the information given in the text;

N (for No) if the statement contradicts the information given in the text;

NG (for Not Given) if the information is not given in the text.

16. The GRE is intended to measure the degree an undergraduate has developed in his or her verbal and quantitative skills in abstract thinking. ________
17. In China the GRE General Test is offered as a computer-based test. ________
18. The GRE consists of five sections which are all objective tests. ________
19. Admission to graduate schools depends on a complex mix of several different factors. However, almost all schools make funding decisions based on GRE score. ________
20. GMAT is a standardized test in mathematics and the English language for measuring aptitude to succeed academically in graduate business studies. ________

Unit 3

Earning and Spending Money

Part 1 Reading Skills

Section A Guessing Unknown Words from the Context III

6. Cause and Effect Relationship

Identifying cause and effect relationship is helpful in figuring out the meaning of unfamiliar words. It's known that the cause is the reason or source of a certain outcome. That is to say, a cause is something that makes something else happen and the effect is the result or consequence of the cause. From this relationship, it's probable for us to make a logical inference.

Signal words introducing the cause such as *because, since, as, for, result from, follow from, attribute...to, base...on..., reason, because of, thanks to, owe to, due to, blame mainly on* can be helpful when you are reading.

Signal words introducing the effect will also help you guess the meaning of unknown words, for example, *as a consequence, as a result, therefore, hence, so, thus, that's why, consequently, result in, contribute to, produce effects on, affect, cause, lead to.* Here are some examples:

1) *Because* she has a great need for privacy, she loathes the public appearances demanded of her as a leading literary figure.

From the cause "She has a great need for privacy", we can infer that she doesn't like publicity. So the word "loathe" most probably means "dislike" or "hate".

2) Amelia Earhart, recognized as a pioneer in aviation, garnered praise *for* her successful solo flights as well as her efforts to open the male-dominated field to other women.

We can infer that there is a cause-effect relationship in the above sentence. Amelia's successful flights and her efforts to open the field to other women are the causes why she was praised. So it's reasonable to guess that the word "garner" has the meaning "get" or "earn".

8. Common Knowledge

Common knowledge is knowledge that is known by everyone or almost everyone. Good readers often try to make sense out of what they read with the help of their prior knowledge, which is an essential reading strategy. Readers' common knowledge helps improve their comprehension of the reading material and do better on reading tests. It will be illustrated below.

1) It's reported that Bill Gates is the most affluent person in the world.

As we all know that Bill Gates is the richest man in the world, we may infer that the word "affluent" means "rich".

2) As a scientist, Edison is very famous for his contrivances.

According to our prior knowledge, Edison was referred to as the Father of invention. So it is reasonable to make the guess that "contrivances" means "inventions".

3) In the figure below, if PQRS is a quadrilateral and TUV is a triangle, what is the sum of the degree measures of the marked angles?

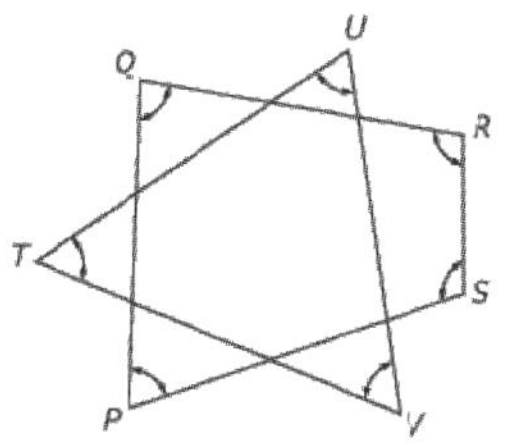

With the help of the figure and our prior knowledge, we can guess the meaning of the words "quadrilateral" and "triangle", and we also share the knowledge that the sum of the degree measures of a triangle is 180 and that of a quadrilateral is 360, so we can make an accurate inference that the sum of the marked angles is 540.

Section B Practice

Directions: Choose the word that best fits the sentence to practice the reading skills discussed above.

1. When he was five years old, the boy scribbled on the bedroom wall with a permanent marker, leaving a/an ________ mark that would still be there even after he grew up and moved away.

   A. inerasable B. mobile C. erasable D. immobile

2. The addition of descriptive details to the basic information serves to ________ the book by producing a fuller account.

   A. objectify B. celebrate C. enrich D. discolor

3. A right angle is an angle of 90 degrees formed by two lines ________ each other.

   A. perpendicular to B. parallel to C. intersecting D. overlapping

4. Sometimes when I'm reading a book in English, I use my ________ to find new vocabulary words.

   A. sketch B. map C. lexicon D. notebook

5. Since the two legislators had a long history of major disagreements, the senator considered his colleague's enthusiastic assurances that they would be in agreement on a forthcoming piece of legislation ________.

   A. fatuous B. precious C. prestigious D. famous

6. Because he felt threatened in his new position, he was ________ exposing his frank opinions of company proposals.

   A. careless about B. indifferent to C. curious about D. chary of

7. To fully understand the impact of global warming on the environment, we should recognize that the components of the problem are ________ and, therefore, a change in any one component will ________ the others.

   A. distinct...influence B. unique...clarify
   C. linked...affect D. unclear...negate
   E. growing...worsen

8. Hoping to ________ the dispute, negotiators proposed a compromise that they felt would be ________ to both labor and management.

   A. enforce...useful B. end...divisive
   C. overcome...unattractive D. extend...satisfactory
   E. resolve...acceptable

9. Because King Philip's desire to make Spain the dominant power in 16th-century Europe ran counter to Queen Elizabeth's insistence on autonomy for England, ________ was ________.

   A. cooperation...assured B. warfare...avoidable

C. ruin…impossible D. conflict…inevitable

E. diplomacy…simple

10. Confident that her own political platform would ________ at election time, the mayor considered her opponent's sudden popularity less a threat than ________.

A. collapse…a blessing B. strengthen…a support

C. prevail…a distraction D. alter…an error

E. shake…a diversion

Part 2 Idioms, Proverbs and Sayings

Directions: The following are idioms, proverbs or sayings by famous people about money. Choose what you think is correct and compare with the right ones.

1. Before gold, even ________ take off their hats. (proverb)

A. presidents B. billionaires C. kings D. emperors

2. Money makes the ________ go. (proverb)

A. rich B. poor C. mare D. ghost

3. Money is not everything, but without money, everything is ________. (proverb)

A. something B. everything C. anything D. nothing

4. I would rather have my people ________ my economies than weep for my extravagance. (Oscar II)

A. laugh at B. smile at C. shout at D. sneer at

5. If rich, it is easy enough to conceal our ________, but, if poor, it is not so easy to conceal our poverty. (Charles C. Colton)

A. money B. wealth C. ignorance D. prejudice

6. Don't tell me where your priorities are. Show me ________ you spend your money and I'll tell you what they are. (James W. Frick)

A. when B. what C. why D. where

7. ________ spend your money before you have earned it. (Thomas Jefferson)

A. Always B. Frequently C. Rarely D. Never

8. There is only one thing to do for a man who is married to a woman who enjoys spending money, and that is to ________ earning it. (Edgar Watson Howe)

A. hate B. enjoy C. protest D. constitute

9. One must ________, in life, between making money and spending it. There's no time to do both. (Edouard Bourdet)

A. tolerate B. outweigh C. choose D. confine

10. Old men are always advising young men to save money. That is bad advice. Don't save every nickel. ________ in yourself. I never saved a dollar until I was forty years old. (Henry Ford)

A. Invest B. Stimulate C. Rally D. Systemize

Part 3 Reading Passages

Section A Breaking the Cycle of Borrowing Money and Paying Interest

For the first fifteen years of my adult life, I borrowed money for every major purchase. Three years ago, I decided to stop borrowing money and get out of debt. As you can imagine, going from a 'borrower' to a 'non-borrower' (Is that a word?) can be a difficult process. Here's how I did it.

1. I created two lists. List A was a list of my monthly expenses—by priority. List B was a list of monthly income. I realized, after making the lists, that I could live without using a credit card or borrowing money, but only if I reduced the number of items in list A.

2. After establishing the fact that I COULD live without borrowing money, I then created a plan to insure that I WOULD live without borrowing money. So, I took the numbers from List A and List B and created a monthly budget.

3. Once the budget had been created, I began to look for additional ways to reduce debt and increase savings. I quickly established an emergency fund of \$1000. Throughout the ensuing debt reduction process, I always maintained an emergency fund balance between \$800 and \$2000. The emergency fund served as my new 'credit card'. When an unexpected expense reared its ugly head—I would dip into my emergency fund, deal with the expense, and move forward.

4. After creating the budget and establishing the emergency fund, I began to attack my debts. I used the debt snowball and in less than 10 months, I was debt free.

Now, if you've made it this far, you'll note that these four steps cover the 'financial side' of the process. But, what about the 'personal side'? What changes took place, internally? How did a compulsive borrower become a competent saver?

1. I began to consider the long-term ramifications of my spending/borrowing habits. I found a few online calculators and calculated how much money I was paying in interest—and how much money I was 'losing' by not contributing to my retirement accounts. Seeing these

calculations had a profound effect—emotionally and psychologically.

2. After realizing that 'something' had to be done—I sat down with my wife and we talked about what we wanted out of life. We both realized that we had 'everything' we wanted—except for financial security. We dedicated ourselves to a life of saving and frugality.

3. I did not cut-up my credit cards or freeze them in the freezer or hide them in a sock drawer. I simply left them in my wallet—and refused to use them. I made up my mind that I would be different. Also, I made a promise to myself (and my readers) that I would do my level best to live without borrowing money. Making this promise 'changed' me.

4. Instead of hiding my struggles, I began to seek the advice and council of money-smart folks. I asked questions and I listened to answers. Admitting my failures allowed me the freedom to accept constructive criticism. By the way—most successful people are happy to share their methods, opinions, and time. All I really had to do was ask.

Getting out of debt feels great. Living debt free feels even better. But, the entire process started when I made some 'financial' AND 'personal' changes. Instead of continuing the same behaviors—and foolishly anticipating different results—I radically changed my lifestyle—and enthusiastically anticipated progress.

(572 words, taken from *http://www.ncnblog.com/2008/02/28/ by NCN.*)

I. Reading Comprehension

Questions 1-8

Directions: Choose the best answer to each question according to the passage.

1. After the author created his monthly expenses and income lists, he ________.
   A. realized that it was possible for him to stop being a money borrower.
   B. realized that he couldn't live without a credit card.
   C. still borrowed a large amount of money for some of his major purchases.
   D. thought that he couldn't reduce his want list because it could be a difficult process.
2. What is the function of the emergency fund created by the author?
   A. To pay his debts
   B. To pay his monthly expenses
   C. To increase savings
   D. To serve as a credit card and cover unexpected expenses
3. The word "reared" in Paragraph 4 is closest in meaning to ________.
   A. tossed B. rose C. scorned D. shook
4. The word "frugality" in Paragraph 8 most probably means ________.
   A. poverty B. density C. economy D. indulgence
5. What attitude does the author's wife hold toward his plan to stop borrowing money from people?
   A. supportive B. indifferent C. ambivalent D. opposed
6. Which of the following statements is NOT a reason for the author's seeking suggestions

from money-smart people?

A. He was open to constructive criticism.

B. What he needed to do was to ask and it was not hard.

C. They would create a monthly budget for him.

D. Most money-smart people are ready to share their good ideas.

7. The word "constructive" in Paragraph 10 is closest in meaning to ________.

A. poor B. dense C. economic D. helpful

8. The word "radically" in Paragraph 11 is closest in meaning to ________.

A. fundamentally B. gradually C. swiftly D. temporarily

9. Directions: Look at the four squares [■] marked A, B, C and D in **Paragraphs 8-9** that indicate where the following sentence can be added. Where do you think the sentence **"Instead of 'removing' the temptation, I faced it head-on."** would best fit?

After realizing that 'something' had to be done—I sat down with my wife and we talked about what we wanted out of life. We both realized that we had 'everything' we wanted—except for financial security. A■We dedicated ourselves to a life of saving and frugality. B■

I did not cut-up my credit cards or freeze them in the freezer or hide them in a sock drawer. I simply left them in my wallet—and refused to use them. I made up my mind that I would be different. C■Also, I made a promise to myself (and my readers) that I would do my level best to live without borrowing money. Making this promise 'changed' me. D■

10. Directions: Complete the table below by indicating which of the answer choices go to the "financial side" of the author's transformation process and which go to the "personal side" of the process.

Financial Side	Personal Side
●	●
●	●
●	●

Answer Choices

A. creating an emergency fund

B. talking with his wife about what they really wanted in life

C. making a promise that he would live without borrowing money

D. paying off all his debts

E. hiding his credit cards

F. making a monthly budget

G. asking money-smart people for suggestions

II. Vocabulary

Directions: Fill in each blank with an appropriate word from the box below. Change the form where necessary. Each word can be used only once.

priority	budget	ensuing	rear	compulsive
ramification	frugality	constructive	radically	anticipate

1. China's 12th Five-Year Plan gives strategic __________ to boosting the tertiary industry for industrial restructuring and upgrading.
2. The stock investors should be fully educated on how the processes work, and what the potential __________ are.
3. The first priority for the EU now is to balance its __________, pay off its debt, resume growth and improve international competitiveness.
4. For the first time in two years, there seems to be movement, or at least a __________ dialogue in the Six-Party Talks.
5. Professionals must realize that the job will never be exactly as you expect and that if you __________ the challenges ahead, your transition into the new organization can be much smoother.
6. The bursting of the real estate bubble and the __________ credit crisis forced American consumers to do something that they had little experience in trying: reduce their debt.
7. There's no need for the central government to change its existing domestic policies __________ to respond to the worsening EU debt crisis as long as the country's rate of GDP growth remains above 7 percent.
8. Some famous hospitals have opened rehabilitation centres for children suffering from Internet Addiction Disorder (IAD), the __________ use of the Internet.
9. It's reported that the Obama Administration will take some measures if race and religion __________ their heads in America.
10. Many Chinese enterprises do not want to become luxury brands, since luxury is not a positive word in Chinese culture, as __________ is advocated.

III. Discussion

Directions: Discuss what money can buy and what money can not buy and find the proper words to fill in the blanks.

1. Money can buy exquisite books but can't buy ______________.
2. Money can buy numerous certificates but can't buy ______________.
3. Money can buy excellent cosmetics but can't buy ______________.
4. Money can buy expensive medicine but can't buy ______________.
5. Money can buy passionate sex but can't buy true ______________.
6. Money can buy luxurious houses but can't buy a cozy ______________.

Section B Needing and Wanting Are Different

"Mom, can I have some money?" Those are the words my mother used to hear all the time. In return, I heard, "Why don't you get a job? Not to make me happy, but so that you have your own money and gain a bit more responsibility." So last year I got a job with Montgomery Ward's photo studio, working about 25 hours a week. For $5 an hour, I was a telephone salesman, trying to persuade people to come in for a free photograph.

All this was during football season and I was on the team as a kicker. To do football and homework and my job at the same time became really hard. I was burning out, falling asleep at school, not able to concentrate. My first class was physics and I hated it. I'd just sit there with my hand on my cheek and my elbow on the desk, and start dozing. One day the teacher asked my partner what I was doing and she said, "Oh, he's sleeping." The teacher came to the back of the class and stared at me. The whole class looked at me for about two minutes and laughed.

My third-period history teacher was really concerned. She was cool. A lot of times, I'd fall asleep in her class. She'd scream, "Wake up!" and slam her hand on my desk. I'd open my eyes for about two minutes, pay attention and go back to sleep. She asked me if I could handle school, football and work. I said, "Yeah. I'm doing OK so far." She said, "Why? Why all this?"

I told her it was for the things I need, when actually it was for the things that I wanted. Needing and wanting are different. Needing something is like your only shoes have holes in them. But when a new pair of sneakers came out and I liked them, I'd get them. My parents didn't feel it was right, but they said, "It's your money. You learn to deal with it." Within two years I had bought 30 pairs. My parents would laugh. "You got your job, you got your money—but where's your money now?" They didn't realize how much my job was hurting my schoolwork.

My priorities were screwed up. On a typical night I did about an hour of homework. A lot of times it was hard for me to make decisions: do I want to be at work or do I want to be at practice? Do I want to worry about what I'll have today or what I'll have in the future? One week in the winter I had to work extra days, so I missed a basketball game and two practices. (I'm on that team, too.) When a substitution opportunity came at the next game, the coach looked at me and said, "OK, we're running 1-5," a new play they had developed during the practices I had missed. I told him I didn't know it, so he told me to sit back down. I felt really bad, because there was my chance to play and I couldn't.

I really did resent work. If I hadn't been so greedy, I could have been at practice. But I kept working, and the job did help me in some ways. When you have a lot of responsibilities, you have to learn how to balance everything. You just grow up faster. At home, your parents always say, "I pay the bills so while you're here you're under my rules." But now with my money I say, "No, no no. You didn't pay for that, I did. That's mine."

Slowly, I've come to deal with managing money a lot better. At first, as soon as I had money, it was gone. Now it goes straight into my bank account. This year I decided not to work at all during football season. I have a lot more time to spend with other players after the game and feel more a part of the team. I've only fallen asleep in class once so far. I'm more confident and more involved in the classes. My marks are A's and B's, a full grade better than this time last year. I'm hoping that will help me get into a better college. I don't go shopping as much. I look at the sneakers in school and think, "I could have those," but I don't need them. Last year I thought that being mature meant doing everything. But I'm learning that part of growing up is limiting yourself, knowing how to decide what's important, and what isn't.

(769 words, taken from *Newsweek*, Nov. 16, 1992 by Jimmy Carrasquillo)

I. Reading Comprehension

*Directions: Choose the best answer to **Questions 1-8** according to the passage.*

1. Why did the author take the job with a photo studio?
   A. Because he was eager to earn some money by himself.
   B. Because he was tired of asking his mother for money.
   C. Because his mother wanted him to earn some money to learn to take on responsibilities.
   D. Because his mother would be happier to see him work.
2. According to the passage, all of the following statements are true of the author after he took the job EXCEPT that ________.
   A. he couldn't concentrate well and fell asleep in class
   B. he could manage well to do his job, homework, and football at the same time
   C. his job exerted some negative influence on his schoolwork
   D. his history teacher was concerned about him and had a talk with him
3. The phrase "burning out" in Paragraph 2 is closest in meaning to ________.
   A. exhausted B. detected C. excited D. intrigued
4. The word "slam" in Paragraph 3 is closest in meaning to ________.
   A. pat softly B. touch softly C. push violently D. hit forcefully
5. What's the purpose of the author to mention the sneakers in Paragraph 4?
   A. To prove it worthwhile to keep himself busy working and studying at the same time
   B. To show off the sneakers he bought
   C. To give an example of the things he wanted but not needed
   D. To give an example of the things he needed but not wanted
6. The phrase "screwed up" in Paragraph 5 is closest in meaning to ________.
   A. inspired B. forgotten C. cherished D. ruined
7. The word "resent" in Paragraph 6 is closest in meaning to ________.
   A. appreciate B. hate C. anticipate D. enjoy
8. From taking on a job, the author learned to ________.

A. limit his desires and know about his priorities

B. manage his money the way his parents did

C. get straight A's for all the courses he took at school

D. be more generous with money

9. Directions: Look at the four squares [■] marked A, B, C and D and decide where the sentence **"Sometimes I felt there was no right choice."** can be added in Paragraph 5 and would best fit.

My priorities were screwed up. A■On a typical night I did about an hour of homework. A lot of times it was hard for me to make decisions: do I want to be at work or do I want to be at practice? Do I want to worry about what I'll have today or what I'll have in the future? B■One week in the winter I had to work extra days, so I missed a basketball game and two practices. (I'm on that team, too.) When a substitution opportunity came at the next game, the coach looked at me and said, "OK, we're running 1-5," a new play they had developed during the practices I had missed. C■I told him I didn't know it, so he told me to sit back down. I felt really bad, because there was my chance to play and I couldn't. D■

10. Directions: An introductory sentence for a brief summary of the passage is provided below. Complete the summary by selecting the THREE answer choices that express the most important ideas in the passage. Some sentences do not belong to the summary because they express ideas that are not presented in the passage or are minor ideas in the passage.

The author decided to take a part-time job and attended school at the same time.

Answer Choice

A. He was so greedy he bought 30 pairs of sneakers with the money he earned.

B. Gradually from the job he learned to take responsibilities and started to mature faster.

C. Finally he realized that being mature meant doing everything.

D. Although at first the part-time job interfered with his schoolwork a lot, he kept doing it.

E. He also realized that being mature meant controlling his desire and being able to distinguish what is important from what is not in his life.

Part 4 Reading Comprehension Test

Directions: Read the 4 passages below and choose the best answer to each question.

Passage 1 No Free Rides, Kid

Christabel Lee was 12 years old and had just saved up $90 for a new bicycle when her wallet disappeared with all her cash in it. She asked her parents if they would buy the bike for her, but they refused. It's not that they couldn't afford to help. Lee's father is vice chairman of a major Hong Kong conglomerate; her family is rich. Lee, now 36 and the managing director of a printing company, remembers crying about the injustice of it all. But today, she recognizes that she gleaned a valuable lesson from the incident: money does not necessarily grow on family trees. "[My dad] instilled strict financial discipline on us when we were young," she says. "It taught me that it's good to plan and save, and that no one's going to come save you if you screw up."

Lee's experience shows how one family answered a common question facing wealthy (and some not-so-wealthy) parents: When children grow up amid plenty, how can they be taught to be sensible about money? We're not talking about checkbook-balancing skills. There is a plethora of practical advice for that, just as there's no shortage of guidance when it comes to transferring assets from one generation to the next. Harder to come by is advice for parents on how to bequeath to their children not just a fat inheritance, but also the values and work ethic that produced their nest eggs in the first place. "So many wealthy families don't know anything about raising kids in a healthy environment," says Thayer Willis, author of *Navigating the Dark Side of Wealth: A Life Guide for Inheritors*. The daughter of multimillion-dollar parents herself, Willis says she was a "spoiled brat" in her youth. She quit jobs whenever things didn't go her way and spent money without limits—until she realized this was not the path to a satisfying existence. "Outsiders think, 'If I just had financial wealth, life would be so easy and I would be happy,'" says Willis, who now counsels wealthy families. "But none of us is given a meaningful life. We're meant to build a meaningful life."

Of course, the children of wealthy parents don't always grow up to be self-indulgent, feckless adults, just as deprived children don't always become driven overachievers. But literature and media are stuffed with rich-kids-gone-bad stories, and there's plenty of anecdotal evidence that cosseted offspring can lack the thrift, independence, ambition, persistence and entrepreneurial spirit that contributed to their parents' success. Most people have heard of the "shirtsleeves to shirtsleeves" curse, which holds that family wealth, once accumulated, is typically dissipated by the third generation because trust-fund babies, having little regard for the money that has come to them without toil, lack the motivation to strive. It's a worry even to—perhaps especially to—the superrich. In a recent interview in London's *Sunday Times* newspaper, Indian-born steel tycoon Lakshmi Mittal said flatly that "money is a curse," and that he was concerned that extreme wealth might be spoiling his young kids. In June, Microsoft founder Bill Gates reiterated that he would donate most of his $58 billion to charity, rather than give it to his three children. That's tough love.

According to Willis, money alone isn't the problem. Rather, it's that kids in wealthy families often are given too much freedom, which leads to a sense of entitlement and a lack of accountability. Underlying the selfishness is insecurity, say Jon and Eileen Gallo, co-authors of the book *Silver Spoon Kids: How Successful Parents Raise Responsible Children*. "They grow up worried inside, thinking, 'Do people like me for who I am?'" says Jon. "It's about developing an identity of their own that's separate from their parents and their parents' money." Being born into wealth often means having a nanny, maid, driver and bank trust officer—in other words, having a staff of people to solve all of your problems. "Sometimes very wealthy parents use money to fill in potholes in the roads so that kids don't have to deal with problems," says Jon. "But dealing with the potholes is how you learn about life."

Parents don't have to be child psychologists to help their kids become responsible adults. Some common parenting set pieces can lay a good foundation. In homes with nearly limitless assets, the challenge is to create limits, so that children can learn that money is something to be earned and husbanded. One of the first steps parents should take is setting up an allowance for kids as soon as they start school, according to the Gallos. "The purpose [of an allowance] is to learn how to budget, to be able to plan for things to buy—to postpone gratification," says Eileen. When the kids reach high school, parents may want to introduce debt into their financial vocabularies by allowing them to use credit cards. But the Gallos recommend training wheels first, in the form of debit cards or cards with a low spending limit.

(830 words, taken from *Time*, Nov 13, 2008 by Ling Woo Liu)

1. From the incident, Chirstabel Lee learned all of the following from her parents EXCEPT that ________.
   A. if she messed things up, nobody would save her but herself
   B. she needed to plan and save.
   C. she could always turn to her parents for help in case of trouble.
   D. money doesn't grow on family trees.
2. When did Willis decide not to be a "spoiled brat" any more?
   A. When she realized that many rich families don't know how to raise kids in a healthy environment
   B. When she realized that she didn't spend money sensibly and wanted to live a meaningful life
   C. When things didn't go her way
   D. When her parents urged her to live a satisfying life

3. Why did Lakshmi Mittal say straightly that "money is a curse"?
   A. Because he believed all rich kids would go bad.
   B. Because he was worried that his great fortune might do harm to his children.
   C. Because he wanted to donate his money to charity.
   D. Because he thought money was the root of all evil.
4. The word "husbanded" in Line 4 of Paragraph 5 is closest in meaning to ________.
   A. withdrawn B. deposited carefully
   C. loved D. spent economically
5. Look at the four squares [■] marked A, B, C and D and decide where the sentence **"It is not a birthright that they are free to squander at will."** can be added in paragraph 5 and would best fit.

   Parents don't have to be child psychologists to help their kids become responsible adults. Some common parenting set pieces can lay a good foundation. A■In homes with nearly limitless assets, the challenge is to create limits, so that children can learn that money is something to be earned and husbanded. B■One of the first steps parents should take is setting up an allowance for kids as soon as they start school, according to the Gallos. C■ "The purpose [of an allowance] is to learn how to budget, to be able to plan for things to buy—to postpone gratification," says Eileen. When the kids reach high school, parents may want to introduce debt into their financial vocabularies by allowing them to use credit cards. But the Gallos recommend training wheels first, in the form of debit cards or cards with a low spending limit. D■
6. An introductory sentence for a brief summary of the passage is provided below. Complete the summary by selecting the THREE answer choices that express the most important ideas in the passage. Some sentences do not belong in the summary because they express ideas that are not presented in the passage or are minor ideas in the passage.

   Many wealthy families are worried that their kids might be spoiled but have no idea how to raise their kids in a healthy environment.

   Answer Choice

   A. Many rich kids usually enjoy too much freedom, lack accountability, and don't have to deal with problems to learn about life.
   B. Rich parents often lack guidance on how to pass their wealth to their kids.
   C. It is advised that rich parents should start with giving their kids allowances to help their kids learn to manage money and to be responsible.
   D. Rich parents should allow their kids to use credit cards on their own freely.
   E. Wealthy parents should teach their kids values and work ethic which contribute to success.

Passage 2 How to Reach Teens in a Recession? Ask Aéropostale

Can a recession actually cause teenage daughters and their moms to shop peacefully together at the mall? Believe it or not, yes. At a New York City shopping center one recent June evening, Adina Armstrong, 13, and her mother Tracy sauntered out of teen retailer Aéropostale, Adina cheerily chirping away on her cell phone, Tracy happily holding a bag full of T shirts. Mom just got Adina two stylish shirts through a buy-one, get-one-free promotion. "What I like about Aéropostale is that when they have a sale, they have a sale," says Tracy. Even better, Adina actually approves of the inexpensive clothes—"They're popular, hip, and fit really well," she says. After Adina explains all this, she goes back to talking on her phone.

Teen retailers, once thought recession-proof, have suffered in this downturn. For example, Abercrombie & Fitch, which has maintained its premium price points, saw same-store sales dip an incredible 28% in May. But amid such carnage, two stores stand out. Buckle, a Nebraska-based retailer that offers a wide range of brand-name selections at its 393 stores across the country, saw first-quarter profits jump 43.5%. Then there's Aéropostale, which targets 14-to-17-year-old boys and girls and operates more than 900 locations in 47 states. Same-stores sales increased 11% in the first quarter, and the company's first-quarter profits rose an eye-popping 81%, to $31.5 million, as it continues to steal share from Abercrombie & Fitch, American Eagle Outfitters and other more upscale chains. In fact, in 9 of the past 11 quarters, the company's profits grew by better than 30%.

Buckle benefits from geography (many of its stores are located in small Midwestern locations with little competition), and the company is relatively underexposed to crashing economies like Florida's and Southern California's. Aéropostale has won because of price. So if teens are shopping at cheaper places or permitting their parents to buy clothes from these outlets, does that mean teens, like, get it? Are they fully aware that their summer-job prospects are dim, that their parents' employment prospects may be dimmer and that it's unfair to guilt Mom and Dad into spending money on expensive clothes? Are kids these days actually acting responsibly? "More than ever, we're seeing that teens are responding to value," says Jeffrey Klinefelter, an equity-research analyst at Piper Jaffray who has written a semiannual research report, "Taking Stock in Teens," for the past eight years. "They seem to be taking on some personal responsibility and discipline in spending money."

According to Klinefelter's research, teens are making fewer trips to the store; teen spending on fashion products fell 13% this spring. Only 35% of the teens Piper Jaffray surveyed had part-time work this spring, compared with 50% four years ago. "Teens definitely have much greater awareness of what's going on around them now than they did eight years ago," says Klinefelter. "They're seeing the news on their computers and cell phones, and are very aware that we're in a recession."

If today's teenagers are indeed spending more responsibly, how long can this attitude last? While retail analysts repeatedly claim that adults will never again consume like they did in prior years, they don't make the same claim about kids. Klinefelter says there's plenty of pent-up demand in the teen sector. Yes, teens aren't spending because of the recession, but that's also because retailers have failed to create a hot new trend. Denim has been the default teen look for the past few years, and nothing has knocked it off its perch. "Once the dominant new fashion trend emerges, teens will rush back out to the stores," says Klinefelter. "The resurgences will require some economic relief, but the segment will make a comeback."

Klinefelter predicts teens will start spending at high levels again in six months to a year. So before then, enjoy the sight of young shoppers scouring for discounts. Teens won't stay thrifty forever. Down economy or not, they're still teens.

(654 words, taken from *Time*, June 21, 2009 by Sean Gregory.)

7. What does Adina mean when she says "when they have a sale, they have a sale." in Paragraph 1?
   A. Adina would go to the sale whenever there is one.
   B. Whenever Adina wants something, they would have a sale.
   C. Aéropostale really offers cheap promotional items during a sale.
   D. Other retailers are all cheating their customers on sales.
8. The word "eye-popping" in Paragraph 2 is closest in meaning to ________.
   A. artificial B. imaginary C. amazing D. proportional
9. Which of the following factors is the key to Aéropostale's outdoing many other retailers in sales?
   A. Price B. A wide range of brand-name selections
   C. Pleasant shopping environment D. Good services
10. The following are all the findings of Klinefelter's research EXCEPT that ________.
    A. teenagers spend less on fashionable goods than before
    B. teenagers go to the store less frequently than before
    C. teenagers are more aware of what is happening around them than before
    D. more teenagers have part-time jobs than 4 years ago
11. Why is denim mentioned in Paragraph 5?
    A. To illustrate that teenagers are living more frugally than before.
    B. To illustrate that retailers are unable to create a dominant new fashion trend.
    C. To illustrate that the recession still exerts great impact on people's life.
    D. To argue that it will lead to the emergence of a new trend soon.
12. It can be inferred from the passage that ________.
    A. teenagers will continue to spend money reasonably even though there will be some economic relief in six months to a year.
    B. teenagers don't care about fashion at all in the recession.
    C. teenagers won't be too concerned about the recession and be thrifty for a very long time because they are just teenagers.
    D. teenagers haven't displayed much self-restraint when they are shopping.

13. What is the main idea of this passage?

A. Today's teenagers are spending money more reasonably because of the recession.

B. In the recession retailers Aéropostale and American Eagle Outfitters stand out in sales.

C. Nowadays teenagers love to go shopping with their parents.

D. Parents want their teens to continue to take on responsibility and discipline in spending money after the recession.

Passage 3 Why Has Everything Become a Costly Milestone Event?

The average Briton spends about £500 on four milestone celebrations a year, from "baby showers" to 30th birthdays to ruby wedding anniversaries. But why have people started celebrating everything so lavishly?

It is a truth universally acknowledged that weddings cost the earth. And they are not just expensive for the bride and groom and their parents. From the hen party in Brighton, to the new frock and the department store gift, guests are also forking out a fortune. But what about all those other rites of passage and affirmations—the christenings, the 60th birthdays and the silver wedding anniversaries? And they are just the traditional events. Money is also being spent on baby showers, 16th birthday parties and school proms (formerly known as the end-of-exams disco).

There are plenty of wildly extravagant tales reported in the newspapers, such as Topshop boss Philip Green spending £4 million on a three-day bar mitzvah celebration for his teenage son, and Elton John wearing a £73,000 Louis XIV costume for his 50th birthday party. This still represents an unusual level of effort for a birthday. Gone are the small gatherings at home and cheap keepsakes such as the 21st key to the door. Even granny's 80th birthday is more likely to be held in a posh hotel with guests travelling half around the world to be there, with everyone pitching in to buy her a cruise around the Mediterranean.

A survey by NS&I Savings suggests Britons attend on average four milestone events each year, spending £120 on each one. Almost a third said they were worried about the cost, while 50% believed such celebrations had become increasingly expensive. Cultural historian Christopher Cook says the fundamental change is that these celebrations used to be family affairs, private and inward-looking. "Now they have become huge public events. And this seems to have marched step in step with an increasing affluence and emergence of a consumer-led society".

He traces it back to the 1980s, or the "me generation" as he calls it, when "for the first time in British society, people thought money was intrinsically good". Essentially people started flashing their cash as "spending money demonstrated one's status, worth and value", he adds. Certainly there were big society parties in the 1920s and 1930s, he says, but they were the preserve of the ruling classes. The trend for huge celebrations has "extended socially from middle and top down to bottom" and "now we all expect these events to be big and lavish". He believes the growth of the celebrity has also encouraged people to splash out on milestone events. "It gives you the opportunity to become as near a celebrity as you can in your own life."

Cook does not throw the blame across the Atlantic and says Britain has developed its own distinct style of showing off. But there can be no doubt that some of the more recent milestones—baby showers, 16th birthdays and proms—have been inspired by America. The 16-year-olds of bygone years used to celebrate finishing their exams with a disco in the assembly hall, drinking weak orange cordial and eating stale crisps, while dancing along to the tape recorder or gramophone in the corner. Now it's all about spray tans, big dresses, even bigger hair and 16-seater limousines. Nine out of 10 secondary schools in Essex will reportedly be hosting a prom or graduation ceremony for their students in the next six weeks.

Justine Roberts from Mumsnet says the growing popularity of proms and 16th birthday parties is down to US TV shows such as My Super Sweet 16, Prom Queen and High School Musical.

Baby showers are also an American import, she says, and they split the parents who use her website. "Some people think it is a nice way to mark a new beginning, while others think it's too commercial and don't like the idea of inviting a load of people around and demanding a gift. "There's nothing wrong with these events in themselves but they are just another way of getting us to spend a lot of money. And in these cash-strapped times, there is a lot of pressure on families." Most people love a bit of a party, but does it need to have such grandeur?

(711 words, taken from *BBC News Magazine*, June 20, 2011 by Caroline McClatchey)

14. The phrase "cost the earth" in Paragraph 2 is closest in meaning to ________.

A. devalue B. soar in expenses C. are very expensive D. inflate

15. Why does the author mention "baby shower, 16th birthday parties and school proms" in Paragraph 2?

A. To give examples of non-traditional events on which people spend much money

B. To give examples of traditional events on which people spend much money

C. To illustrate that parents are spending a fortune for their kids

D. To blame today's teenagers for being too wasteful

16 Look at the four squares [■] marked A, B, C and D and decide where the sentence "**But it is not just tycoons and celebrities who are pulling out all the stops.**" can be added in Paragraph 3 and would best fit.

A■There are plenty of wildly extravagant tales reported in the newspapers, such as Topshop boss Philip Green spending £4m on a three-day bar mitzvah celebration for his teenage son, and Elton John wearing a £73,000 Louis XIV costume for his 50th birthday party. B■This still represents an unusual level of effort for a birthday. C■Gone are the small gatherings at home and cheap keepsakes such as the 21st key to the door. D■Even granny's 80th birthday is more likely to be held in a posh hotel with guests travelling half around the world to be there, with everyone pitching in to buy her a cruise around the

Mediterranean.

17. According to Christopher Cook, what was the basic change that the Britons' celebrations went through?
    A. The celebrations turned from family affairs to public events.
    B. The celebrations turned to be more inward-looking.
    C. The celebrations made people start to think money was intrinsically good.
    D. The celebrations became increasingly meaningful.
18. According to Christopher Cook, which of the following is NOT a contributing factor to the phenomenon that people started to spend more money than before in the 1980s?
    A. The growth of the celebrity
    B. The belief that the way people spend money indicated their status, worth and value
    C. The emergence of a consumer-led society
    D. Britain style of showing off.
19. Why does the author think that America should be partially responsible for Briton's increasingly lavish celebrations?
    A. America has developed its own unique way of showing off.
    B. Americans convinced Britons of spending money generously on celebrations.
    C. Britons want to be close to Americans in every possible way in their life.
    D. Some recent milestones events in Britain were inspired by America.
20. Which of the following statements sums up the main idea of the passage?
    A. Britons have started to celebrate events lavishly and there are several contributing reasons.
    B. American cultural invasion is serious in Britain.
    C. Celebrities play a major role in encouraging people to spend a lot of money on celebrations.
    D. Britons have developed their distinct ways to show off their wealth.

Passage 4 The Smell of Money

For many years large supermarkets have been encouraging us to spend money by pumping the smell of freshly-baked bread into their stores. Now Dale Air, a leading firm of aroma consultants, has been approached by Barclay'S Bank to develop suitable artificial smells for their banks. Researchers have suggested surrounding customers with the "smell of money" will encourage them to feel relaxed and optimistic and give them added confidence in the bank's security and professionalism.

But before a smell can be manufactured and introduced into bank's air conditioning systems, it must be identified and chemically analyzed, and this has proved to be difficult. The problem is that banknotes and coins tend to pick up the smell of their surroundings. So cash that has been sitting in a cash register at a fishmonger's will smell of fish, and banknotes used to pay for meals in restaurants will tend to smell of food.

It may be a challenge, but aroma experts have little doubt that the use of artificial smells can be an effective form of subconscious advertising. Lunn Poly, a British travel company, introduced the smell of coconuts into its travel agencies and saw a big increase in spending by holiday makers. Many cafes now have electric dispensers that release the smell of freshly roasted coffee near their entrances, subtly encouraging customers to come in and have a drink or snack. Even prestigious car maker Rolls-Royce has been spraying the inside of its cars to enhance the smell of the leather seats.

"The sense of smell is probably the most basic and primitive of all human senses." explains researcher Jim O'Riordan. "There is a direct pathway from the olfactory organs in the nose to the brain. "It is certainly true that most people find certain smells incredibly strong, stirring memories and feelings in a way that few other stimulants can rival. It is a phenomenon marketing consultants have long recognized, but until recently have been unable to harness. "We've made great progress but the technology of odor production is still in its infancy," says o'Riordan, "Who knows where it will take us."

(374 words)

21. Which of the following places has a long history of using smells in business?
   A. Restaurants B. Barclay's Bank C. Supermarkets D. fish markets
22. According to the researchers, adopting artificial smells in banks will encourage customers ________.
   A. to be more friendly to the bank staff B. to have more confidence in banks
   C. to spend more time in banks D. to deposit more money in banks
23. Why did the author mention fish in the second paragraph?
   A. To illustrate that money will pick up smells of the surrounding.
   B. To explain the process of analyzing the smell of money.
   C. To prove that adopting smells in banks will not be effective.
   D. To prove that introducing smells in the restaurant works well.
24. It can be inferred from the last paragraph that ________.
   A. just until recently did people start to find out about the use of artificial smells
   B. the technology to produce artificial smells is far from mature
   C. some customers dislike the use of aromas in public places
   D. researchers think using aromas will turn out to be a disaster in the end
25. What does the passage mainly discuss?
   A. The use of smells has the capacity to influence customers in a subtle way
   B. Smell is the most basic and primitive of all human senses
   C. Supermarkets encourage its customers to spend money by using smells
   D. Researchers recommend banks to surround customers with the money smell

Unit 4

Time and Punctuality

Part 1 Reading Skills

Section A Guessing Unknown Words from Word Formation I

Besides context clues, some knowledge about word formation will also contribute to the understanding of unfamiliar words or familiar words but with different meanings, thus improving reading comprehension.

In English, there are several ways to form new words based on other words or morphemes, among which the most important are clipping, blending, conversion compounding, affixation, etc.

Clipping is a type of word formation by which words are formed by deleting parts of the base words, for example, *ad* for advertisement, *lab* for laboratory, *chute* for parachute, *quake* for earthquake, *biz* for business.

Blending is a combination of parts of different words, such as *smog* (smoke + fog), *motel* (motor + hotel), *infoport* (information + airport), *sitcom* (situation + comedy), *netizen* (internet + citizen).

Conversion is to assign an already existing word to a new word class (part of speech). The knowledge of one word will help you to define the same word which is of a different part of speech. For example the word "down" is commonly used as an adverb or preposition. When it is used as a verb like in "Without saying a word, the man *downed* a glass of beer" it is not difficult to infer that it may mean "drink down".

Compounding is the process of combining two or more words to create a new word with a meaning of the sum of the parts. Compounds are written sometimes as one word like *rainfall*, *fingerprint*; sometimes as two or more hyphenated words such as *passer-by*, *weather-beaten chief-in-editor*; and sometimes as two separate words, for example, *heart attack*, *movie star*. However, sometimes a compound word is not just the sum of the meaning of two words. For example, "black market" means "illegal selling and buying" rather than "a market which is black in colour".

Affixation is the process of forming a new word by adding a morpheme (or an affix) to an already existing word. Affixes which are placed before the stem of a word are called prefixes, and those that follow are referred to as suffixes. Usually prefixes alter the meaning of the words while suffixes tend to change the parts of speech. Since affixation is the most frequently used way to form new words, it will be discussed in more details in this book. This unit will deal with prefixation and suffixation will follow up in the next unit.

1. Prefix

A prefix is a letter or a group of letters attached to the beginning of a word that partly indicates its meaning. Understanding the meanings of the common prefixes can help you deduce the meanings of new words you come across while reading.

There are more than 50 prefixes in English. The most frequently used prefixes will be listed below according to its meaning.

1) Prefixes used to give a negative or opposite meaning

Prefix	Meaning	Examples
un-	negation or opposite	unsociable, uncertainty, undo, uncover
dis-	negation or opposite	dissatisfied, disorder, disarm, distract
non-	negation or opposite	non-aggressive, non-violence, non-claim
im-	negation or opposite	imbalance, immoral, impartial, impolite
in-	negation or opposite	inaccurate, incorrect, indirect, inefficient
il-	negation or opposite	illegal, illiterate, illogical, illiteracy
ir-	negation or opposite	irregular, irresponsible, irrelevant
anti-	opposite or against	antipathy, anti-corruption, antiforeign
contra/o-	opposite or against	contraseasonal, controversy, contradict
counter-	opposite or against	counterpart, countermeasure, counteract

2) Prefixes indicating number

Prefix	Meaning	Examples
uni-	one	unicorn, uniform, unilateral, unilingual
mono-	one, alone, single	monocyclic, monographic, monologue
bi-	two, twice	bilateral, bilingual, bimonthly, bisexual
di-	two, twice	dialogue, diphthong, didactyl, dioxide
tri-	three	triangle, tricycle, tripod, trisect
quar-	four	quarterly, quadrangle, quadrilateral
quin/t-	five, fifth	quintuplets, quintuple, quinquennium
dec/a-	ten	decadal, decade, decameter, decagram
cent/i-	one hundred, hundredth	century, centigrade, centimeter
kilo-	thousand	kilogram, kilometer, kilolitre, kiloton
milli-	one-thousandth	millimeter, milliwatt, milligram
semi-	half	semi-circle, semi-final, semicolony
multi-	many	multicultural, multimedia, multiply
poly-	many, much	polysynthetic, polynuclear, polysyllable
re-	again	rechargeable, recollection, recycle

3) Prefixes indicating position or direction

Prefix	Meaning	Examples
over-	over, above, beyond	overflow, overbridge, overlap
up-	upwards, above	upcoming, uprising, update, upgrade
sub-	down, under, close to	subconscious, submarine, subtract
under-	below	underlined, underground, underestimate
de-	off, from, removal	devalue, degrade, derail, decentralize
in-	into	inborn, input, income, insert, inscribe
out-	outside, beyond	outdoor, outline, outgoing, outburst
ex-	out	exclusive, exclosure, exclaim, extract
en-/em-	put in or on	endanger, empower, enclose, enlarge
fore-	in front, before	forehead, forefront, forelimb, foreface
inter-	between	interpersonal, internet, interview
intra-	between, inside, within	intravenous, intra-linguistic, intramural
trans-	across	transatlantic, transaction, transplant

4) Prefixes indicating size or amount

Prefix	Meaning	Examples
micro-	small	microscope, microwave, microcopy
macro-	large, long	macroeconomics, macroscopic
mini-	small, short	miniskirt, minicab, minidisk
maxi-	large, long	maxiskirt, maximin, maxicoat
nano-	very small	nano-scale, nano-pants, nanosecond
out-	surpassing	outlive, outnumber, outstanding, outlast
over-	beyond, too much	overestimate, overcrowded, overdue
super-	over, beyond	superman, superpower, supernatural
hyper-	over, beyond	hyperactive, hypercharge, hypercriticize
extra-	beyond, more than	extraordinary, extracurricular

5) Prefixes indicating time

Prefix	Meaning	Examples
pre-	before, forward	prehistorical, precaution, prescribe
ante-	before	antecedent, antecessor, antedate
pro-	before	proactive, procreation, proclaim
fore-	beforehand, in advance	forefather, forerunner, forecast
post-	after, behind	postwar, postgraduate, postmodern
ex-	former	ex-wife, ex-president, ex-convict
neo-	new, recent, modern	neoclassical, neo-Nazi, neo-type
syn-	same time, together	synchronize, syndrome, synchronic

6) Prefixes with other meanings

Prefix	Meaning	Examples
mis-	wrong, bad	misleading, misfortune, misjudge
mal-	ill, badly	malcontent, malformation, maltreat
hetero-	different	heterosexual, heterogenetic
homo-	same	homosexual, homonym, homophone
auto-	self	automatic, autobiography, autotype
co-	with	cooperative, coauthor, coexist
com-, con-	with, together	commensurable, concur, concelebrate

Section B Practice

Directions: Read the following passage and fill in each blank with the word given in brackets, adding a suitable prefix and in its proper form.

Punctuality is one of the characteristics that 1) _________ (able) to complete a required task or fulfill an obligation before or at a previously designated time. "Punctual" is often used synonymously with "on time." It is a common 2) _________ (conception) that "punctual" can also, when talking about grammar, mean "to be accurate."

Punctuality is an important constituent of good character. A person who is always on time for his appointments shows real consideration for others while a person who is always late shows selfishness and thoughtlessness and it will bring him bad effects. For example, calling on a friend five minutes later than the appointed time may cause him some 3) _________ (expected) troubles. It also proves him to be 4) _________ (trustworthy).

According to each culture, there is often an understanding about what is considered an acceptable degree of punctuality. Usually, a small amount of lateness is acceptable; this is commonly about ten or fifteen minutes in Western cultures, but it is 5) _________ (acceptable) in such instances as doctor's appointments or school lessons. In some cultures, such as Japanese society, or in the military there basically is no allowance.

Some cultures have an 6) _________ (spoken) understanding that actual deadlines are different from stated deadlines; for example, it may be understood in a particular culture that people will turn up an hour later than advertised. In this case, since everyone understands that a 9 a.m. meeting will actually start around 10 a.m., no one is 7) _________ (convenient) when everyone turns up at 10 a.m.

In cultures which value punctuality, being late is equivalent to showing 8) _________ (respect) for another's time and may be considered insulting. In such cases, punctuality may be 9) _________ (forced) by social penalties, for example by excluding low-status latecomers from meetings entirely. Such considerations can lead on to considering the value of punctuality in econometrics and to considering the effects of 10) _________ (punctuality) on others in queueing theory.

Part 2 Idioms, Proverbs and Sayings

Directions: The following are idioms, proverbs or sayings by famous people about time. Choose what you think is correct and compare with the right ones.

1. Time and ________ waits for no man. (Proverb)
   A. money B. chance C. tide D. knowledge
2. What may be done at any time will be done at ________ time. (Proverb)
   A. any B. some C. no D. every
3. An idle youth, a ________ age. (Proverb)
   A. needy B. hard C. miserable D. regretful
4. Ordinary people merely think how they shall spend their time; a man of talent tries to ________ it. (Arthur Schopenhauer)
   A. kill B. value C. save D. use
5. To choose time is to ________ time. (Francis Bacon)
   A. value B. kill C. use D. save
6. The ________ age is before us, not behind us. (Mark Twain)
   A. golden B. silver C. valueless D. invaluable
7. Punctuality is the stern virtue of men of ________, and the graceful courtesy of princes. (Edward Bulwer Lytton)
   A. law B. business C. letters D. sports
8. Fish and visitors smell ________ days. (Benjamin Franklin)
   A. one B. two C. three D. four
9. Weep no more, no sigh, nor groan. ________ calls no time that's gone. (John Fletcher)
   A. Regret B. Sorrow C. Worry D. Fear
10. The time of life is short; to spend that shortness basely, it would be too ________. (William Shakespeare)
    A. long B. hard C. bitter D. economical

Part 3 Reading Passages

Section A Punctuality Tips and Strategies

Punctuality tips and strategies can increase the ease and speed with which we build this important character trait. Most adults understand the basic meaning of punctuality. We know that punctual people meet obligations or complete necessary tasks before a previously named time.

Punctuality involves more than that, however, and only as we see the rest of the picture can we build solid punctuality. Only by employing vital tips and strategies can we build this character trait effectively.

Who Needs These Tips and Strategies?

Punctuality is a growing need in every arena. This list contains just five of them:

- **Employers** long for greater punctuality among employees.
- **Employees** wish they could improve their punctuality quotient (PQ).
- **Parents** yearn for children and teenagers to exhibit promptness.
- **Teachers** at every level, including tertiary, want greater punctuality.
- **Speakers** want punctual audiences who do not interrupt their speaking.

If we completed the list, it would include every person on earth who was capable of understanding—because punctuality is a character trait. It is an absolute value, tied to other absolute values.

The universal need for punctuality creates a common need for these tips and strategies. We all need to teach punctuality—to ourselves first, and then to others if we are in such a position.

Teaching Yourself to Be Punctual

Teaching punctuality to the person in the mirror is vital if you aspire to be a man or woman of high moral values. It is essential, too, if you expect to teach this character trait to others. As with every character trait, you must practice what you preach. Credibility hangs on actions. An employer, teacher, or parent who is perpetually tardy, for example, will earn little more than disrespect by teaching punctuality to others.

Once you have taught yourself to be punctual, you can apply the same tips and strategies to teach punctuality to others.

Strategies and Tips

With that in mind, here are six strategies and tips that can help you:

1. Admission: Admit that you need to build punctuality. Many people think they are already punctual enough. They tell you that punctuality is relative. As long as you come within 10 minutes of the deadline, you are punctual. The same people tend to believe that driving within 10 miles above a posted speed limit is lawful. If you have always thought 10-15 minutes of tardiness is well within the limits of punctuality, you are wrong. Employ the strategy of admission. Admit that you do not exercise true punctuality. You will work to build or polish a trait only if you know you do not already possess it in polished form.

2. Respect: Tardiness is tantamount to disrespect and you must recognize it for what it is: an insult. It is a slap in the face. Your lateness says that you and your schedule are more important than the other person and his or her schedule. Some politicians, presidents, and other leaders have consciously employed lateness to send that very message: "It is right for ME to be late and keep YOU waiting because I am more important than you!" Wrong. The other person is always more important. Exercise respect for others as an incentive to punctuality. Think about the value—the worth of that other person. Make it the "carrot" that keeps you reaching out for punctuality.

3. Love: This absolute value requires doing what is best for others. This is sure to include punctuality. I cannot remember an instance in my own life when it would have been best for the other person to have me arrive late. You may disagree, but think it through to logical conclusions. Even when punctual arrivals catch others unprepared, such arrivals urge them to develop this character trait of well-mannered people. Lateness on your part often causes others to adjust schedules, which is usually less than best for them. Exercise love in the form of deadlines and appointments satisfied.

4. Responsibility: One facet of the character trait responsibility is that the task or duty often has a deadline. Johnny's responsibility to clean the classroom hamster cage during lunch hour every day has a deadline—the end of lunch hour. If Johnny has not completed it by then, he has not exercised punctuality and has not fulfilled his responsibility. Karen's responsibility to prepare 50 binders for a May 3 seminar that begins at 9 a.m. has a deadline—the seminar's scheduled time. If Karen fails to have the folders prepared by then, she has not exercised punctuality and has not fulfilled her responsibility. Remind yourself firmly that responsibility requires punctuality. Emphasize punctuality to yourself whenever you accept a responsibility. Write the deadline as part of the responsibility.

5. Self-Control: A big part of exercising punctuality is taking power over yourself. You must crack the whip over your own head. Control self's desire to put off preparation; to sleep a few more minutes; to talk to a friend a little longer; or to do one more thing before leaving for an appointment. Control self's choice of activities so that you meet deadlines. Harness your leisure time to be sure you can be punctual. Self-control is a mighty character trait, and can make the difference between being prompt and being tardy.

6. Be Realistic: Most tardiness results from willful decisions. Yes, there are accidental causes. The car pool driver may have forgotten that this was her day. Dad may have forgotten to waken you. The bus may have missed your stop. Your husband may have forgotten to set the alarm clock. More likely causes are the decisions you made. You decided to stay up late last night and had trouble getting yourself in gear. You decided to watch television for 30 minutes more instead of preparing for tomorrow morning. You decided to stop for coffee and a donut when you were already running late. You decided to work on a project you liked instead of the one that was due. Get real. Take action to make yourself punctual.

Teaching Punctuality to Others

Teaching punctuality is appropriate in nearly every setting.

Employers do not need to be told that tardiness is costly. That fact has been documented through various economic studies. Employers should institute a program that will help employees in practical ways. Give them practical tips that will help them arrive at work on time—and return from lunch breaks on time. Teach them how to structure their work to be sure deadlines are met.

Character education teachers, and indeed teachers at every level, should help students develop this character trait. Tardiness is a *hindrance* to efficient education. It reduces academic achievement. It affects the progress of not only the individual student but of the entire class. Even in a school that does not list character education on its curriculum, teaching punctuality is vital to successful schooling.

Parents should teach children, and insist on promptness around the home, establishing a valuable life skill. Even a young child is able to help lay out tomorrow's clothing before going to bed; to have everything ready for an early departure on vacation; to work toward deadlines.

Warning

In conclusion, please note that punctuality, like every other quality on the list of character traits, must never be built for selfish reasons. Asking "What's in it for me?" is not a valid incentive. Build punctuality because it is an absolute value. It is the right thing to do.

(1,238 words, taken from *http://character-in-action.com*)

I. Reading Comprehension

Directions: Choose the best answer to finish the incomplete statements below according to the above passage.

1. According to the passage, punctuality is increasingly necessary for ________.

   A. employers and employees B. students and children
   C. speakers and audiences D. everybody

2. "The person in the mirror" refers to ________.

   A. the writer B. the employer C. you yourself D. the teacher

3. The phrase "is tantamount to" most probably means ________.

   A. is equivalent to B. lies in C. leads to D. results from

4. You can be punctual if you ________.
   A. crack the whip over your own head B. sleep a few minutes less
   C. talk with your friend a little shorter D. can control your bad desires
5. According to the passage, the statement which is NOT true is ________.
   A. Politicians, presidents, and other leaders are more likely to be late because they think they are more important than others
   B. You should be aware that there are accidental causes that may stop you from carrying out your plan
   C. The boss should tell the employees that tardiness is costly
   D. The habit of punctuality should be developed both at school and at home

II. Vocabulary

Directions: Fill in each blank with an appropriate word from the box below. Change the form where necessary. Each word can be used only once.

trait	obligation	arena	quotient	yearn
tertiary	preach	tardy	polish	tantamount
incentive	facet	harness	document	hindrance

1. Researches show that emotional __________ plays a more important role than IQ in one's success.
2. I believe that every right implies a responsibility; every opportunity, an __________; every possession, a duty.
3. The post-1990 generation __________ for both a flourishing career and a colorful personal life.
4. In the past decade, the two countries have constantly upgraded their coordination and cooperation in the international __________.
5. The Chinese government is working on a new __________ to guarantee the stable growth in its economy.
6. The ethics and values that Confucius __________ in ancient times are still instructive in the modern, competitive society today.
7. Some experts suggested that China should creatively __________ and maximize its resources and become more actively engaged in international affairs and make its voice heard.
8. Undoubtedly many parents have good intentions, and only want to help their children, but they may prove to be more of a __________ than a help.
9. The majority of Chinese people agree that lending a helping hand to Africa today is __________ to helping ourselves tomorrow.
10. Some Chinese agencies help applicants who want to study abroad "__________ the language" in applications but they are unaware it is cheating.

11. The government should make efforts to create jobs in the __________ industry, which absorbs most graduates, and should also encourage young people to start their own businesses.
12. The Chinese economy at present showed a __________ of stability, with little risks of the economy overheating or a sharp decline in economic growth.
13. Migrant workers sometimes get lower pay than what was promised, and __________ payment still exists in some places.
14. The passage introduces ten tips in details on how to __________ valid marriage for immigration purposes.
15. Many Chinese TV reality shows discuss almost every __________ of romantic love and what achieving personal happiness means.

III. Discussion

Directions: Discuss and decide which words to fill in so as to make the following sentences sound logical about the value of time.

1. To realize the value of one year, ask a __________ who has failed an __________ exam.
2. To realize the value of one month, ask a __________ who has given __________ to a premature baby.
3. To realize the value of one week, ask an __________ of a __________ newspaper.
4. To realize the value of one hour, ask the __________ who are waiting to meet.
5. To realize the value of one minute, ask the person who has __________ the train, bus or plane.
6. To realize the value of one second, ask a person who has survived an __________.
7. To realize the value of one __________, ask a __________ who has won a __________ medal in the Olympics.

Time waits for no one. So treasure every moment you have.

Section B The Date Father Didn't Keep

By Robert Zacks

Directions: Read the passage below and decide whether the statements that follow are true or false according to it. Write T for True and F for False.

It happened in one of those picturesque Danish taverns that cater to tourists and where English is spoken. I was with my father on a business-and-pleasure trip, and in our leisure hours we were having a wonderful time.

"It's a pity your mother couldn't come," said Father. "It would be wonderful to show her around."

He had visited Denmark when he was a young man. I asked him, "How long is it since you were here?"

"Oh, about 30 years. I remember being in this very inn, by the way." He looked around, remembering. "Those were gracious days—" He stopped suddenly, and I saw that his face was pale. I followed his eyes and looked across the room to a woman who was setting a tray of drinks before some customers. She might have been pretty once, but now she was stout and her hair was untidy. "Do you know her?" I asked.

"I did once," he said.

The woman came to our table. "Drinks?" she inquired.

"We'll have beer," I said. She nodded and went away.

"How she has changed! Thank heaven she didn't recognize me," muttered Father mopping his face with a handkerchief. "I knew her before I ever met your mother," he went on. "I was a student, on a tour. She was a lovely young thing, very graceful. I fell madly in love with her, and she with me."

"Does Mother know about her?" I blurted out, resentfully.

"Of course," Father said gently. He looked at me a little anxiously. I felt embarrassed for him.

I said, "Dad, you don't have to..."

"Oh, yes, I want to tell you. I don't want you wondering about this. Her father objected to our romance. I was a foreigner. I had no prospects, and was dependent on my father. When I wrote Father that I wanted to get married he cut off my allowance. And I had to go home. But I met the girl once more, and told her I would return to America, borrow enough money to get married on, and come back for her in a few months."

"We know," he continued, "that her father might intercept a letter, so we agreed that I would simply mail her a slip of paper with a date on it, the time she was to meet me at a certain place; then we'd get married. Well, I went home, got the loan and sent her the date. She received the note. She wrote me: "I'll be there." But she wasn't. Then I found that she had been married about two weeks before, to a local innkeeper. She hadn't waited."

Then my father said, "Thank God she didn't. I went home, met your mother, and we've been completely happy. We often joke about that youthful love romance."

The woman appeared with our beer.

"You are from America?" she asked me.

"Yes," I said.

She beamed. "A wonderful country, America."

"Yes, a lot of your countrymen have gone there. Did you ever think of it?"

"Not me. Not now," she said. "I think so one time, a long time ago. But I stay here. It's much better here."

We drank our beer and left. Outside I said, "Father, just how did you write that date on which she was to meet you?"

He stopped, took out an envelope and wrote on it. "Like this," he said. "12/11/73, which was, of course, December 11, 1973."

"No!" I exclaimed. "It isn't in Denmark or any European country. Over here they write the day first, then the month. So that date wouldn't be December 11 but the 12th of November!"

Father passed his hand over his face. "So she was there!" he exclaimed. "And it was because I didn't show up that she got married." He was silent a while. "Well," he said, "I hope she's happy. She seems to be."

As we resumed walking I blurted out, "It is a lucky thing it happened that way. You wouldn't have met Mother."

He put his arm around my shoulders, looked at me with a heart-warming smile, and said, "I was doubly lucky, young fellow, for otherwise I wouldn't have met you, either!"

(699 words, taken from *Readers' Digest*)

1. The writer was on a business trip to Europe with his father. ________
2. The writer's grandfather strongly objected to his father's relationship with a girl he met in Europe. ________
3. The writer was angry because his father did not tell his romance to his mother honestly. ________
4. It is the different writing order of the date and month between America and Europe that led to the misunderstanding between the two lovers. ________
5. The writer's father felt regretful that he didn't marry the Danish woman. ________

Part 4 Reading Comprehension Test

Part A

Directions: Read the following four texts. Answer the questions below each text by choosing A, B, C or D.

Text 1

The most precious commodity today is "time". We buy "time-saving" devices; we never seem to have enough "time"; we buy on "time" (credit) because we want the item NOW and will pay for it later. "TIME" is the most precious commodity we have.

Interestingly enough, it would appear that most people think THEIR time is more important than the time that belongs to others. Physicians are busy, using their time to care for patients. Is the waiting patient's time any less valuable? Employees may think their "OFF HOURS" are more important than their "WORK HOURS".

Actually time is equally important to everybody. So it's important to observe the rule of punctuality in all walks of life, especially in workplaces. Punctuality in the workplace is essential to gain respect from employer and coworkers alike.

Punctuality first reflects courtesy and consideration for employer and coworkers. Continually tardy employees gain a reputation from employers that they cannot be trusted to honor their "start" time. Coworkers learn whether a fellow employee is "early", "late" or "right on time", which helps determine when to expect them. If something as simple as "start time" cannot be honored, can they be trusted to accomplish more difficult assignments during the day?

Secondly, punctuality reflects the importance and value placed on the job. Reporting to work early gives the employee time to "catch their breath" before starting the job. Rushing in, hurrying to "punch the clock", and hoping the boss will not see when the employee is late, reflect a lack of importance placed on the job.

Occasionally, every employee will be caught in traffic, or have some unexpected delay at home, but the frequency of such tardiness will usually be minimal.

Thirdly, punctuality is a habit learned by valued employees and honored by employers. I once knew a man who reported to the break room 1 hour before his "punch in" time. Everyday, people knew that he would be there drinking coffee, reading the paper, waiting time to start. He was a maintenance man who people knew could be counted on to be at work, on time, and ready to go. When people needed something fixed, they knew he was dependable, due to his punctuality AND work habits.

Earning the respect of your employer and fellow employees is usually related to work performance. The missing element however, is that the reputation for work performance begins with punctuality or tardiness. Punctuality gains respect in the workplace. Try it and you'll see that people (and your boss) will notice.

(419 words, based on a passage written by Ron Zamkus)

1. Which of the following can not support the idea that time is the most precious commodity today according to the writer?

   A. People buy many devices so as to help them to save time.

   B. People always feel that they don't have enough time.

   C. People tend to loan more money before they have.

   D. People think that their time is more important than that of others.

2. Being punctual in work can show all of the following EXCEPT ________.

   A. politeness and consideration　　B. respect for others

   C. respect for work　　D. respect for work performance

3. The word "minimal" (Line 2, Paragraph 6) most probably means ________.

   A. maximum　　B. minimum　　C. minimized　　D. maximal

4. The writer's attitude toward the man who would arrive an hour early but drink coffee, read newspaper and wait time to start is ________.

   A. critical　　B. neutral　　C. positive　　D. negative

5. Which of the following may be the most suitable title for this passage?

A. The Importance of Punctuality
B. Punctuality in Workplaces
C. How to Get Respect from Others
D. Time—a Commodity

Text 2 The Politics of Punctuality

CEDAR RAPIDS, Iowa—The crowd was already getting a little restless here tonight at a campaign rally for Senator Barack Obama, when a woman walked to the front of the room and offered her apologies.

"How many political campaigns do you know that run on time? None" said Linda Langston, a local Democratic official tasked with keeping the crowd of several hundred people entertained as they waited for Mr. Obama. "We are sorry. He will be here soon."

Soon was not soon enough for Kay and Tom Lammers, who were among the smattering of people who headed for the doors in the gymnasium of Kirkwood Community College. They said they had been told that Mr. Obama would arrive at 6:30 p.m. and it was already more than an hour later and still no sign of the senator.

As the Lammers zipped up their coats and walked away, a young campaign worker approached them and implored their patience. "We would love for you to stick around for five more minutes!" the aide said. "He's on his way! He's on his way!"

Here in Iowa, punctuality in politics can be important. As candidates are aggressively working to court voters, any slight—even appearing late at a rally—can turn off voters. (Even so, John Edwards still has among the worst on-time records of Democratic candidates, just like he did four years ago, and he still came in second place.)

It turns out that Mr. Obama apparently was flying in from Chicago, and blustery winds in Cedar Rapids delayed his plane. But that explanation was of little solace to Mr. Lammer, who seemed far angrier than his wife at Mr. Obama's tardiness.

"If he would have been here on time," Mr. Lammers said, "I would have stayed and listened."

Despite the panicked look on the faces of some Obama aides, the vast majority of people remained in the audience, waiting for the senator. As for the Lammers, will tonight's delay influence their decision at the Iowa caucuses on Jan. 3?

"Oh, no. I really think he's one of the few people who can actually turn this country around," said Mrs. Lammers, volunteering the fact that she is leery of Senator Hillary Rodham Clinton. "As much as I respect Hillary Clinton, I don't feel she's what the country needs."

About 15 minutes after the Lammers' car pulled from the parking lot, the music started playing and Mr. Obama appeared on stage for the opening stop of a four-day Iowa tour. The first words out of his mouth? "I do apologize for being late," he said, speaking to a several hundred people who remained in the room and welcomed him with applause.

(447 words, taken from *New York Times*, Nov. 6, 2007 by Jeff Zeleny)

6. "Soon was not soon enough for Kay and Tom Lammers, who were among the smattering of people who headed for the doors" implies that ________.

A. no matter how soon he would appear, they would not wait for him
B. no matter how soon he would come, he was already late for one hour
C. it's meaningless although he would arrive soon
D. it's impossible for him to be there sooner than they left

7. The word "implore" in Paragraph 4 most probably means ________.
A. require B. order C. plead D. recommend

8. The following are all reactions of Mr. and Mrs. Lammers to Mr. Obama's tardiness EXCEPT that ________.
A. both of them were angry at his being late
B. they couldn't accept his reason for his lateness
C. they became impatient and drove for home
D. they would not vote for him

9. The word "leery" in Paragraph 9 is closest in meaning to ________.
A. respectful B. distrustful C. distasteful D. trustful

10. When did Mr. Obama finally show up at the campaign rally?
A. At about 6:30 p.m. B. After 7:30 p.m. C. At about 7:35 p.m. D. After 7:45 p.m.

Text 3

Contrary to what some people may think about punctuality and attendance in the modern workplace, the situation has improved. Although the Great Recession had many downsides, a CareerBuilder survey shows that this economic event caused many more worried workers to report to work on time than in 2008 and 2009. CareerBuilder conducted the survey over the final two months of 2010 and published results online in February 2011. The article adds a bit of humor by including some of the "most outrageous tardiness excuses" heard by hiring managers. However, when employees craft apologies, they should do so with the utmost seriousness and respect.

Defer to the Employee Handbook

Many companies, even small businesses, provide new hires with an employee handbook during orientation. Before formulating an apology, workers should defer to the instructions in this policy manual that explain the procedures for addressing tardiness and absenteeism. In some office places, employees might compose an email and send it off to a supervisor or department manager. Archived emails or saved voice mails about apologizing for being tardy provides the employer and employee with an accurate record in the event disciplinary action or termination.

Be Honest

Workers should tell the truth when creating a verbal or written apology about being late for the job. This seems obvious, especially in small businesses in which employees and managers might have a close personal and professional relationship. Workplace consultant B.J. Gallagher states that repeatedly lying and using the same excuse, such as an alarm clock did not go off, can damage a relationship and rapport that has built up over time between the worker and the manager.

Make Up for Potential Losses

Employees might preemptively suggest to managers how they can make up for potential losses to the business because of lack of punctuality. Workers might offer to stay to make up for the minutes or hours that were missed with another employee who sacrificed his day off. Other options might include taking work home in the evening or coming into the office on the weekend. The manager might appreciate your thought and concern for the business.

Explain Your Corrective Actions

The onus is on the employee to avoid being late in the future. Managers may issue a warning or other disciplinary notice about attendance infractions, but this is a formal business process. In your apology, state what you are capable of doing to prevent being late again. For example, if an unexpected traffic accident caused your tardiness, state in your apology that you will try to leave for work 30 minutes earlier than normal to avoid congestion.

(432 words)

11. During the Great Recession, more and more workers report to work on time mainly because ________.
    A. there are many downsides in economy
    B. they are worried about the downsides in economy
    C. the situations of their workplaces have been improved
    D. they are worried that they might lose their jobs if they are tardy
12. The word "formulate" in Line 11 is similar to the word "________" in Paragraph 1.
    A. conduct　　B. publish　　C. include　　D. craft
13. The purpose of this passage is to ________.
    A. describe the most outrageous excuses employees have made for tardiness
    B. introduce how to make convincing excuses for tardiness
    C. introduce how to make utmost serious and honest apologizes for tardiness
    D. introduce how to avoid tardiness
14. The word "archived" in Line 14 is closest in meaning to ________.
    A. composed　　B. saved　　C. formulated　　D. sent
15. Which of the following statements is NOT true according to the passage?
    A. One should read the employee manual first to know the procedures to apologize for his tardiness.
    B. One might not tell the truth of his tardiness in a big company because the boss may not know him.

C. One should tell the manager to compensate for the losses he has caused.

D. One should promise that he would not be late again.

Text 4 An obsession with being on time

Anywhere else in the world, a train running 90 seconds late would perhaps be considered on time. But in Japan, 90 seconds would foil commuters who depend on trains' connecting to one another with balletic precision, often with only a couple of minutes to spare.

And so to make up for a lost 90 seconds, a 23-year-old train engineer was speeding when his train jumped off the tracks at a curve in western Japan and hurtled into a nine-story apartment building on Monday morning. The death toll of the most serious accident in Japan in four decades rose to 94.

Across the country, the accident has already caused much soul-searching over Japan's attention to—some would say obsession with—punctuality and efficiency. To many, the engineer's single-minded focus on making up the 90 seconds seemed to reveal the weak points of a society where the trains really do run on time, but where people have lost sight of the bigger picture.

Yasuyuki Sawada, 49, a railway worker, saw deeper problems hidden in the accident. "There is no flexibility in our society; people are not flexible, either," he said. "This disaster was produced by Japanese civilization and Japanese people."

The Japanese search for rail perfection is relentless, from the humble commuter train to the country's most famous tracks. In 2004, on the 40th anniversary of the bullet train, there was much hand-wringing over the fact that a year earlier the trains on that line had registered, on average, a delay—of six seconds.

Train companies are secretive about delays. But any regular rider notices that they tend to be caused, not by engineering mishaps, but by causes beyond human control, like typhoons and people's jumping before oncoming trains.

So confident is Japan in its trains' safety that there are no restrictions on how close residential buildings can be erected next to tracks: It is not rare to see them only a meter, or three feet, away.

Keeping to increasingly packed and tight schedules has become all-important. This month, the West Japan Railway had for the first time issued a written statement to its employees stating that delays would betray customers' confidence. It was perhaps with this in mind that the 23-year-old engineer, Ryujiro Takami, headed for Osaka on Monday morning. Takami, believed to have died in the crash, had only 11 months of experience, and he had been reprimanded once for overshooting a platform by 100 meters.

Apparently aware that he would be reprimanded again, he sped up. The train, carrying about 580 passengers, began running abnormally fast, so much so that the scenery outside whizzed by. The engineer had made up 30 seconds, so that the train was running only 60 seconds late when it derailed at a curve and slammed into the building a little more than three meters away from the railway tracks.

(476 words, adapted from *The New York Times*, by Norimitsu Onishi)

16. The word "hurtle" in Paragraph 2 is closest in meaning to ________.

    A. slam B. run C. flow D. flip

17. According to the passage, the reason that led to the collision of the train is ________.

    A. the choosiness of the commuters

    B. the carelessness of the train engineer

    C. the single-mindedness of the engineer

    D. the relentless search for perfection

18. The delays of the trains in Japan are mainly caused by ________.

    A. engineering breakdowns

    B. the weather

    C. the passengers in a hurry

    D. secretive rules

19. Why are there no restrictions on the distance between residential buildings and tracks in Japan?

    A. Because the schedules are increasingly packed and tight.

    B. Because the Japanese have excessive confidence in the safety of the trains.

    C. Because the Japanese have confidence in their civilization.

    D. Because space is limited and precious in Japan.

20. The word "reprimanded" most probably means ________.

    A. criticized B. punished C. dismissed D. eliminated

Part B

Directions: For Questions 21-25 choose the most suitable paragraph from the list **A to G** and fill them into the numbered boxes to form a coherent text. Paragraph D has been correctly placed. There is one paragraph that does not fit in with the text.

A Therefore the issue of punctuality seems almost like a simple, insignificant consideration and yet it is fundamentally important to your career well being. It might seem like a very basic thing, but your ability to get to work on time could have a bearing on your entire professional career.

B When everybody makes an effort to get to work on time, constant lateness doesn't sit well with your peers. They understand that if everybody was late, nothing would get done properly and the chances are that while you are late, somebody else is covering your work. The workplace requires that teams work together, supporting and respecting one another and a fundamental part of this comes from everybody working to the same rules and processes.

C Punctuality is an attribute that employers prize highly. Employees that are regularly late cause a number of issues for their employers by disrupting the workplace. Punctuality is a combination of attitude and capability. Some individuals seem patently incapable of attending work on time. Others just seem unwilling. In either case, anybody that maintains a good record of punctuality gains a great deal of respect.

D You have a contractual obligation to your employer to attend work for a certain number of hours per week and according to specific start and end times. Maintaining that commitment demonstrates that you are professional and understand the importance of the employment contract that you have signed. Your ability to accept and understand this commitment on a very basic level demonstrates your potential to do so with more significant matters, and could therefore result in promotion or other rewards. In order for your career to advance, your employer must respect your skills and capabilities.

E He initially will get respect from his line managers. Managers want to see that their team members take their work seriously. Punctuality is a strong indicator that the employee is committed. It demonstrates that the employee is willing to manage his/her team, balancing work and personal commitments, to maintain a regime in line with the manager's expectations. It is a sign also of mutual respect. Employees that are able to attend work punctually demonstrate a capability to work under direction and follow leadership instruction. Effective working requires individuals that are able to work in this manner.

F Focusing on completing a work deadline can be a stressful and strenuous task, especially as the decisive time and date draws ever closer. However, simply by focusing on the task at hand, you can subsequently eliminate the stress and worry associated with meeting work deadlines and not only meet them, but also complete them with time to spare, thus granting you some extra freedom and time to yourself to focus on completing other tasks in advance in the midst of setting a great impression for your quality of work and ethic in the work place. If you are looking for ways in which you can focus on completing a work deadline, there are many tips that can be offered.

G The respect earned from others will boost your self-respect, which is critical to both your personal and professional lives. Your family will want to admire somebody that is well-respected at work and has a good professional reputation. As an individual, you will want to feel that you are recognized as being good at what you do, through the respect of others. A strong degree of self-respect helps boost career-minded individuals, who grow in confidence through the respect of others.

(582 words)

21. ________ 22. ________ 23. ________ D 24. ________ 25. ________

Unit 5

Attitudes towards Life and Death

Part 1 Reading Skills

Section A Guessing Unknown Words from Word Formation II

2. Suffix

A suffix is a letter or a group of letters which are added after the stem of a word to form a new word. Usually a suffix is not to modify the meaning of a stem, rather, to change the grammatical function of a stem, that is, to change the word-class or the part of speech of the base though there are a few exceptions.

Suffixes can be divided into noun suffixes, adjective suffixes, adverb suffixes and verb suffixes according to the function. The most frequent suffixes will be listed in the tables below. They are very helpful in your reading comprehension.

1) Verb Suffixes

Suffix	Meaning or Function	Examples
-ify, -fy	to make or become	intensify, terrify, simplify, beautify
-ize, -ise	to make or become	civilize, sympathize, normalize, organize
-ate	to make or become	accumulate, consolidate, eradicate
-en	to make or become	fasten, quicken, strengthen, worsen
-ish	to lengthen the stem	abolish, banish, establish, vanish

2) Noun Suffixes

Suffix	Meaning	Examples
-ance, -ence	state or quality of	maintenance, eminence, prominence
-sion, -tion	state of being	concession, corruption, destruction
-ness	state of being	goodness, heaviness, hopefulness
-acy	state or quality	accuracy, bankruptcy, democracy
-ment	condition of	argument, retirement, treatment
-sure, -ture	act or process of	departure, expenditure, exposure
-al	act or process of	disposal, proposal, refusal, survival
-dom	rank or condition	freedom, kingdom, wisdom
-ity, -ty, -y	quality of	curiosity, poverty, safety, modesty
-ship	position held	fellowship, membership, scholarship
-th	state of being	breadth, depth, stealth, warmth
-ism	doctrine, belief	capitalism, feudalism, Marxism
-ology	subject of study	biology, ecology, sociology, zoology
-er, -or	one who, something that	interpreter, opener, reactor, translator
-ar	one who	beggar, liar, pedlar, scholar
-ee	one subject to an action	examinee, interviewee, refugee
-eer	one concerned with	mountaineer, profiteer, volunteer
-ist	one who is an expert in	chemist, dentist, pianist, physicist
-an, -ian	a native of or	Korean, Iranian, magician, physician
-ese	a native of or style of	Cantonese, Portuguese, officialnese
-ish	a native of	Irish, Jewish, Scottish, Turkish
-ess	a female of	actress, airhostess, empress, princess
-ant	one acting as an agent	assistant, celebrant, deodorant
-logist	one who studies	anthropologist, biologist, geologist

3) Adverbial Suffixes

Suffix	Meaning	Examples
-ly	in a…manner	casually, hurriedly, swiftly, worriedly
-ward	toward	backward, downward, westward
-wise	in the manner of	clockwise, likewise, otherwise
-ways	relating to direction	edgeways, lengthways, sideways

4) Adjective Suffixes

Suffix	Meaning	Examples
-able, -ible	capable of being	reliable, respectable, responsible, visible
-ious, -ous	characterized by	envious, mysterious, simultaneous
-ic, -ical	pertaining to,	economic, heroic, economical, systematic
-ful	notable for, full of	colorful, forgetful, plentiful, respectful
-less	without	endless, fearless, jobless, hatless, hateless
-ive	having the nature of	creative, positive, aggressive, progressive
-ant, -ent	having the quality of	resistant, tolerant, consistent, prominent
-al, -ial	pertaining to	natural, regional, sexual, presidential
-ish	having the quality of	bookish, childish, foolish, selfish
-ary	connected with	arbitrary, contrary, elementary, military
-y	characterized by	cloudy, gloomy, hearty, sleepy, weighty
n.+-ly	having the nature of	brotherly, costly, motherly, quarterly
-ar	of the kind of	angular, lunar, molecular, solar
-like	similar to	catlike, childlike, doglike, ladylike
-proof	against, resistent	shockproof, soundproof, waterproof
-an, -ian	belonging to	Chilean, Christian, Russian, sylvan, urban
-esque	reminiscent in style of	arabesque, picturesque, Romanesque

Section B Practice

Directions: Read the following passage and fill in each blank with the word given in brackets, adding a suitable suffix and in its proper form.

Greet This Day with Love

I will greet this day with love in my heart. For this is the greatest secret of success in all ventures. Muscle can split a shield and even destroy life but only the unseen power of love can open the hearts of men. I will make love my greatest weapon and none can defend against its force.

And how will I do this? Henceforth will I look on all things with love and I will be born again. I will love the sun, for it warms my bones; yet I will love the rain, for it 1) __________ (pure) my spirit. I will love the light, for it shows me the way; yet I will love the 2) __________ (dark), for it shows me the stars. I will welcome happiness, for it 3) __________ (large) my heart; yet I will endure sadness, for it opens my soul. I will acknowledge rewards, for they are my due; yet I will welcome obstacles, for they are my challenge.

And how will I speak? I will laud my enemies and they will become friends; I will encourage my friends and they will become brothers. Always will I dig for reasons to applaud; never will I scratch for excuses to gossip. When I am tempted to 4) __________ (critic) I will bite on my tongue; when I am moved to praise I will shout from the roofs.

Is it not so that birds, the wind, the sea and all nature speaks with the music of praise for their 5) __________ (create)? Cannot I speak with the same music to his children? Henceforth will I remember this secret and it will change my life.

And how will I act? I will love all manner of men, for each has qualities to be admired even though they be hidden. With love I will tear down the wall of 6) __________ (suspect) and hate which they have built round their hearts and in its place will I build bridges so that my love may enter their souls.

I will love the 7) __________ (ambition), for they can inspire me! I will love the 8) __________ (fail), for they can teach me. I will love the kings, for they are but humans; I will love the meek, for they are divine. I will love the rich, for they are yet 9) __________ (lone).

I will love the poor, for they are so many. I will love the young, for the faith they hold; I will love the old, for the 10) __________ (wise) they share. I will love the 11) __________ (beauty), for their eyes of sadness; I will love the ugly, for their souls of peace.

But how will I 12) __________ (act) to the actions of others? With love. For just as love is my weapon to open the hearts of men, love is also my shield to repulse the arrows of hate and the spears of anger. 13) __________ (adverse) and 14) __________ (courage) will beat against my new shield and become as the softest of rains.

And how I confront each whom I meet? In only one way. In silence and to myself I will address him and say, "I Love You." Though spoken in silence these words will shine in my eyes, 15) __________ (wrinkle) my brow, bring a smile to my lips, and echo in my voice; and his heart will be opened.

(By Og Mamtino)

Part 2 Idioms, Proverbs and Sayings

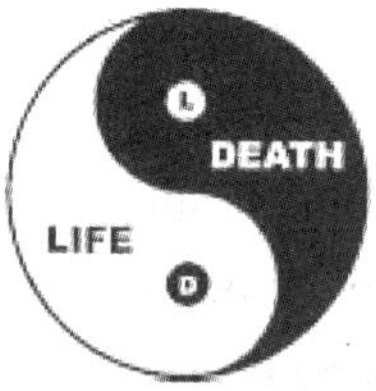

Directions: The following are idioms, proverbs or sayings by famous people about life and death. Choose what you think is correct and compare with the right ones.

1. Life is full of ________, loneliness, and suffering—and it's all over much too soon. (Woody Allen)
   A. misery B. happiness C. joy D. honesty
2. Life is ours to be spent, not to be ________. (D. H. Lawrence)
   A. killed B. saved C. bought D. sold
3. We make a living by what we get, we make a life by what we ________. (Churchill)
   A. have B. obtain C. own D. give
4. The value of life lies not in the ________ of days, but in the use we make of them. (Montaigne)
   A. length B. circle C. vacancy D. span
5. We can't all be heroes. Somebody has to sit on the curb and ________ as they go by. (W. Roger)
   A. salute B. shout C. clap D. cheer
6. The important line in life is not the ________ which stands, but the ________ which faces.
   A. direction, position B. line, place
   C. spot, line D. position, direction
7. A(n) ________ death honors the whole life. (Proverb)
   A. honest B. fair C. free D. happy
8. As a day ________ brings happy sleep, so life well-used brings happy death. (Leonardo da Vinci)
   A. good-cost B. well-cost C. good-ent D. well-spent
9. Life does not cease to be funny when people die any more than it ceases to be serious when people ________. (George Bernard Shaw)
   A. laugh B. cry C. smile D. wrinkle
10. Must not all things at the last be ________ up in death? (Plato)
    A. destroyed B. attacked C. swallowed D. ruined

Part 3 Reading Passages

Section A Legal Systems Handle Euthanasia Differently Around the Globe

The World Medical Assn. regards euthanasia as unethical, but anecdotal evidence suggests the practice is quietly carried out in many countries. The World Right to Die Federation lists pro-euthanasia societies in nearly 20 countries. Here is a look at euthanasia and physician-assisted suicide and the laws governing them in some countries:

UNITED STATES: Euthanasia is regarded as a crime, generally murder or manslaughter. There have been unsuccessful efforts in several states to legalize it, dating as far back as the 1930s, when proposals were turned down by legislators in Nebraska and New York.

More recently, with concern over rising health care costs and improvements in medical technology that help forestall death, there has been renewed debate. In 1989, a group of distinguished medical ethicists published an article in the *New England Journal of Medicine* in which they concluded it is "not immoral for a physician to assist in the rational suicide of a terminally ill person." Last year, voters in California turned down a ballot initiative that would have permitted doctor-assisted suicide, and in 1991 Washington voters did the same. Meanwhile, authorities in Michigan are threatening to prosecute Dr. Jack Kevorkian, who has gained notoriety by helping 15 terminally ill patients to kill themselves.

CANADA: Euthanasia and assisted suicide are outlawed, but a 42-year-old British Columbia woman dying of Lou Gehrig's disease is fighting a highly publicized court battle for permission to have her doctor attach her to a suicide device that would pump lethal medication into her. As it stands now, any doctor helping Sue Rodriguez carry out this death wish could be sentenced to up to 14 years in prison.

JAPAN: Euthanasia is legally murky, left to the discretion of regional courts with no official guidelines regarding the practice. A landmark 1962 decision by a high court in Nagoya declared euthanasia legal under certain circumstances, specifying that it be performed by a medical doctor. A Yokohama doctor is standing trial for giving a lethal injection to a coma patient whose family, authorities say, did not request it.

A 1990 survey for the Japan Medical Society found 87% of its members would honor a patient's desire to "die with dignity."

MEXICO: Euthanasia is regarded as murder, but there is no specific legislation covering it because it simply is not an issue in this largely Roman Catholic society. There have been no cases reported.

BRITAIN: Euthanasia and physician-assisted suicides are illegal, treated as homicide. But unofficial estimates suggest the number of unreported cases run in the thousands, and vehement pro- and anti- euthanasia groups are active.

GERMANY: Euthanasia and physician-assisted suicide are illegal, punishable by up to five years in prison. The latest statistics show six cases were prosecuted in 1990; one defendant was acquitted, two were given probation, and three were fined. In 1989, a nurse was sentenced to 11 years in prison for euthanizing five patients.

The term "death help" is used instead of "euthanasia" in Germany, to avoid comparisons to the Nazi era, when Hitler used the word to describe his campaign of genocide.

FRANCE: Euthanasia is considered homicide. However, now there are French doctors who specialize in what is called "helping the patient to die," which in medical circles is regarded as easing a patient's suffering but not deliberately causing death.

ITALY: Euthanasia is treated as willful murder. There are a few movements lobbying for legalization, but the issue has not reached Parliament. There are no statistics on euthanasia deaths, but when mercy killing comes to light, the law usually takes the view that the practitioner was acting under extenuating circumstances, and sentences are meted out accordingly.

ISRAEL: Euthanasia is not strictly legal, but courts acknowledge that there are situations in which a doctor may take into consideration a patient's expressed wishes not to have his or her life prolonged by artificial means.

SOUTH AFRICA: Euthanasia and physician-assisted suicide are considered murder, though a doctor who gave his cancer-stricken father an overdose of Pentothal in 1975 received only a suspended sentence and had his medical license reinstated after two years.

(674 words, March 14, 1993, *Times* staff writers and researchers)

I. Reading comprehension

Directions: Read the following statements and countries. Fill in the blanks in each statement with the letter that stands for the correspondent country.

***NB**: You may use any country more than once or not use it at all.*

A. Mexico	B. Isreal	C. Germany	D. France
E. Britain	F. Japan	G. Italy	H. Canada
I. United States	J. South Africa		

1. Euthanasia is not permitted by law and doctors who help patients to commit suicide are to be punished by up to 5 years in prison in __________.
2. A British Columbia woman is battling with the court for a permission of committed suicide assisted by her doctor in __________.
3. Though some states try to legalize euthanasia, it is still generally considered to be illegal in __________.
4. Heated disputes are going on about whether euthanasia is legal or not in __________.

5. If a patient wishes not to prolong his or her life by artificial means, doctors can take it into consideration to help him or her to take euthanasia in __________.
6. Euthanasia is considered to be homicide in __________ and __________.
7. Euthanasia is considered to be murder in __________, __________ and __________.
8. Though euthanasia is declared legal under certain circumstances, there is not clarified decision whether Euthanasia is legal or not in __________.

II. Vocabulary

Directions: Fill in each blank with an appropriate word from the box below. Change the suffix where necessary. Each word can be used only once.

legalization	ethicists	terminally	notoriety	publicize
murky	defendant	deliberately	vehement	lethal

1. Beijing has been notified abroad for its urban pollution, including __________ smog, sandstorms and exhaust emissions.
2. There was intentional and __________ targeting of the civilian houses," said deputy foreign minister during a visit to the site shortly after reporters arrived.
3. __________ rains and hail storms battered the city of Shaoguan in Guangdong province, which is located to the Southeast of Guizhou, on Sunday.
4. He was pronounced dead at 6:21 p.m., 10 minutes after the __________ drugs began flowing into his arms.
5. The player was once a shining gymnastics star at the age of 18, when he won two gold medals at the 2001 Beijing Universiade. But in 2007, he gained __________ fame with a scrics of theft cases. He confessed he had committed about 10 thefts because of financial strains.
6. Aircraft carriers are essential for China primarily to __________ its territory and territorial waters and bring a semblance of parity among the world's big powers.
7. Food scandals in recent years in China indicated that a lack of business __________ had caused the problem.
8. It's time for the Chinese to embrace the concept of 'natural death', which is already widely recognized in the West, because the __________ ill patients need more psychological care.
9. The State Council, or the cabinet, has repeatedly called on its ministries to __________ their budget information and provide greater details regarding how they spend public funds.
10. New York is the sixth and also the largest state in the US to __________ gay marriage.

III. Debate

Directions: In some countries, such as in the United States and Italy, ***euthanasia*** is illegal and regarded as a crime or even a murder, while in some other countries, it is considered to be legal and doctors are permitted to help patients to take euthanasia. What is your opinion about it? Have a debate on ***euthanasia***. One group argues for it and the other group refutes its point.

Section B "Am I To Love Life Less?"

By Mary Manachi

Directions: Read the story and fill in each blank with ***NO MORE THAN THREE WORDS****.*

"We'd just cut the watermelons at a Sunday-school picnic and I was laughing at the kids' antics–playing" the sweet pink slices like harmonicas, making big green grins with the rind, spitting the seeds.

"You seem so happy," said a woman next to me. "How do you do it after...after all that's happened to you?"

Again and again, people ask me that question—people who know that Louis and I had three children who died of Cooley's anemia. First Rosemarie, then Marylou, then George.

How can I be happy? Well...

Marylou was born in 1955. She was our second child, two years younger than our healthy daughter, Ann. At first I thought Marylou's pale skin merely meant she took after me. Although Louis and I are both of Mediterranean descent, he's the one with the olive complexion. Marylou's pediatrician wasn't so sure. "She seems to be anemic," he said, and had her tested. Afterward, the doctor called Louis and me in for a consultation.

"I'm sorry," he said, "but your baby has thalassemia major." In this rare genetic disorder, commonly known as Cooley's anemia after the doctor who discovered it, the bone marrow does not manufacture the proper type of adult hemoglobin, the blood protein that carries oxygen to body tissues.

"It mainly affects people of Mediterranean heritage," the doctor told us. Wanting a second opinion, we took Marylou to the Children's Blood Foundation clinic at the New York Hospital-Cornell Medical Center. There, a doctor confirmed the diagnosis. He also said that Marylou would have to come back to the clinic every two weeks for a blood transfusion.

From then on, I drove my daughter into New York City from West Paterson, N.J., regularly. After a few months, she got used to it. And she had company; 19 other children were being treated there for the same illness.

Louis and I wanted more children, but now we wondered.

"Don't worry," our own doctor assured us. "This very rarely happens twice in a family."

Rosemarie was born in 1959. She looked fine—bright blue eyes and fine brown hair like Marylou's but something was wrong. One day she'd seem perfectly normal, the next her head would be sweating. The pattern had been the same with Marylou. Finally, when she was six months old, doctors confirmed that Rosemarie would also need transfusions.

So now I was driving two little girls into the city. It was easy to see how much they depended on the transfusions. As the time for a treatment neared, they would tire easily and become irritable. But after their hospital visit—grueling as it was—they seemed happy again. Meanwhile, Louis and I tried to hide our anguish by giving our three daughters a normal life, with music lessons, games and family outings.

In 1961 our son, George, was born. We had yearned for a boy, and had been assured our chances of having another child with the same affliction were virtually nil. But from the first moment I held my little boy, I knew. Soon I was taking George into New York along with two-year-old Rosemarie and six-year-old Marylou.

Even so, Louis and I were grateful for our four lovely children. As the years passed, the transfusions became part of our lives, and we went on hoping that a medical breakthrough would make them unnecessary.

Then came our shocking discovery. One morning at the hospital one of the other mothers handed me a newspaper clipping headlined BAFFLINF, FATAL BLOOD DISORDER. It was about children coming to that very clinic. "*Many die before they are 20*," the article said.

I couldn't believe it. I asked our doctor, "Is it true?"

"Yes," he sighed. "I'm afraid it is." There was no known medical help to prevent my children's death at a young age.

For years Louis and I lived in a daze. His reaction was to say little and concentrate on his work as a garment designer. Mine was to cry whenever I was alone or with the other mothers at the clinic.

We couldn't bring ourselves to discuss it with the children, though I knew that from talking with the other patients, they understood the seriousness of those small but significant moments that change the way you see things.

I'd walked into nine-year-old Rosemarie's room one evening and found her making a jeweled butterfly pin. "How beautiful," I said as I watched her carefully set a rhinestone. She was already selling her work at craft shows.

"Thanks, Mom," she murmured. "I'm going to earn all I toward college."

College?

I cleared my throat. "Uh… what are you planning to study, Honey?"

She looked up, eyes shining. "Nursing, Mom. I want to be like those nice women at the hospital."

She turned back to her work, and I walked slowly out of the room, trying to take it all in. Rosemarie was not thinking about death; she was focusing on life.

At Thanksgiving, one of her teachers phoned me. The students had been asked to write about what they were most thankful for. "I thought you'd like to hear Rosemarie's answer," the teacher said. Her voice trembled as she read, "I thank God for my good health."

Good health? How could she write that? Then I remembered the other children Rosemarie saw in the hospital, the ones with amputations or cancer. Rosemarie could walk, go to school, skip rope.

Rosemarie had filled our house with Scripture plagues that she made. In her own room she'd hung one that read: This is the day which the Lord has made; let us rejoice and be glad in it (Psalms 118:24).

I saw then that our house was not a house of shadows and sorrow; our children filled it with cheer. Marylou's piano music rang through the rooms. Rosemarie busily crafted jewelry and plaques. Little George had an extensive rock collection; he was already talking about becoming a geologist. Slowly, I began to see that my children, all of them were rejoicing in life.

On July 4, 1969, Rosemarie, now ten, was in the hospital with a cardiac problem, a side effect of Cooley's. "You seem better, Honey," I said to her that night as I kissed her good-by. "I'll be back in the morning with Daddy."

Just after I got home, the telephone rang. Rosemarie was gone. "Peacefully," the hospital said.

We mourned. My faith was profoundly shaken. I fought battles with God, kicking and screaming, trying to find answers. Then, little by little, I came to a true understanding and discovered life can go on.

Marylou and George had known their lives would be short, but with Rosemarie gone they were forced to face that fact head-on. Marylou, four years older than Rosemarie, began carefully tending her sister's grave. I knew she must be contemplating her own death. And yet she took up life with new vitality. She began making the honor roll in high school and was very popular. And she made a suggestion that gave new directions to our lives.

In 1973 Marylou graduated from high school as a member of the National Honor Society. She had undergone surgery for removal of her spleen, so had worked extra hard for this honor. In the fall, she entered William Paterson College as a fine-arts major. Soon she made the dean's list. She worked part-time in a TV-repair shop, and her civic activities—collecting for charity, and other volunteer work—put her in touch with almost everyone in town.

The following year she volunteered for an experimental drug treatment of Cooley's anemia. She had to be hospitalized for three weeks. "But if it helps other kids, it's worth it," she said.

On January 20, a heavy snow kept us all at home. Marylou practiced her piano in the morning, but she was exhausted. "I think I'll rest for a while," she said as she went to bed. Later I brought her some lunch.

"Oh, this soup is so good!" she exclaimed. Then the light went out of her eyes, and she fell back on her pillow.

Marylou's funeral was one of the largest ever in West Paterson. The mayor and the entire city council were there. In the words of the Cooley's volunteer group who honored her, she had "lived and understood life better in her 19 years than most of us could possibly hope to if we lived to be a hundred."

Our oldest daughter, Ann, was busy with her career. George, a typical teenager, kept our house lively. His friends came and went, and the telephone rang constantly. He dated and had an after-school job at a restaurant. After graduation from high school, George went on to William Paterson College. He continued working, and the summer he was 19 he bought a Chevrolet Monza sports car, shiny black with fire-engine-red trim—a young man's dream. He kept it carefully garaged and in showroom shape.

That's why, one night in September 1980, I knew something was wrong. George came home from a date, and after he went to bed I noticed that his Monza was pulled into the garage at a careless angle. A few days later he told me, "Mom, I just can't make it anymore. I'm so tired."

That night he said, "I know I'm going, Mom." He looked at me. "Promise me you won't cry? You know where I'll be."

"No, George, I won't cry."

My son smiled, shook his head and lay back, eyes closed. Then he took a deep breath and was gone.

Rosemarie.

Marylou.

George.

And so, again and again, people ask, "How can you be happy after all that's happened?"

I'll tell you how.

My children understood that life is a holy gift. They loved each day they were given, and their enjoyment and gratitude were like sunlight, warming and brightening our time together. In the face of early death, they embraced life. If they loved life so much—honoring it, reaching out to soothe their stricken friends, using their days creatively—am I to love life less?

No! I will not dishonor God—or my children—with gloom and self-pity. I will embrace life as they did. I shall rejoice and be glad in it.

(1,715 words, From *Readers' Digest* May 1985)

1. After she was confirmed by the doctor that her second child Marylou had the disease of Cooley's anemia, the author had to take Marylou to the clinic regularly for ____________________.
2. The author and her husband decided to have another child even though she had had two daughters suffering Cooley anemia because they were told by the doctor that the chances of having another child with the same affliction were ____________________
3. When they got the news from an article that her sick children were to die before they were 20, the author and her had lived ____________________.
4. After Rosemarie's death, Marylou and George knew they had to face that fact that they would also die young, but they still led a ____________________ life.
5. Marylou's funeral was one of the largest ever in West Paterson because her ________________ attitude to life had moved and influenced so many people.

Part 4 Reading Comprehension Test

Passage 1

Directions: Read the following passage and the statements after it, mark

Y (for Yes) if the statement agrees with the information given in the text;

N (for No) if the statement contradicts the information given in the text;

NG (for Not Given) if the information is not given in the text.

I'll never forget her—in fact, I still have dreams about the look on her children's faces after she died. Her name was Claire, and she came into the Emergency Room (ER) where I was working as an emergency physician. She had an old neck collar on upside down and was complaining of neck pain and a bad headache. She was about 60 years old, and I thought she might have a mental handicap because she had difficulty describing her symptoms. Her son and daughter were with her, and they also seemed a bit slow.

This ER was always busy, and the administration had been pressuring us to move patients through more quickly.

I examined Claire briefly and saw no obvious worrisome signs. X-rays of her neck showed nothing wrong; I assumed she had slept wrong or pulled a muscle. So I discharged her with some pain medication and picked up the next chart in the bottomless stack.

The next morning we received a call from an ambulance transporting a female who had suffered cardiac arrest. She was brought into the resuscitation room, where we continued CPR. I didn't recognize her at first, but then I noticed a familiar-looking son and daughter sobbing in the hallway. I looked at the lifeless patient and almost broke into tears myself. In my rush the day before, I hadn't listened carefully to Claire's complaint of severe headache. Now it seemed clear to me that I'd overlooked a symptom of an impending stroke.

We did everything we could, but I knew our efforts were hopeless.

After I pronounced her dead, I met her son and daughter in the small chapel near the emergency department.

I started to explain—in way too technical terms—what happened. Then I paused, and tears came to my eyes.

"I'm so sorry," I said. "I wish I had ordered a CT scan yesterday. I must have missed something. I'm so sorry."

"That's okay," Claire's daughter replied. "We know you did your best. Mom said you were a good doctor."

I couldn't stop my tears now.

A few days later, I went to the funeral, where I sat with Claire's children.

Even though 20 years have passed and I'm now a medical-school professor, I haven't forgotten. I try to impress upon physicians-in-training that medicine is more than using advanced technology to move an endless flow of patients.

Every person in the exam room, regardless of social status, is a human with a family, and our duty is to act in that person's best interest—not in the best interests of insurance companies and hospital administrators, the way I did.

We also need to ease the burden on the ER. Between 1997 and 2006, emergency department visits increased by 32 percent, while reimbursement to hospitals hasn't kept up. We need more retail health clinics and urgent-care centers.

And we need to educate people so they trust these new clinics and use them for all but the direct emergencies.

(520 words, taken from *Readers' Digest* 2009 (4) by Bryan E. Elesoe)

1. The author examined the patient Claire briefly and found no obvious worrisome signs because Claire had difficulty describing her own symptoms and her son and daughter also seemed a bit slow. ________
2. The hospital administration pressures physicians to discharge patients more quickly because there are too many patients in the ER. ________
3. The author has not forgotten the incident of Claire even though 20 years has passed because she felt sorry and regretful for not examining Claire carefully. ________
4. According to the author, the hospital administrations do not act in the patients' best interest but in the best interest of insurance companies and hospitals. ________
5. The author believes that more new clinics and urgent-care centers are needed to ease the burden on the ER. ________

Passage 2

Directions: Read the following passage carefully and complete the summary with ***no more than three words*** for each blank.

Shi Tiesheng, 59, donated his spinal marrow and brain for medical research, and his liver to a patient in need, said Ling Feng, director of the neurosurgery department of Xuanwu Hospital of the Capital Medical University.

"The recipient of Shi's liver was found in Tianjin at the right time, and the transplant operation was successfully done this morning," Ling said.

"In addition to his liver, Shi also donated his spinal marrow and brain for medical research.

"He looked as serene as if he had been asleep," said Ling who, with many of Shi's friends from the Chinese Writers Association, said farewell to Shi in the hospital's mortuary on Friday morning.

"He made a contribution to others in an honorable way. As long as the person he donated his liver to survives, he is still alive."

Born in Beijing in 1951, Shi was sent to rural Shaanxi province as an educated urban youth during the "cultural revolution" (1966-1976).

Paralyzed in both legs after an accident at 21, he was sent back to Beijing and worked in a neighborhood factory. From 1998, he suffered from kidney failure and had to undergo dialysis treatment three times a week.

Shi began to publish in 1979. He is best known for his short stories *My Faraway Clear Peace River* and *Strings of Life*, essays *The Temple of Earth and I* and *Fragments Written at the Hiatuses of Sickness*, and novels *Notes on Principles* and *My Sojourn in Ding Yi*.

A collection of his short stories was translated into English and published as *Strings on Life* in 1991.

He won many of the country's literature prizes, including the Lu Xun Literature Prize, the Lao She Essay Prize and the National Excellent Short Story Prize.

"Physical affliction made him more keenly conscious of his existence," friend and fellow writer Chen Cun said.

Shi admitted in *The Temple of Earth and I* that he was constantly seized by depression and mental turmoil.

But the tortured soul managed to transcend his personal predicament and he meditated in his writings on the existence of the invalid and men in general.

"Shi survived a setback, which either devastates a person or pacifies him," friend and fellow writer Jiang Zidan said.

Arguably one of the few Chinese writers with a serious religious sense, Shi had long been preparing to bid farewell to the world. He wrote in *The Temple of Earth and I*: "Death is a thing one never needs to be anxious to seek—it is a festival bound to arrive."

(427words, taken from *www.chinadaily.com.cn/china/2011-01/01* by Yang Guang)

Shi Tiesheng, a Chinese famous writer, decided to donate his 6. ________________, including his spinal marrow, brain for medical research and his liver to a patient in need. Shi was born in 1950 and 7. ________________ in an accident at the age of 21. He began to publish in 1979 and was best known for his 8. ________________ for which he won many of the country's literature prizes. He was tortured by the physical affliction but his soul managed to transcend his 9. ________________. In his opinion, death is a natural destiny; it is 10. ________________ that is to come to everybody eventually.

Passage 3 Life without Death

Directions: Read the following passage and match each paragraph with the facts or opinions which are expressed in the correspondent paragraphs.

A: Until recently, the thought that there might ever be a cure for aging seemed preposterous. Growing older and more decrepit appeared to be an inevitable and necessary part of being human. Over the last decade, however, scientists have begun to see ageing differently. Some now believe that the average life expectancy may soon be pushed to 160 years; others think that it may be extended to 200 or 300 years. A handful even wonder whether we might one day live for a millennium or more.

B: Behind this new excitement is the theory that the primary cause of ageing lies in highly reactive molecules called free radicals, left behind by the oxygen we breathe. Free radicals react with the molecules in our bodies, damaging DNA, proteins and other cell tissues, and are known to be implicated in diseases as diverse as cataracts, cancer and Alzheimer's. The body does its best to protect itself against free radicals by producing its own chemicals to prevent ageing, such as vitamins E and C, but it is always fighting a losing battle.

C: A year ago Gordon Lithgow of the University of Manchester discovered a way to help combat free radicals. Using one of these anti-ageing chemicals, he managed to increase the lifespan of one species of earthworm 50 percent. Despite cautionary words from the scientists, many welcomed this as the first step towards a drug which would extend life. Research involving the mutation of genes has also thrown up fascinating results: after identifying two of the genes that appear to control how long the earthworm lives, similar genes were found in organisms as various as fruit-flies, mice and human beings. When one considers the vast evolutionary distances that separate these species, it suggests that we may have discovered a key to how ageing is regulated throughout the entire animal kingdom.

D: Some scientists, however, are quick to discourage extravagant speculation. "There is no evidence whatsoever that swallowing any chemical would have an effect on mammals", says Rich Miller of the University of Michigan. "And those people who claim it might need to go out and do some experimenting". Some research, moreover, has produced alarming results. As well as controlling ageing, these genes also partly control the hormones which regulate growth. The upshot of this is that although the lives of mutant micc can be extended by up to 80 percent, they remain smaller than normal.

E: Quite apart from these sorts of horrors, the ethical implications of extending human lifespan are likely to worry many people. Even if the falling birthrates reported in the world's developed nations were to be repeated throughout the world, would this be sufficient to compensate for massively extended life expectancy, and would we be willing to see the demographic balance of our society change out of all recognition? David Gems, the head of the Centre for Research into Ageing at University College, London, is enthusiastic about the opportunities opened up by extended life, but even he observes. "If people live much longer, the proportion of children would, of course, be very small. It strikes me that it might feel rather claustrophobic: all those middle-aged people and very few children or young people."

F: The philosopher John Polkinghorne emphasizes that any discussion of the merits of life-extending therapies must take into account the quality of the life that is lived: "One would not wish to prolong life beyond the point at which life ceased to be creative and became just repetition. Clearly, there are only so many rounds of golf one would want to play."

(598 words, From *The Spectator*, 9th February, 2002 by Duncan Turner)

NB: *There are more opinions than paragraphs, so you will use some paragraphs more than once.*

Paragraph A	Paragraph B
Paragraph C	Paragraph D
Paragraph E	Paragraph F

11. ________ A new way to fight against free radicals is discovered.
12. ________ Research shows that the genes, which can help controlling ageing, are likely to control hormones.
13. ________ Some scientists believe that life span may soon be extended.
14. ________ Some scientists worry that the extension of lifespan would bring problems such as the break of the demographic balances of the society.
15. ________ It has been discovered that the free radicals work with molecules in our bodies to cause humans to become ageing.
16. ________ Some people believe that the quality of life is more important than the extension of lifespan.
17. ________ The key to how ageing is regulated throughout the entire animal kingdom seems to have been discovered.

Passage 4 Facts about Suicide

Directions: Read the passage and choose the best answer to each question.

You've decided to do it. Life is impossible. Suicide is your way out.

Fine—but before you kill yourself, there are some things you should know. I am a psychiatric nurse, and I see the results of suicide—when it works and more often, when it doesn't. Consider, before you act, these facts:

Suicide is usually not successful.

You think you know a way to guarantee it? Ask the 25 year old who tried to electrocute himself. He lived. But both his arms are gone.

What about jumping? Ask John. He used to be intelligent, with an engaging sense of humor. That was before he leaped from a building. Now, he's brain-damaged and will always need care. He staggers and has seizures. He lives in a fog. But, worst of all, he KNOWS he used to be normal.

Even less violent methods can leave you crippled. What about pills? Ask the 12 year old with extensive liver damage from an overdose. Have you ever seen anyone die of liver damage? You turn yellow. It's a hard way to go.

No method is foolproof. What about a gun? Ask the 24 year old who shot himself in the head. Now he drags one leg, has a useless arm and has no vision or hearing on one side. He lived through his "foolproof" suicide. You might, too.

Suicide is not glamorous. You may picture a movie star in a slinky negligee drifting off to eternal sleep from an overdose of pills, but your picture omits a likely sickening reality: as she dies, her beautiful gown is soiled with her excrement.

Who will clean your blood off the carpet or scrape your brains from the ceiling? Commercial cleaning companies may refuse that job—but SOMEONE has to do it. Who will have to cut you down from where you hanged yourself or identify your bloated body after you've drowned? Your mother? Your wife? Your son?

The carefully worded "loving" suicide note is no help. Those who loved you will NEVER completely recover. They'll feel regret and an unending pain. And rage, because at that moment, you cared only about yourself.

Suicide is contagious. Look around at your family: sons, daughters, brothers, sisters, husband, wife. Look closely at the 4-year-old playing with his cars on the rug. Kill yourself tonight, and he may do it 10 years from now. It's a fact that suicide often follows suicide in families, and kids are especially vulnerable.

You do have other choices. There are people who can help you through this crisis. Call a hot line. Call a friend. Call your minister or priest. Call a doctor or hospital. Call the police.

They will tell you that there's hope. Maybe you'll find it in the mail tomorrow. Or in a phone call this weekend. Or when you meet someone shopping. You don't know—no one does. But what you're seeking could be just a minute, a day or a month away.

You say you don't want to be stopped? Still want to do it? Well, then, I may see you in the psychiatric ward later. And we'll work with whatever you have left.

(532words, taken from *Readers' Digest*, September 1992 by Renee T. Lucero)

18. What is the author's tone of writing the article?

A. pessimistic and depressed B. peaceful and indifferent

C. relaxed and joyful D. humorous and concerned

19. What does the author mean when he writes "Suicide is not glamorous"?

A. Suicide can result in bad damage.

B. Suicide can bring much grief and trouble.

C. Suicide can destroy all the beauty of one's decent life.

D. Suicide can be unsuccessful.

20. What is the author's purpose of writing this article?

A. To threaten readers the brutal facts of suicide

B. To amuse readers

C. To inform and offer help for those who want to commit suicide

D. To argue how to commit suicide successfully

Passage 5 Three Passions

Directions: Read the passage and complete the table below with the answers A-E.

Three passions, simple but overwhelmingly strong, have governed my life: the longing for love, the search for knowledge, and unbearable pity for the suffering of mankind. These passions, like great winds, have blown me hither and thither, in a wayward course, over a deep ocean of anguish, reaching to the very verge of despair.

I have sought love, first, because it brings ecstasy—ecstasy so great that I would often have sacrificed all the rest of life for a few hours of this joy. I have sought it, next, because it relieves loneliness—that terrible loneliness in which one shivering consciousness looks over the rim of the world into the cold unfathomable lifeless abyss. I have sought it, finally, because in the union of love I have seen, in a mystic miniature, the prefiguring vision of the heaven that saints and poets have imagined. This is what I sought, and though it might seem too good for human life, this is what—at last—I have found.

With equal passion I have sought knowledge. I have wished to understand the hearts of men. I have wished to know why the stars shine. And I have tried to apprehend the Pythagorean power by which number holds sway above the flux. A little of this, but not much, I have achieved.

Love and knowledge, so far as they were possible, led upward toward the heavens. But always pity brought me back to earth. Echoes of cries of pain reverberate in my heart. Children in famine, victims tortured by oppressors, helpless old people a hated burden to their sons, and the whole world of loneliness, poverty, and pain make a mockery of what human life should be. I long to alleviate the evil, but I cannot, and I too suffer.

This has been my life. I have found it worth living, and would gladly live it again if the chance were offered me.

(322 words, by Bertrand Russell)

Longing for love	Searching for knowledge	Pity for suffering
brings ecstasy 21. ________ 22. ________	23. ________ 24. ________	25. ________

A. relieves the evil
B. understands the hearts of man
C. apprehends the mystery of the universe
D. alleviates the loneliness
E. prefigures the vision of the heaven

Unit 6

Love, Marriage and Family

Part 1 Reading Skills

In the previous five units, the reading skills of guessing unknown words have been illustrated. You can learn to figure out the meaning of unfamiliar words both from the context and from the word formation. However, understanding the meaning of words is only a prerequisite to understanding the text. The next step is how to understand sentences.

English is known as a hypotactic language which focuses on the language cohesion in form. And there are some laws governing the elements and the construction of sentences. Thus some knowledge about the syntactic structure is necessary for the comprehension of reading materials.

Section A Understanding Sentences

As we know English sentences can be divided into three kinds grammatically: simple sentences, compound sentences and complex sentences.

A simple sentence contains a subject and a verb and an object (if any), and it expresses a complete thought. A compound sentence is made up of two independent clauses joined by a coordinator. Such conjunctions as *and, nor, but, or, yet, so* will show different relationships between the pieces of information. A complex sentence has an independent clause joined by one or more dependent clauses. A complex sentence always has a subordinator such as *because, since, after, although*, or *when* or a relative pronoun such as *that, who*, or *which*.

Usually the structure of an English sentence can be compared to a tree. If the subject and the verb as well as the object make up the trunk, then the modifiers like adjectives, adverbs, prepositional phrases together with all kinds of clauses constitute the branches, small and large.

It's acknowledged that a simple sentence is relatively easier to understand. However, sometimes a comprehensive analysis is still needed. Here is an example:

1) *Widely regarded as the greatest American chess player in history, Bobby Fischer's prominence came as a child, winning the U.S. Open at the age of thirteen and becoming a grandmaster at age fifteen.*

In the above sentence, we can only find one subject (Bobby Fischer's prominence) and a verb (came). So it is a simple sentence which informs us that Bobby Fischer earned his fame when he was still a child (*as a child*). However, much detailed information can be attained from the modifiers. "Widely regarded as the greatest American chess player in history", "winning the U.S. Open at the age of thirteen" and "becoming a grandmaster at age fifteen" are all used to modify Bobby Fischer and there is an implied cause-effect relationship between the modifiers and the modified, that is, because when Bobby won the U.S. Open he was only thirteen and when he became a grandmaster he was only fifteen, it led to a conclusion that he became famous as a child. From this example it can be said that simple sentences sometimes are not simple.

A compound sentence is a combination of two simple sentences and the relationship itself between them is uncomplicated. For example,

2) *Helen Keller learned to read by the Braille system, and she learned to write by using a specially constructed typewriter.*

In this sentence, there is a parallel relationship between "Helen Keller learned to read" and "she learned to write". Usually the relationship between the simple sentences in a compound sentence tends to be obvious. Once you understand the simple sentences, the whole structure is not hard to grasp.

However, complex sentences are far more complicated and difficult. A complex sentence often contains more than one clause, parallel structure, inversion, infinitive, participle, gerund, ellipsis, etc. The components are dependent on each other and they won't work without the other. Basically, in a complex sentence there are conjunctions to join clauses together. Some of these clauses might be complete short sentences, but in a complex sentence at least one of them will depend on the conjunction for its meaning. In other words, if the conjunction is taken away, the two sentences won't make sense by themselves. Take the following sentence as an example:

3) *Chilean novelist and short-story writer María Luisa Bombal wrote innovative and influential stories featuring heroines who create fantasy worlds in order to escape from unfulfilling love relationships and restricted social roles.*

In the example sentence, the main structure is: María Luisa Bombal + wrote + stories. "*María Luisa Bombal*" is modified by "*Chilean novelist and short-story writer*"; "*stories*" is modified by "*featuring heroines who create fantasy worlds in order to escape from unfulfilling love relationships and restricted social roles*" and "*featuring heroines*" is followed by an attributive clause "*who create fantasy worlds in order to escape from unfulfilling love relationships and restricted social roles*".

The example sentence contains the following information:

a. María Luisa Bombal is a Chilean novelist and short-story writer.

b. She wrote innovative and influential stories.

c. In her stories, the featuring heroines experienced unfulfilling love relationships and were restricted by the society.

d. So they created fantasy worlds to escape from them.

From the analysis process of the above examples, some strategies can be recommended in order to make a full understanding of sentences, whether they be simple, or compound or complex ones:

First, identify the main structure: that is, identify the **subject + predicate (verb) + (object)**.

Second, examine the modifying parts of the main parts and clauses.

Third, examine the full understanding of the complex sentence.

Following these steps contributes to a comprehensive understanding of a variety of sentences that experienced writers are likely to use to make their writing interesting and lively.

Section B Practice

Directions: A part of each of the following sentences is underlined; beneath each sentence are five ways of phrasing the underlined material. Select the option that produces the best sentence. If you think the original phrasing produces a better sentence than any of the alternatives, select choice A.

1. <u>They are smaller than their counterparts in Africa, so Asiatic lions</u> can be found only in Gir, a forest region in northwest India.

   A. They are smaller than their counterparts in Africa, so Asiatic lions

   B. Its counterparts in Africa are bigger, but the Asiatic lion

   C. The Asiatic lion is smaller than their counterparts in Africa, they

   D. The counterparts of African lions in Asia are smaller, although they

E. Smaller than their counterparts in Africa, Asiatic lions

2. The gong, believed to have originated in Western Asia, reached China in the sixth century, where it continues to be used for a wide range of purposes, including as a military signal, a rhythmic accompaniment for vocal performance, and a ritual instrument.

A. including as B. which include C. which includes D. including

E. they include as

3. Since William the Conqueror in 1066, every British sovereign has been crowned in Westminster Abbey except Edward V and Edward VIII, neither of them were crowned.

A. neither of them were B. neither were

C. neither of whom was D. with neither being

E. with neither who had been

4. The modern recreational canoe closely resembles the Native American bark canoe in shape, length, weight, and carrying capacity, differing only in the materials of which they are made.

A. they are made B. they make them C. they made it D. it is made

E. its making

5. About 35 percent of the world's orange juice is produced by Florida, comparing it with nearly 50 percent produced by Brazil, the world's largest orange producer.

A. comparing it with B. but C. whereas D. although

E. compared with

6. In just a couple of years, low-carbohydrate diets have accomplished what the government has failed to do in decades of trying: it has convinced the public of refined grains, that they are bad and whole grains are good.

A. it has convinced the public of refined grains, that they

B. convincing the public about refined grains, which

C. convince the public that refined grains

D. convinces the public of refined grains, they

E. convincing the public that refined grains

7. Woody Guthrie wrote and adapted more than a thousand songs, many of them are about the struggles of workers and the poor in the United States.

A. many of them are B. many of which are

C. many are D. which are, many of them,

E. and many of them that are

8. A Raisin in the Sun won for its author Lorraine Hansberry the distinction of being the first African American to receive the New York Drama Critics' Circle Award.

A. of being the first African American to receive

B. to be the first African American receiving

C. of the first African American to receive

D. that she had been the first African American to receive

E. that she was to be the first African American having received

9. Though its early history is not fully known, origami, the art of folding objects out of paper without cutting, pasting, or decorating, <u>seems that it had developed from</u> the older art of folding cloth.
   A. seems that it had developed from
   B. seems to have developed from
   C. seems to have been developed out of
   D. had developed, it would seem, out of
   F. developing, it seems, out of

10. Lady Day, as Billie Holiday was usually called, was the finest jazz singer of her generation, <u>and it was the opinion of her fans, she was</u> the greatest jazz singer of the twentieth century.
   A. it was the opinion of her fans, she was
   B. the opinion of her fans was of her as
   C. her fans had this opinion, she was
   D. for her fans, the opinion was of her as
   E. in the opinion of her fans, she was

Part 2 Idioms, Proverbs and Sayings

Directions: The following are idioms, proverbs or sayings by famous people about love, family and marriage. Choose what you think is correct and compare with the right ones.

1. Beauty is in the eye of the ________. (Proverb)
   A. lover B. beholder C. partner D. spouse
2. No words are necessary between two ________ hearts. (Proverb)
   A. loving B. sweet C. warm D. passionate
3. Absence to love is what ________ is to fire. It extinguishes the small; it inflames the great. (Roger de Bussy-Rabutin)
   A. water B. oil C. wind D. sand
4. Man's love is of man's life a thing apart, it is woman's ________ existence. (Byron)
   A. whole B. apart C. a part D. complete
5. Marry in haste, ________ at leisure. (Proverb)
   A. regret B. repent C. disappointed D. satisfied
6. Keep your eyes wide open before marriage, ________ afterwards. (Proverb)
   A. half open B. half shut C. wide open D. completely shut
7. Happy families are all ________; every unhappy family is unhappy in its own way. (Tolstoy)
   A. the same B. similar C. different D. alike

8. By all means marry; if you get a good wife, you'll be happy. If you get a bad one, you'll become a ________. (Socrates)

   A. prisoner　　B. professor　　C. philosopher　　D. politician

9. A mother only does her children harm if she makes them the only ________ of her life. (W. Somerset Maugham)

   A. love　　B. care　　C. concern　　D. responsibility

10. It is a ________ father that knows his own child. (William Shakespeare)

   A. loving　　B. careful　　C. responsible　　D. wise

Part 3 Reading Passages

Section A Liking, Loving and Lust

1 The family cycle begins, naturally enough, with "boy meets girl." It's the attraction of opposites that sparks the explosion that kicks along the whole wheel of life. But attraction is a complicated thing. It has many levels to it, and understanding these levels is vital to a happy love-life.

2 Nor everyone gets together in the same way. For instance, some couples are first attracted at the mind level—liking the other person's ideas, finding him or her funny, interesting, stimulating. Other couples may find that they connect initially from the heart level; that warm affection and loving feelings arise easily between them. And of course many couples begin with an obvious sexual attraction, that tantalizing tingling excitement that is pure lust! To complicate it more, the way you feel about the other person is not always mirror-reflected—you can lust after someone who only likes you, or love someone who is only capable of lust, and so on. It can be tricky, especially when you are young and inexperienced (or, for that matter, old and stupid).

3 Levels of attraction are especially important to be aware of in the early stages of finding and choosing a partner. It's important, especially for teenagers, to distinguish these three levels of need and, in handling personal relationships, to be honest with yourself about which is what. Knowing yourself well enough to tell love from lust, liking from loving, is the real sex education and can help avoid countless problems.

4 Now let's explore how the three levels of attraction work, and then what to do when they stop working. Even if you've been married for fifty years, you'll enjoy reading this part, to reminisce and understanding the journey you have already made. If you're a little younger than that, it might even help you to power our love-life along!

Liking: A Meeting of Minds

5 Liking is the safest, easiest kind of human attraction. You can like all kinds and all ages and sexes of people—you can even like people you don't approve of, or would never buy a used car from. Often you will like some things about a person, and dislike other parts of them. (If you like everything about someone, stick around; something you won't like is bound to show up.)

6 As you get more involved with a person, either as a friend or as a lover, then you might ask them to change behavior you don't like. Relationships involve changing ourselves all the time. It's no big deal: if you are giving your lover a back rub, you might do it vigorously, because that's what you enjoy. They explain they like a gentler massage, and so you change. If you live together, you might like to make the kitchen spotlessly clean and tidy after every meal. They might prefer to leave the dishes for big once-a-week cleanup. Committed partners sometimes make big requests of their partner: to give up drinking or smoking or living a life of crime, for instance! Our partners may change, or they may not. We are all aiming to get more of what we like, and less of what we don't.

7 A trap with liking, especially when we are starting out in a relationship, is that we will tend to like people just because they like us, especially if we are inexperienced or, let's face it, a bit desperate. In fact, it might be their liking us that is the main attraction. If their enthusiasm for our wonderful qualities fades, as well it might, then we might discover we do not like them after all.

8 A note of caution. Our hormones can be our worst enemy at this stage. From the mid-teens on, nature wants us in love and breeding fast, so a certain amount of applying the brakes is needed. You make the best choices when you are not in such a hurry. That's why it's a good idea at any age to fill up your need to like and be liked with friendships of many kinds, before you get into the tangle of involving yourself in a couple. Loneliness blurs your judgment—believe it.

Loving: The Heart Connection

9 Liking usually comes first, but loving can soon follow, and everyone over the age of ten knows that this is a different and more powerful emotion. Love requires a certain kind of openness and trust, a willingness to be vulnerable.

10 Love can be expressed in words, but it is not about words. The human heart aches, it sings and it soars, but it doesn't talk much! Loving actually causes alarm in some people because it is part of a domain that is unfamiliar—the domain of emotion. Don't panic—feelings are simple!

11 With increasing honesty as you voice your feelings, a couple can begin to understand and clear up the obstacles to closeness one by one. Love grows through the vulnerability you show, as well as the strength of feelings you admit to. Your real self comes out more and more—and guess what? They still like you! You begin to feel that you can say anything, discuss anything, be completely yourself. It's a great feeling. (Though there's always

something new dark and murky arising from deep down, to make you start all over again.)

12 The good news is that love between two people may take decades to reach its fullest peak, so you have plenty to look forward to.

13 So in a growing relationship, men and women find attraction growing from head to head, and also heart to heart. But there's another level too, so let's rock on down to the basement.

Lust: The Fire Down Below

14 Sexual attraction is a lifelong, powerful tide which either adds energy and magnetism to relationships, or constantly blasts us apart, depending on our skill and awareness in navigating it. You will often hear sex denigrated as the "animal" part of our make-up, a Stone Age leftover which disturbs out rational mind. In fact human beings are more dedicatedly and enduringly sexual than any other animal species.

15 In human beings, the original purpose of the sex drive—to motivate reproduction—has been partly diverted to serve an equally important role, that of social connection. Although sex often seems to be a disrupting influence on our social fabric, it is nonetheless the force that creates and holds families and therefore communities together. Obligation and duty wear thin very quickly; they are recent and advanced concepts in evolution: nature counts on much stronger glues to cement us. Our biology has ensured that we will not rely on abstract ideas of loyalty and live, but that commitment will be deeply felt, that these feelings will give us more pleasure and reward than any other path in the long run. Therefore sex, love, communication and long-term bonding are all deeply intertwined in human beings. We make love with our brains, which is why sex is so special and important-and difficult.

(1,171 words)

I. Reading Comprehension

Directions: Choose the best answer to each of the following questions.

1. What is the main point the writer intends to illustrate in Paragraph 2?
   A. The writer intends to state that different people have different understandings of sexual attraction.
   B. The writer intends to state that people attract each other in different ways and at different levels.
   C. The writer intends to state that the way you feel about the other person is not always mirror-reflected and is complicated.
   D. The writer intends to state young and inexperienced people are more easily tricked by other persons.

2. Which of the following is NOT the reason why it is especially important to distinguish the levels of attraction?
   A. It helps young people to handle personal relationships better.
   B. It helps young people to know themselves better.
   C. It helps young people to avoid many problems.

D. It helps young couples to understand each other better.

3. Which of the following sentences can serve as the topic sentence of Paragraph 6?

   A. Relationships involve changing ourselves all the time.

   B. Committed partners sometimes make big requests of their partner.

   C. Our partners may change, or they may not.

   D. We are all aiming to get more of what we like, and less of what we don't.

4. What is the trap with liking according to the writer's opinion in Paragraph 7?

   A. Our hormones can cheat us in the period of mid-teen.

   B. People's liking us may be the reason we like them.

   C. we feel desperate when we find our lovers' enthusiasm to us fades

   D. We cannot make the best choice when we are in a hurry or when loneliness blurs our judgment.

5. Which of the following is NOT the feature of loving?

   A. Love requires openness and trust, a willingness to be vulnerable.

   B. Love is a more powerful emotion than liking.

   C. Love is the domain of each others' emotion.

   D. Love is the force that creates and holds families and therefore communities together

6. Which of the following is NOT the correct understanding of sex according to the writer's opinion?

   A. The original purpose of the sex drive is to motivate reproduction.

   B. Sex plays a special and important role in families and social connections.

   C. One of the important functions of sex is to help and hold families and communities together.

   D. Sex should be separated from love because sex is one part of the animal species.

7. The purpose of this article is ________.

   A. to inform B. to argue C. to advise D. to entertain

II. Vocabulary

Directions: Fill in each blank with an appropriate word from the box below. Change the form where necessary. Each word can be used only once.

spark	tantalize	reminisce	bound	committed
blur	vulnerable	magnetism	domain	fabric

1. The French designer—famed for developing Madonna's Conical bra for her 1990 Blonde Ambition Tour—has said his collaboration with the *Wedding Style* magazine was __________ to happen because he loved the magazine very much.
2. The Chinese ambassador to Ethiopia said that China has always been __________ to enhancing relations with Ethiopia and Africa in general.
3. The display of the movie "Sex and the City II" is sure to __________ women everywhere who love fashion.

4. Chinese basketball player Yao Ming's retirement has __________ hot discussions on the micro blog.
5. In recent years, TV talent shows such as Super Girls have "created" many gender-neutral stars. One such example is female singer Li Yuchun, who neither looks nor behaves like a woman. These shows __________ gender differences and tend to reverse the standards of aesthetics.
6. Sea has already become the important space to extend national interests, while sea safety has become a major __________ of national security.
7. The stability of a country's social __________ largely depends on the sound development of the nation's economy.
8. For thousands of years, the lunar New Year has been the most widely celebrated festival for the majority of Chinese people. It is a time for families to gather, __________ about the previous year's joys and remember its sorrows. It's a time to wish everyone the best in the upcoming year.
9. Inflation has emerged as one of the key social and economic challenges confronting the Chinese government this year. Increases in prices reduce purchasing power, particularly for the poor and most __________ in society.
10. The 29-year-old bride Kate Middleton has enough __________ to attract top fashion designers to design her wedding dress.

III. Discussion

1. Read the following lines from *A Chinese Odysse*y: *A Pandora's Box* and try to learn them by heart. Do you believe in everlasting love?

   You ought to kill me, and I ought to die. Once, I let a true love slip away before my eyes, only to find myself regretting when it was too late. Nothing in the world can be as painful as this. Just let your sword cut into my throat! Don't hesitate! If the God would give me another chance, I would tell the girl I love her. If our love had to be set a time limit, I wish it would be 10,000 years!
2. "Naked wedding" is a popular catch phrase in China coined amid the background of skyrocketing property prices. It refers to a marriage without a house, a car, diamond ring, or fancy wedding ceremony—but a nine-yuan marriage certificate. What's your attitude toward "naked wedding"?

Section B Story of Regret

Directions: Read the following passage and the statements after it, mark

Y (for Yes) if the statement agrees with the information given in the text;

N (for No) if the statement contradicts the information given in the text;

NG (for Not Given) if the information is not given in the text.

There was a guy who believed very much in true love and decided to take his time to wait for his right girl to appear. He believed that there would definitely be someone special out there for him, but none came.

Every year at Christmas, his ex-girlfriend would return from Vancouver to look him up. He was aware that she still held some hope of rekindling the past romance with him. He did not wish to mislead her in any way. So he would always get one of his girl friends to pose as his steady whenever she came back.

That went on for several years and each year, the guy would get a different girl to pose as his romantic interest. So whenever the ex-girlfriend came to visit him, she would be led into believing that it was all over between her and the guy.

The girl took all those rather well, often trying to casually tease him about his different girl friends, or so, as it seemed! In fact, the girl often wept in secret whenever she saw him with another girl, but she was too proud to admit it. Still, every Christmas, she returned, hoping to rekindle some form of romance. But each time, she returned to Vancouver feeling disappointed.

Finally she decided that she could not play that game any longer. Therefore, she confronted him and professed that after all those years, he was still the only man that she had ever loved. Although the guy knew of her feelings for him, he was still taken aback and had never expected her to react that way. He always thought that she would slowly forget about him over time and come to terms that it was all over between them. Although he was touched by her undying love for him and wanted so much to accept her again, he remembered why he rejected her in the first place—she was not the one he wanted. So he hardened his heart and turned her down cruelly. Since then, three years had passed and the girl never returned anymore. They never even wrote to each other. The guy went on with his life—still searching for the one but somehow deep inside him: he missed the girl.

On the Christmas of 1995, he went to his friend's party alone. "Hey, how come all alone this year? Where are all your girl friends? What happened to that Vancouver baby who joins you every Christmas?" asked one of his friends. He felt warm and comforted by his friend's queries about her, still he just surged on.

Then, he came upon one of his many girl friends whom he once requested to pose as his steady. He wanted so much to ignore her... not that he was impolite, but because at that moment, he just didn't feel comfortable with those girl friends anymore. It was almost like he was being judged by them. The girl saw him and shouted across the floor for him. Unable to avoid her, he went up to acknowledge her.

"Hi... how are you? Enjoying the party?" the girl asked.

"Sure... yeah!" he replied.

She was slightly tipsy... must be from the whiskey on her hand. She continued, "Why...? Don't you need someone to pose as your girlfriend this year?" Then he answered, "No, there is no need for that anymore..."

Before he can continue, he was interrupted, "Oh yes! Must have found a girlfriend! You haven't been searching for one for the past years, right?" The man looked up, as if he has struck gold, his face beamed and looked directly at the drunken girl. He replied, "Yes... you are right! I haven't been looking for anyone for the past years."

With that, the man darted across the floor and out the door, leaving the lady in much bewilderment. He finally realized that he had already found his dream girl, and she was... the Vancouver girl all along! The drunken lady had said something that awoken him.

All along he had found his girl. That was why he did not bother to look further when he realized she was not coming back. It was not any specific girl he was seeking! It was perfection that he wanted, and yes... perfection!!

Realizing that he had let away someone so important in his life, he decided to call her immediately. His whole mind was flooded with fear. He was afraid that she might have found someone new or no longer had the same feelings anymore... For once, he felt the fear of losing someone.

As it was Christmas Eve, the line was quite hard to get through, especially an overseas call. He tried again and again, never giving up. Finally, he got through... precisely at 12:00 midnight. He confessed his love for her and the girl was moved to tears. It seemed that she never got over him!

Even after so long, she was still waiting for him, never giving up. He was so excited to meet her and to begin his new chapter of their lives. He decided to fly to Vancouver to join her. It was the happiest time of their lives! But their happy time was short-lived. Two days before he was supposed to fly to Vancouver, he received a call from her father. She had a head-on car collision with a drunken driver. She passed away after 6 hours in a coma.

The guy was devastated, as it was a complete loss. Why did fate play such cruel games with him? He cursed the heaven for taking her away from him, denying even one last look at her! How cruel he cursed! How he damned the God! How he hated himself... for taking so long to realize his mistake!! That was in 1996.

(970 words)

1. When his ex-girlfriend came to see him, the boy always got one of his female friends to pose as his girlfriend because he did not want to mislead his ex-girlfriend. ________
2. The boy's ex-girlfriend did not mind when she saw the boy had new girlfriend because she believed he still loved her. ________

3. When his ex-girlfriend professed that she still loved him all those years, the boy was very surprised. ________
4. Although touched by his ex-girlfriend's affection to him, the boy still refused to rekindle with her because he was still waiting for his right girl to appear. ________
5. When his friends queried about his ex-girlfriend on the Christmas of 1995, the boy felt quite awkward. ________
6. The boy behaved impolitely when the drunken girl talked with him and he felt uncomfortable for he once required the girl to pose as his girlfriend. ________
7. It was after the talk with the drunken girl that the boy realized his dream girl was his ex-girlfriend. ________
8. The boy was rather afraid because he was not sure whether his ex-girlfriend was still waiting for him. ________
9. The boy and the girl decided to meet at the airport of Vancouver. ________
10. It was on her way to buy Christmas gifts for the boy that the girl had the traffic accident. ________

Part 4 Reading Comprehension Test

Passage 1 Have I Found Ms. Right?

Directions: Read the passage carefully and finish the summary with the words in the box that follows. Note there are more words than needed.

Choosing your life partner is a decision that requires very careful thought. Getting married is something you do not want to take lightly. Divorce rates around the world are increasing every year, and in some countries they are now as high as 50 percent! If you don't want to end up divorced and heart-broken, take my advice and follow these five rules to help you choose your perfect partner.

First of all, you and your partner should be compatible. You need to know that you share a common purpose in life. You and your partner should have similar goals and ambitions that you can work towards achieving throughout your married life. It will be difficult to keep your marriage together if your partner wants to stay at home and raise a large family, but you want to travel the world instead of having children. Find out what your intended spouse's life goals are long before you tie the knot!

Next, ask yourself this question: Is my partner a person with whom I can share my innermost thoughts and feelings? In other words, can you be completely honest and open with this person, or do you sometimes feel shy and uncomfortable telling her how you feel? If your situation is the former, then you have probably found your true love. If, however, it is the latter take your time before you make plans to walk down the aisle with this person.

Third, only marry someone who has qualities you admire. If you respect people who work hard, you should marry someone who is hard-working, not someone who is lazy or too easy-going.

Fourth, marry a person who is polite and kind to others; they will be polite and kind to you. In my experience, you can learn a lot about the true nature of a person by watching how he or she treats other people. A person who is kind and giving to family and friends will be kind and giving towards to you. Someone who has good manners and is polite and respectful towards others will show you the same consideration. Watch how your partner treats people she does not have to be nice to such as waiters, taxi drivers, or store clerks. Does your partner pay attention to how you and others feel, or does she have a self-centered nature?

Finally, when you enter into a relationship with someone, remember that you should not expect to change that person. If your partner has qualities or faults that you feel you cannot tolerate, then you probably shouldn't marry her. Marriage should be about accepting a person—with all their good and bad points—for life.

Finding your life partner is not always easy. Falling in love is a great feeling, so take time to enjoy all the emotions that go along with it. However, when you decide to marry, use your head and your heart to think about things carefully. Spending the rest of your life with one person takes hard work and effort. Make sure that the person you marry is the right one for you.

(518 words)

A. careful	B. admire	C. rules	D. regulations
E. tolerate	F. compatible	G. change	H. similar goals
I. take efforts	J. attitudes	K. emotions	L. competent
M. kindly	N. free	O. self-supported	P. self-centered

Careful thought is required in order to choose your life partner. Here are some pieces of advice and 1. __________ offered to help you. First, before you get married, you should make sure that you and your partner should be 2. __________ and share 3. __________ and ambitions. Second, you and your partner are 4. __________ to share with each other your deepest and genuine 5. __________. Third, marry a person whose qualities you 6. __________ and who treats other people 7. __________; never expect to 8. __________ your partner. Never marry a person who is 9. __________ and who has qualities that you cannot accept or 10. __________. Enjoy the love emotion with your partner but think carefully when you decide to marry and 11. __________ to spend a happy married life.

Passage 2 The Odd Couple

Directions: Read the passage below and choose the best answer to each question.

I have always wondered how my parents were attracted to each other. Their personalitics, temperaments, and attitudes toward money are all opposite. The saying that "opposites attract" certainly holds true for them.

Their personalities are quite different. My mother is outgoing and friendly. She enjoys people because, to her, they are the most interesting form of life. When she meets new people, she greets them as if they were old friends, whether they are first time clients at her beauty shop or acquaintances of someone she already likes. She loves to socialize. Making conversation with any type of personality comes easily to her—it's a natural quality.

My father, on the other hand, is conservative and shy. Socializing is not easy for him. His shyness may give the impression that he's cold, but once he gets to know you, his warmth and sincerity emerge.

When it comes to controlling one's temper, my mother clearly outdoes my father. She will tolerate a lot before she gets angry and prefers to rationalize rather than lose her temper. However, my father's temper is like a short fuse on a stick of dynamite. He will flare up immediately when something is said or done wrongly. Also very stubborn, he always insists that he is right. Our dinners often turn into debates, with the issue usually being money.

My mother is not a bargain shopper. She does not cut out coupons or compare products or prices; she is impatient—if she likes something, she buys it. My father, therefore, has always done our food shopping. He compares products and prices, looks for sales and bargains, and buys only what he needs. He has also always taken care of our household finances and is the bookkeeper and accountant of the family. My father says that my mother has champagne tastes with a beer pocketbook, and she says that he's cheap, but there is a happy compromise—she spends and he saves.

"It must be love," I say about this odd couple. They may be very different, but they are also very compatible. Learning from each other ensures the success of their partnership.

(356 words)

12. All of the following aspects are the differences between my father and mother EXCEPT ________.

A. temperaments
B. attitudes towards money
C. attitudes towards each other
D. personalities

13. "However, my father's temper is like a short fuse on a stick of dynamite. He will <u>flare up</u> immediately when something is said or done wrongly". Which of the following is closest in meaning to the underlined part?

A. become sad
B. become angry
C. become worried
D. become bitter

14. The reason why the writer's father does food shopping is that ________.
    A. he is the bookkeeper and accountant of the family
    B. his mother is not good at bargaining while shopping
    C. he knows what they need
    D. he buys everything he likes
15. The sentence "my father says that my mother has champagne tastes with a beer pocketbook" means that the writer's father thinks ________.
    A. she likes champagne more than beer
    B. she likes beer more than champagne
    C. she likes to buy things that are too expensive for them to afford
    D. she spends more money than he saves
16. Which of the following statements can serve as the main idea of this passage?
    A. Love between a couple can help them live a harmonious life even though they may have different personalities.
    B. His parents are an odd couple because they love each other but never feel attracted to each other.
    C. Couples of different personalities are less compatible than couples of the same personalities.
    D. "Opposites attract" certainly holds true for everyone.

Passage 3 American Wedding Customs

Directions: Fill in the blanks after a fast reading of the following passage.

Wedding days are often considered the most important day of many people's lives. For this reason alone, throughout the past and into modern day, numerous customs and superstitions have developed around the wedding event, in hopes of creating "The Perfect Day"!

A very common custom still honored today is in reference to a time-old saying, "Something old, something new, something borrowed, something blue, and a silver sixpence inside your shoe". So old is this that tracing it back to its origination is nearly impossible. Some contribute it to Victorian times, others say it is even older than that. The "old" is believed to be the friends and family attending the wedding. The "new" is represented by the couple themselves, as a "new" union. The "borrowed" is something from the families that is to be returned, such as the bride's wedding dress, or the veil, borrowed from her own mother. Something "blue" is often interpreted to represent the bride's virginity, as in the opposite of red, which throughout time has come to represent a woman of many men. Modern day brides often wear a bit of blue material tucked out of sight. The sixpence can be any form of money, tucked into the bride's shoe to bring wealth, both in monetary means and love, to the union.

The veil and the bridesmaids were originated not as decorations or to allow your friends to share in your happy day, but to help confuse the evil spirits that were believed to be lurking about on this holy day. The veil, by hiding the face, particularly the eyes, confused the evil spirits. Bridesmaids would surround the bride, thus confusing the evil spirits as to who was the actual bride. In a similar belief, the best man is supposed to protect the groom from the day the wedding is first set in motion, until he is rightfully married to his impending bride.

Weddings have historically taken place in higher numbers during the month of June than any other month of the year. It ties into the old belief that it was lucky to be married on the day of the full moon. A wedding on the June day of a full moon was considered to be the most prosperous and long lasting union of all. These go together with the belief that a wedding on a bright, sunny day, which June is well known for, foretold good luck for the bride and groom, compared to being married on a rainy day, which foretold bad luck and a short marriage.

People also throw rice at weddings. Why? It shows that the guests wish fertility, prosperity, and long lasting happiness for the newly married couple.

Colors have long played a part in the planning of weddings. While many believe that the white of the wedding dress signified that the bride is a virgin, this is not actually true in all societies. An old saying sums up the colors in a wedding very well:

Marry in white, you will do all right
Marry in blue, your man will be true
Marry in brown, you will live in town
Marry in green, you should be ashamed to be seen
Marry in red, wish yourself dead
Marry in black, better turn back
Marry in yellow, not marrying the right fellow
Marry in gray, sadness will come your way

The day of the week that the wedding is to take place is also steeped in custom, hence the saying:

Marry on Monday for wealth,
Tuesday for health,
Wednesday the very best day of all,
Thursday you will soon be counting your losses,
Friday you cross,
and if married on Saturday, you will have no luck at all!

One tradition that has been around so long is whether or not it is good luck for the bride to make her own wedding dress. Some people believe it is lucky, others feel it is very unlucky for the bride to even help with the making of the dress.

Throwing of the bride's bouquet is good luck for the bride, and foretells the next of her friends to be married. Whoever catches the bouquet should take a small sliver of the wedding cake home with her and place it beneath her pillow just as she goes to sleep that night. She will dream of her future husband on that single night.

Many superstitions also exist for right after the wedding to start the marriage off right. The new couple should borrow a coffeepot for the first three months, then purchase one together. A new broom and frying pan is needed to start the couple off on a road to happiness, never start off a marriage with these two items old, or already used. The bride should cook her new husband and herself their first meal; it should not be eaten at a restaurant or an in-laws house. Never sell the wedding dress. It can be borrowed out, or even given away, but never let money be received for the dress or the marriage will come to a quick end.

Keep in mind these are all just customs and superstitions. Marriage is a union between two people who love each other! (But it never hurts to add a little luck in whatever way you can!)

(880 words)

17. The function of veil in the wedding is ________________.
18. Weddings often take place in higher numbers during June because ________________ ________________.
19. The color "blue" in the wedding represents ________________.
20. The bride's "bouquet" in the wedding represents ________________.
21. To sell the wedding dress means ________________.

Passage 4 Families

Directions: Read the following passage carefully and choose the best answer to each question.

"Family"—the word had different meanings for different people, and even the dictionary gives us several definitions: "a group of people related by blood or marriage, "two adults and their children," "all those people descended from a common ancestor," "a household," and so on. Some people think of a family as a mother, a father, and their children; others include grandparents, aunts, uncles, and cousins. For some of us, family means the group of relatives living far away from home. For others, having a family simply means having children. Some families have long histories, while others know very little about their ancestors. No matter it is young or old, large or small, traditional or modern, every family has a sense of what a family is. It is that feeling of belonging, of love and security that comes from living together, helping and sharing.

There are basically two types of families: nuclear families and extended families. The nuclear family usually consists of two parents (mother and father) and their children. The mother and father form the nucleus, or center, of the nuclear family. The children stay in the nuclear family until they grow up and marry. Then they form new nuclear families.

The extended family is very large. There are often many nuclear families in one extended family. An extended family includes children, parents, grandparents, uncles, aunts, and cousins. The members of an extended family are related by blood (grandparents, parents, children, brothers, sisters, etc.) or by marriage (husbands, wives, mothers-in-law, etc.) they are all related, so the members of extended family are called relatives.

Traditionally, all the members of an extended family lived in the same area. However, with the change from an agricultural to an industrial society, many nuclear families moved away from the family home in order to find work. In industrial societies today, the members of most nuclear families live together, but most extended families do not. Therefore we can say that the nuclear family becomes more important than the extended family as the society industrializes.

In post-industrial societies like the United States, even the nuclear family is changing. The nuclear family is becoming smaller as parents want fewer children, and the number of childless families is increasing. Traditionally, the father of a nuclear family earned money for the family while the mother cared for the house and the children. Today, more than 50 percent of the nuclear families in the United States are two-earner families—both the father and the mother earn money for the family—and in a few families the mother earns the money while the father takes care of the house and the children. Many nuclear families are also "splitting up"—more and more parents are getting divorced.

What will be the result of this 'splitting" of the nuclear family? Social scientists now talk of two new family forms: the single parent family and the remarried family. Almost 20% of all American families are single parent families, and in 85 percent of these families the single parent is the mother. Most single parents find it very difficult to take care of a family alone, so they soon marry again and form remarried families. As social scientists study these two new family forms, they will be able to tell us more about the future of the nuclear family in post-industrial age.

(557 words)

22. What is the definition of "family" according to the passage?

A. A group of people related by blood or marriage

B. Two adults and their children

C. All those people descended from a common ancestor.

D. All of the above.

23. The largest family is ________.

A. the single parent family　　B. The extended family

C. The nuclear family　　D. the remarried family

24. Which of the following about the nuclear family is NOT true?

A. The nuclear family becomes more important than the extended family today.

B. Change of the society makes it necessary for many nuclear families to move away for work.

C. The members of most nuclear families live together today.

D The nuclear family members don't like to live with other extended family members.

25. According to the passage, post-industrial societies refer to ________.

A. developing countries　　B. developed countries

C. underdeveloped countries　　D. the United States

Unit 7

Food and Table Manners

Part 1 Reading Skills

Words are connected with meaning and are used to refer to concepts. Words combined in accordance with some rules make up sentences to convey meaning and message. However, they are separate units which will not provide a whole picture of the ideas that writers are trying to express. Paragraphs, articles, passages textbook chapters and books all have topics and main ideas. As an effective reader, you need to find the topics and the main ideas writers are trying to communicate.

The topic, or the gist, is the larger conceptual framework of a paragraph, an article, a passage or a chapter of a book. Usually the writer will explain, discuss or argue for the topic by telling how, what, when, where, why, how much, or how many etc according to certain patterns. These detail patterns will naturally lead to his conclusion and thus the main idea is clear.

Locating the topic, clarifying the patterns of details that aim to expound the topic will enable you to know about the writer's intention, his purpose of writing, that is, the main idea of his writing. The main idea is the most important piece of information the author wants you to know about the concept of that paragraph, or article, or passage.

Being able to recognize, identify, and understand the relationship between topics, main ideas, and supporting details can be crucial for a reader to have a comprehensive understanding of what he is reading.

Section A Distinguishing Topic from Main Idea

1. What is a Topic?

A topic is the broad, general theme or message. It is what some call the subject. When you read for the meaning, you should begin by looking for the topic. This helps you connect what you read to what you already know. In order to find the topic, ask yourself: "What is this about? What is the general idea?"

2. What is the Main Idea?

The main idea of a paragraph is the author's idea about the topic. In order to find the main idea, ask yourself: "What does the author want the reader to know about the subject or topic of the paragraph?"

3. Distinguishing Topic from Main Idea

A paragraph is a group of sentences that are all about the same thing. They all have the same topic. The general idea or the subject of the paragraph is the topic. The main idea further focuses on the point of the paragraph. So it is the "key concept" being expressed. It is always a complete sentence that includes both the topic and the idea that the author wishes to express about the topic. Now let's look at the following two paragraphs:

Some people believe that money is the source of happiness. In their eyes, only a rich man can live happily. For example, a man with plenty of money can buy delicious food, beautiful dress, luxurious houses, expensive cars—anything required for him to live comfortably and enjoyably.

Other people, however, view money as the root of all evil. As a proverb goes, "Money makes the mare go." Money can drive people into stealing, robbing and even murdering. Many people become criminals just because they are in search of money. For these people, money brings them nothing but evil and misery.

The topic of the above two paragraphs is the same: money. However, the main idea is quite different from, and even opposite to each other. The main idea of the first paragraph is "Some people believe that money is the source of happiness." However, the main idea of Paragraph Two is "Other people view money as the root of all evil." As for the main idea of these two paragraphs, we can conclude that different people hold different attitudes toward money."

Section B Practice

Directions: Read the following paragraphs and write down the topic and the main idea of each exercise.

1. All human beings are able to digest all kinds of fruit, vegetables, and meats. But most people learn to eat only what their cultures teach them is good.

   Hindus are people who follow the religion of Hinduism. Most Hindus live in India. Hindus will not eat beef. They use their cows for milk. They use cows to help fertilize the soil. But they will not eat a cow's meat.

   Religious Jews will not eat pork or shell-fish, such as lobsters and shrimp. But to many other people, lobster is a good food. Americans usually do not consider insects as food. But ants are accepted as food in parts of Africa and Asia. The food people of one culture eat is no more "natural" than that of another.

   Topic: ____

   Main Idea: ____________________________________

2. People in different places eat differently. In some places, such as China, children learn to eat with chopsticks. In other places, people pick up food with the thumb and the third finger. What do most children learn to eat with in our culture?

   Most of us eat sitting on chairs at tables. But many Americans now eat standing up at hamburger counters. In some parts of the world, such as Japan, most people sit on floor to eat, rest on cushions, or squat on their heels.

   We are taught not to make noises when eating. But in some places, noises show appreciation for food, and quiet eating is considered rude. The things we call good manners are really the ways the people of our culture approve of doing things.

   Topic: ____

   Main Idea: ____________________________________

3. We are taught to eat three meals a day—breakfast, lunch, and dinner. In some places in the world, lunch is the main meal of the day. In other places, people eat only breakfast and dinner. When do you think is the best time to give the stomach food? Different people have different answers.

   Topic: ____

   Main Idea: ____________________________________

Part 2 Idioms, Proverbs and Sayings

Directions: The following are some idioms containing fruits, food or drink. Please match Column A with Column B to form complete idioms or proverbs and try to work out the meaning of each one.

Column A	Column B
1. When the monkey can't reach the ripe banana...	a. …over spilt milk
2. The proof of the pudding is…	b. …the broth
3. Too many cooks spoil…	c. …in one basket
4. One man's meat is another man's…	d. …better than none
5. You can't have your cake…	e. …in the eating
6. Don't put all your eggs…	f. …poison
7. It's no use crying...	g. …and eat it too
8. Don't marry a girl who wants…	h. …a kiss without a squeeze
9. A cherry year…	i. …a dumb year
10. An apple-pie without some cheese is like…	j. …a closed mouth
11. A pear will never fall into…	k. …strawberries in January
12. Half a loaf is…	l. …buying melons
13. Beautiful grapes often make…	m. …a merry year
14. A plum year…	n. …he says it is not sweet
15. Marriage is a little bit like…	o. …poor wine

Part 3 Reading Passages

Section A Food Taboos

Taboo food and drink are food and beverages which people abstain from consuming for religious, cultural or hygienic reasons. Most food taboos include the meat of a particular animal, including mammals, rodents, reptiles, amphibians, bony fish, and crustaceans. Some taboos are specific to a particular part or excretion of an animal, while other taboos forgo the consumption of plants, fungi, or insects.

Food taboos can be defined as a codified set of rules about which foods or combinations of foods may not be eaten and how animals are to be slaughtered. The origin of these prohibitions and commandments is varied. In some cases, these taboos are a result of health considerations or other practical reasons. In others, they are a result of human symbolic systems. Some foods may be prohibited during certain festivals (e.g. Lent), at certain times of life (e.g. pregnancy), or to certain classes of people (e.g. priests), although the food is in general permissible.

Various religions forbid the consumption of certain types of food. For example, Judaism prescribes a strict set of rules, called *Kashrut*, regarding what may and may not be eaten. Islam has similar laws, dividing foods into *haraam* (forbidden) and *halal* (permitted). Jains often follow religious directives to observe vegetarianism. Hinduism has no specific proscriptions against eating meat, but Hindus apply the concept of *ahimsa* (non-violence) to their diet and consider vegetarianism as ideal, and largely practice forms of vegetarianism.

Aside from overt rules, there are cultural taboos against the consumption of some animals. One cause is the classification of a food as famine food—the association of a food with famine, and hence association of the food with hardship. Within a given society, some meats will be considered taboo simply because they are outside the range of the generally accepted definition of a foodstuff, not necessarily because the meat is considered repulsive in flavor, aroma, texture or appearance. Dog meat is eaten, in certain circumstances, in Korea, Vietnam, and China, although it is nowhere a common dish. Similarly, horse meat is rarely eaten in the Anglosphere, although it is part of the national cuisine of countries as widespread as Kazakhstan, Japan, and France.

In some instances, a food taboo may only apply to certain parts of an animal.

Sometimes food taboos enter national or local law, as with the ban on cattle abattoirs in most of India, and horse slaughter in the United States. Even after resumption to Chinese rule, Hong Kong has not lifted its ban on supplying meat from dogs and cats, imposed in colonial times.

Environmentalism, ethical consumerism and other activist movements are giving rise to new taboos and eating guidelines. A fairly recent addition to cultural food taboos is that of eating the meat or eggs of endangered species or animals that are otherwise protected by law or international treaty. Examples of such protected species include some species of whales, sea turtles, and migratory birds.

Similarly, sustainable seafood advisory lists and certification consider certain seafood taboo due to unsustainable fishing. Organic certification prohibits most synthetic chemical inputs during food production, or genetically modified organisms, irradiation, and the use of sewage sludge. The Fair Trade movement and certification discourage the consumption of food and other goods produced in exploitative working conditions. Other social movements generating taboos include Local Food and *The 100-Mile Diet*, both of which encourage abstinence from non-locally produced food, and veganism, in which adherents endeavour not to use or consume animal products of any kind.

Cat meat is eaten in China and Vietnam. In desperate times, people of other areas have been known to resort to cooking and eating cats.

In 2008, it was reported that cats were a staple part of the local diet Guangdong, China, with many cats being shipped down from the north and one Guangzhou-based business receiving up to 10,000 cats per day from different parts of China. Protesters in other parts of China have urged the Guangdong provincial government to crack down on cat traders and restaurants that serve cat meat, although no law says it is illegal to eat cats.

Many Hindus, particularly Brahmins, are vegetarian, abstaining from eating meat. Even those Hindus who do eat meat abstain from the consumption of beef, as the cow holds a sacred place in Hinduism. Consumption of beef is taboo out of respect for the cow. Some ethnic Chinese may also refrain from eating cow meat, because many of them feel that it is wrong to eat an animal that was so useful in agriculture. Some Chinese Buddhists discourage the consumption of beef, although it is not considered taboo.

Generally in all Western countries eating dog or cat meat is considered taboo, though that taboo has been broken under threat of starvation in the past.

Horse meat is the culinary name for meat cut from a horse. It is a major meat in only a few countries, notably in Central Asia, but it forms a significant part of the culinary traditions of many others, from Europe to South America to Asia, the top eight countries consuming about 4.7 million horses a year. However, because of the role horses have played as a companion and as a worker, and concerns about the ethics of the horse slaughter process, it is a taboo food in some cultures. These historical associations, as well as ritual and religion, led to the development of the aversion to the consumption of horse meat. The horse is now given pet status by many in some parts of the Western world, particularly in the USA and UK, which further solidifies the taboo on eating its meat.

(934 words, taken from *http://en.wikipedia.org/wiki/Food_taboo*)

I. Reading Comprehension

Directions: Choose the best answer to finish the incomplete statements according to the above passage.

1. All of the following words from the above passage are synonyms EXCEPT ________.
   A. prescribe B. prohibit C. forbid D. ban
2. All of the following are reasons for food taboos EXCEPT ________.
   A. health consideration B. religious belief
   C. unsustainable development D. environmental movements
3. From Paragraph 3 we can infer that ________.
   A. a famine food is usually associated with hardship, thus becomes a taboo
   B. in some countries people don't eat certain meats just because they never consider them as food
   C. in the Anglosphere people don't eat dog
   D. People in Kazakhstan, Japan, and France like to eat horse
4. Hong Kong is cited as an example to show that ________.
   A. China has resumed its rule over it
   B. food taboo is sometimes a result of imposed laws from colonists
   C. dog and cat are forbidden food there
   D. it chooses to carry on the ban on eating cat and dog even though it doesn't need to obey laws of England
5. All of the following statements are true about Chinese EXCEPT that ________.
   A. Some Chinese like to eat cat B. Chinese eat dog
   C. Some Chinese don't eat cow meat D. Nothing is inedible for Chinese

II. Vocabulary

Directions: Fill in each blank with an appropriate word from the box below. Each word can be used only once.

abstain	hygienic	forgo	slaughter	prescribe
repulsive	resumption	aroma	culinary	migratory

1. Nothing pains him more than the decision taken three years back to __________ an opportunity to list his company in the US markets.
2. Swans are __________ birds that are very sensitive to climate change.
3. Friction between doctors and patients has been created as many doctors are willing to __________ unnecessary and expensive medicines in order to increase income.
4. Muslims around the world __________ from eating, drinking and conducting sexual relations from sunrise to sunset during Ramadan, the holiest month in the Islamic calendar.
5. The __________ of talks, the first in 15 months, is the result of joint efforts by all parties involved and hasn't come easily.

6. He didn't mention being sick because of poor __________ condition during the month after his arrival.
7. We are honored and proud to show the essence of China's __________ culture to friends from all over the world.
8. Once the tea is soaked in fresh-boiled water, a sweet woodsy __________ rises out.
9. Nanjing witnessed the mass __________ of 300,000 people in 1937 following the Japanese invasion of the then Chinese capital.
10. Aggressive beggars and those cheating people who take pity on them are no doubt __________.

III. Discussion

Directions: Look at the following pictures and discuss:

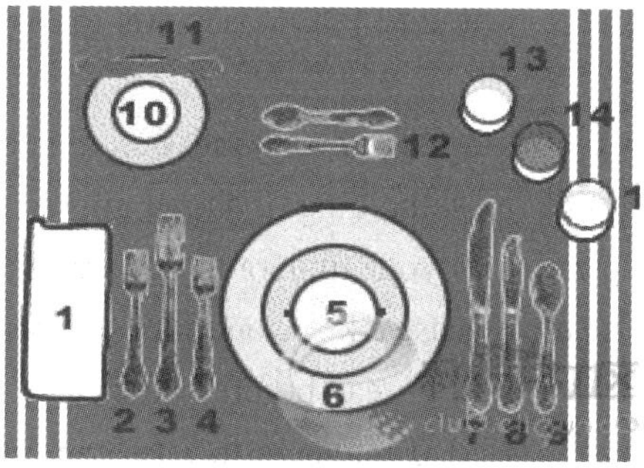

1. What are all these numbered utensils for on a formal western dinner table?

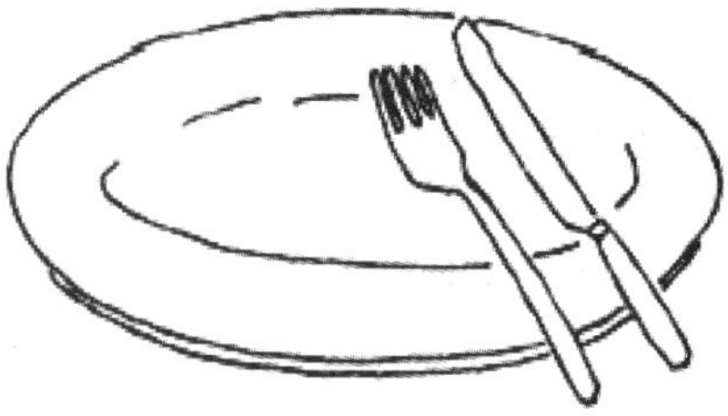

2. What do these two pictures mean?

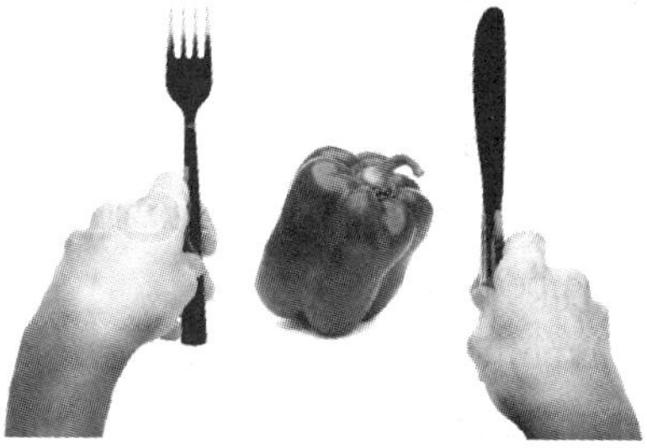

3. Which is the correct way to hold a knife and fork?

Section B Dos and Don'ts when Eating in Britain

Directions: Read the following text and decide whether the statements after it are true or false. Write T for True and F for False.

The British generally pay a lot of attention to good table manners. We eat most of our food with cutlery. The foods we don't eat with a knife, fork or spoon include sandwiches, crisps, corn on the cob, and fruit.

Things you should do:

If you cannot eat a certain type of food or have some special needs, tell your host several days before the dinner party.

If you are a guest, it is polite to wait until your host starts eating or indicates you should do so. It shows consideration.

Always chew and swallow all the food in your mouth before taking more or taking a drink.

Always say thank you when served something. It shows appreciation.

You may eat chicken and pizza with your fingers if you are at a barbecue, finger buffet or very informal setting. Otherwise always use a knife and fork.

When eating rolls, break off a piece of bread before buttering. Eating it whole looks tacky.

On formal dining occasions it is good manners to take some butter from the butter dish with your bread knife and put it on your side plate (for the roll). Then butter pieces of the roll using this butter. This prevents the butter in the dish getting full of bread crumbs as it is passed around.

In a restaurant, it is normal to pay for your food by putting your money on the plate the bill comes on.

When you have finished eating, and to let others know that you have, place your knife and folk together, with the prongs (tines) on the fork facing upwards, on your plate.

Things you should not do:

Never lick or put your knife in your mouth.

It is impolite to start eating before everyone has been served unless your host says that you don't need to wait.

Never chew with your mouth open. No one wants to see food being chewed or hearing it being chomped on.

It is impolite to have your elbows on the table while you are eating.

Don't reach over someone's plate for something; ask for the item to be passed.

Never talk with food in your mouth.

It is impolite to put too much food in your mouth.

Never use your fingers to push food onto your spoon or fork.

It is impolite to slurp your food or eat noisily.

Never blow your nose on a napkin (serviette). Napkins are for dabbing your lips and only for that.

Never take food from your neighbours plate.

Never pick food out of your teeth with your fingernails.

Things that are ok to do

It is ok to pour your own drink when eating with other people, but it is more polite to offer pouring drinks to the people sitting on either side of you.

It is ok to put milk and sugar in your tea and coffee or to drink them both without either.

If not used to eating with a knife and fork, what to do?

We eat continental style, with fork in the left hand and the knife in the right (or the other way round if you are left-handed). At the top of your plate will be a dessert spoon and dessert fork.

If you are eating at a formal dinner party, you will come across many knives and forks. Start with the utensils on the outside and work your way inward with each subsequent course.

How to eat with a knife and fork in England

The fork is held in the left hand and the knife in the right. If you have a knife in one hand, it is wrong to have a fork in the other with the prongs (tines) pointed up. Hold your knife with the handle in your palm and your folk in the other hand with the prongs pointing downwards.

When eating in formal situations, rest the fork and knife on the plate between mouthfuls, or for a break for conversation.

If you put your knife down, you can turn your fork over. It's correct to change hands when you do this, too, so if you are right handed you would switch and eat with the fork in your right hand. If it is your sole eating instrument, the fork should be held with the handle between the index finger and the thumb and resting on the side of your middle finger.

How to eat Soup

When eating soup, tip the bowl away from you and scoop the soup up with your spoon. Soup should always be taken (without slurping of course) from the side of the spoon, and not from the 'end' as in most of the rest of Europe.

How to eat peas

To be very polite, peas should be crushed onto the fork—a fork with the prongs pointing down. The best way is to have load the fork with something to which they will stick, such as potato or a soft vegetable that squashes easily onto the fork. It's sometimes easier to put down your knife and then switch your fork to the other hand, so you can shovel the peas against something else on the plate, thus ensuring they end up on your fork. The fork should not be used as a scoop but held so that the points of the tines face.

How to eat pudding (desserts)

To eat dessert, break the dessert with the spoon, one bite at a time. Push the food with the fork (optional) into the spoon. Eat from the spoon. (Fork in left hand; spoon in right.)

How to use a napkin or serviette

The golden rule is that a napkin should never be used to blow your nose on. This is a definite no-no. Napkins should be placed across the lap—tucking them into your clothing may be considered 'common'.

(972 words, taken from *http://projectbritain.com/*)

1. You can take a drink when there is food in your mouth. ________
2. In any cases it's impolite for you to use your finger to pick up food. ________
3. It is good manners to take some butter from the butter dish with your fork. ________
4. It's bad manners to put a knife in your mouth. ________
5. It's impolite to make noises while chewing food. ________
6. If you want something to eat, you can stand up and fetch it by yourself. ________
7. It's acceptable to use your napkin to rub your hands. ________
8. You can use your fingers to pick food out of your teeth. ________
9. At a formal dinner party use the utensils from the outside to inside. ________
10. It's a correct way to use your spoon and knife to eat desserts. ________

Part 4 Reading Comprehension Test

Passage 1

Directions: Read the following passage carefully and match the topics with all the paragraphs. The first and the last have been done for you. Note there are more paragraphs than topics as some paragraphs deal with the same topic.

1. Healthy eating and living a healthy lifestyle has a lot to do with forming the right habits. Here are seven of the best habits you can develop when it comes to healthy eating. Start by picking one of them and making it a habit of your own before moving on to the next. Before you know it, you will have developed a much healthier eating lifestyle.
2. Your body has to stay well hydrated to perform at its best and to properly process all the nutrients in the food you eat. Drink at least 8 glasses of water a day. You may need even more water if you are in a hot environment—like spending the day at the beach in

95-degree weather, or if you are exercising.

3. If you are trying to lose weight, add plenty of ice to each glass of water. Your body will burn energy to warm the water up to body temperature. Research has shown you can speed up your metabolism by 1/3 by drinking several glasses of ice water each day.
4. You've probably heard this before; breakfast is the most important meal of the day. After not eating for the past ten hours, your body needs fuel to get you going. You will have more energy and will be more alert after eating breakfast.
5. A recent study has shown that women who eat breakfast will consume an average of 100 calories less during the day than their counterparts who skipped breakfast. If you are trying to lose weight, eating breakfast is a definite must.
6. Make sure your children eat breakfast as well. They will be more alert in school and able to concentrate better.
7. There are many days when we are tempted to skip lunch. We are trying to lose weight and want to save some calories; we don't have the time and end up working through our lunch break, or have errands to run. Let's take a look at what happens when we skip lunch. Blood sugar levels drop, metabolism slows down to compensate for the missing fuel and when you get home you are starving and eat everything you can get your hands on.
8. Eat a light lunch each day. If you don't have time to go out, pack a brown bag lunch. Fix a turkey sandwich and some carrots or grapes in the morning and take them with you for a quick lunch at your desk.
9. We all need to snack from time to time. In fact, it's a good idea to eat two healthy snacks in addition to your three main meals. This doesn't mean that you can stop by the snack machine and grab a bag of chips or a candy bar.
10. Choose healthy snacks like fruits and vegetables, low fat yogurt, cottage cheese with applesauce, some whole-wheat crackers with cheese, or some trail mix.
11. There is a good reason the 5-a-day campaign was started. We should eat at least 5 servings of fruits and vegetables a day, yet many of us get hardly any servings in at all. Grab a piece of fruit for a snack, add some banana and raisins to your favorite breakfast cereal, have a salad with lunch, and make it a habit to fix at least one vegetable side with dinner each night. A simple fruit salad of cut up fruit dressed with a touch of lemon juice and honey makes for a quick and delicious desert any night of the week.
12. With our busy lives we are always tempted to put of dinner until the last minute. Try to eat dinner at least 3 hours before you go to bed. This will give your body a chance to digest most of the food before you rest for the next 8 hours.
13. A strategy that has worked well for me is to plan dinner for the week ahead of time and making sure I have every thing I need in the house. It allows me to get dinner started as soon as I get home and cuts out the extra time it takes to dig through the cupboards trying to find something to make and then running to the store to get the remaining ingredients.
14. Take a few minutes one day a week and plan the entire menu. Make a grocery list and shop

for everything you need for the next few days. You may even want to post your menu on the fridge so other family members can get a head start on dinner if you have a late meeting at the office.

15. Do you really know what you are eating each day? We often snack and eat more at regular meals than we realize. To get a better idea of what you are eating on a daily basis keep a food journal for a few days. All you need is a notebook and a pen. Write down everything you eat and drink in a given day. It is also a good idea to make notes about any emotions related to what you eat. For example, if you had a bad day at the office, and you have 2 slices of cheesecake after you get home as a result, write it down. You'll be able to analyze what causes you to choose unhealthy foods and at what times of the day you are most likely to grab unhealthy foods. Recognizing what your bad eating habits are is the first step toward correcting the behavior.

16. You will be amazed how much better you will feel by incorporating these seven habits of healthy eating. Give them a try and see for yourself. Over the next few months we will be discussing many other health related topics. Don't miss next month's issue about easy ways to incorporate exercise into your daily routine.

(980 words)

Topics	**Paragraph(s)**
Introduction	1
Eating Breakfast	1. ________
Having Lunch	2. ________
Avoiding Late Dinners	3. ________
Choosing Snacks Carefully	4. ________
Keeping a Food Journal	5. ________
Eating Fruit and Vegetables	6. ________
Drinking Plenty of Water	7. ________
Conclusion	16

Passage 2

Directions: Read the following passage and choose the best answer to complete each statement.

A broader view of food should regard it essentially as including all things that go to nourish us, just as a broader view of house should include everything pertaining to living conditions. As we are all animals, it is but common sense to say that we are what we eat. Our lives are not in the lap of the gods, but in the lap of our cooks. Hence every Chinese gentleman tries to befriend his cook, because so much of the enjoyment of life lies within his power to give or to take away as he sees fit. Chinese, and I suppose Western, parents always try to befriend the wet-nurse and treat her royally, because they realize that the health of their baby depends on the temper and happiness and general living conditions of the wet-nurse. *Pari passu*, we should give our cooks who feed us the same royal treatment, if we care as much for our own health as we care for that of our babies. If a man will be sensible and one fine morning, when he is lying in bed, count at the tips of his fingers how many things in this life truly give him enjoyment, invariably he will find food is the first one. Therefore it is the invariable test of a wise man whether he has good food at home or not.

The tempo of modern city life is such that we are giving less and less time and thought to the matter of cooking and feeding. A housewife who is at the same time a brilliant journalist can hardly be blamed for serving her husband with canned soup and beans. Nevertheless, it is a pretty crazy life when one eats in order to work and does not work in order to eat. We need a certain kindness and generosity to ourselves before we learn kindness and generosity to others. What good does it do a woman to do some muckraking for the city and improve general social conditions, if she herself has to cook on a two-burner range and allow ten minutes for eating her meal? Confucius undoubtedly would divorce her, as he divorced his wife for failure in good cooking.

The story is not exactly clear as to whether Confucius divorced her or she just had to run away in order to flee from the demands of this fastidious artist of life. For him "rice could never be white enough and mince meat could never be chopped fine enough." He refused to eat "when meat was not served with its proper sauce," "when it was not cut square," "when its color was not right" and "when its flavor was not right." I am quite sure that even then his wife could have stood it, but when one day, unable to find fresh food, she sent her son Li to buy wine and cold meat from some delicatessen and be through with it, and he announced that he "would not drink wine that was not homemade, nor taste meat that was bought from the shops," what else could she do except pack up and run away? This insight into the psychology of Confucius' wife is mine, but the severe conditions that he imposed upon his poor wife stands there today in the Confucian classics.

(551 words, taken from *The Importance of Living* by Lin Yutang)

8. The word "invariable" in Paragraph 1 most probably means ________.

A. reliable B. changeless C. unchangeable C. unsteady

9. The word "tempo" in Paragraph 2 is closest in meaning to ________.

A. temper B. quality C. pace D. frequency

10. The writer's attitude toward the woman journalist is ________.

A. understanding B. reproachful C. sympathetic D. complimentary

11. According to the writer, Confucius and his wife got divorced most probably because of all of the following reasons EXCEPT that ________.

A. his wife failed in good cooking

B. his wife thought Confucius was too choosy about food

C. his wife couldn't get their son to find the proper food for cooking

D. his wife had no choice but escape

Passage 3

Directions: Reading the following passage and fill in each blank with ***no more than three words*** *from the text.*

Many countries in Latin America and the Caribbean (LAC), most of them with well-developed systems of food control, have prepared contingency plans to support their actions during an emergency. However, currently there is no reference to document best practices to use during the development of such plans, or what they should contain. Emergency management of food safety is rarely the responsibility of a single national authority, and requires a timely and coordinated collaboration among all stakeholders to ensure effective intervention.

Population growth, global trade, climate change and crisis in emergency situations, challenge the control systems of food safety, jeopardizing an adequate supply of safe food and compliance with SPS requirements at both national and international level for food marketing. The capacity building in emergency situations is promoted in response to these concerns.

During 14 to 16 June 2012, was presented the "Regional Workshop for developing national intervention plans for emergency situations related to food safety" for countries of South America (Bolivia, Brazil, Ecuador, Colombia, Chile, Paraguay, Peru, Uruguay and Venezuela) in Santiago, Chile. Among conclusions of this workshop was considered working on a new workshop, focused on realities and emergency situations of countries in Central America, Mexico and the Caribbean.

Since, at present, food chains and the threats to food safety are often global in nature, FAO is in a unique position to evaluate these vulnerabilities, from production to consumption, and to provide advice on potential threats and guidance, and how to cope with them. In addition, it is also very important that all countries count on mechanisms to respond to crises related to food safety quickly and coordinated, because not all threats can be anticipated.

FAO has a solid experience in the efficient implementation of programs of food safety.

Collaboration with the World Health Organization (WHO) on issues related to food safety is sound. FAO and WHO ensure, by working together, that the agricultural and health sectors work jointly at national level to deal with crises and threats to food safety.

Moreover, the International Regional Organization for Plant and Animal Health (OIRSA) is an intergovernmental organization specialized in plant and animal health, founded over 59 years, to provide technical cooperation to the Ministries and Departments of Agriculture and Livestock of the nine member States: Mexico, Central America and the Dominican Republic in the protection and development of agricultural resources, aquaculture and forestry, through a safe food production for the welfare of the population.

Disasters such as earthquakes, tsunamis, hurricanes, tropical storms or volcanic eruptions, specific events, continous dangers, such as outbreaks of Escherichia coli in Germany and Salmonella in the U.S.A, or other crises that arise as cholera in Haiti and the Dominican Republic are all situations that make evident the need to be prepared to intervene in an organized and coordinated manner. Therefore it is important to establish a National Emergency Intervention Plan related to Food Safety, based on science and risk analysis. To strengthen preparedness, in addition to recognition and quick response to deal with these emergencies are key elements of the emergency programs in food safety of FAO and WHO, specifically the Emergency Prevention System for Food Safety (EMPRES food safety) and the International Food Safety Authorities (INFOSAN).

In this context, FAO, in collaboration with the Pan American Health Organization (PAHO) and OIRSA, organized and presented the "Regional workshop for developing national intervention plans for emergency situations related to food safety" convened in Panama City, between 13 and 15 March 2012.

(580 words)

12. Emergency management of food safety requires a timely and coordinated collaboration to ensure ______________________________.
13. The "Regional Workshop for developing national intervention plans for emergency situations related to food safety" was held in ______________________________.
14. Faced with the globalization of food chains and the threats to food safety, FAO takes its unique responsibilities to evaluate these weaknesses and to ____________________ _________ on potential threats and guidance.
15. FAO and WHO ensure that the agricultural and health sectors work jointly at ______________________________ to deal with crises and threats to food safety.
16. Disasters that have happened made it clear that it's necessary to have international intervention in an ______________________________ way.

Passage 4 Food safety is top item on the menu

Directions: Read the following passage and decide whether the statements after it are true or false. Write T for true and F for false.

Temptation. It wasn't a chunky wedge of rich, dark chocolate cake. Or a juicy, marbled slab of medium rare Wagyu tenderloin or even a deep fried onion blossom fat-bomb.

Floating inside the thick glass jar were small cubes of fermented tofu. My fork speared a square and dropped it into the bowl of rice porridge. A swirl of red-flecked slime rose to the surface. Bits of black gelatinous preserved eggs popped up as I stirred and the distinctive scent of sulfur and ammonia wafted up. I knew I was taking a risk eating it—was this the menu for a proverbial "last meal" or the ingredients that would make it so?

A recent poll showed 73 percent of respondents felt food safety in China was suspect. A further 27 percent viewed it as extremely unsafe. The majority of those surveyed said they believed the danger comes mainly during the unregulated production and processing of domestic foods.

I came upon such a "factory" once. While walking through a maze of hutong, I saw a small group of people around a long table. It seemed they were at an afternoon social. There was boisterous chatter, a haze of cigarette smoke hung above their heads, empty beer bottles littered the dusty ground and when I got closer I could see they were picking little black bits of dried fruit out of a cracked straw basket and wrapping them with their bare hands. Their dirty, bare hands.

Seeing that I was a foreigner, they generously gave me a couple of pieces to take with me. I looked at the paper wrapper and recognized it as one of the more popular brands of preserved plums—that was the moment I bid dried fruit adieu.

I admit I'm not usually concerned with the back-story of the things I eat. The chances are that a car, bus or scooter will send me to hospital way before the accumulated nitrate levels will. Even so, wary of the extra hormones and hot flashes my family was getting from the nightly servings of chicken, we started to raise our own hens for meat and eggs.

Lessons learned? Never name an animal you want to end up in the frying pan and DIY eggs cost 50 times as much as store bought.

Eating healthy in China doesn't mean a balanced diet of the four food groups, as much as avoiding foods with carcinogenic properties: pork with clenbuterol, milk with melamine, century eggs and mushroom soy sauce with industrial salt, gutter oil, expired foods re-packaged, and now Shandong apples coated with toxic pesticides.

The problem is: these and other yet-to-be discovered tainted foods don't come with warning labels. We often find out after the fact, like in the case of those perfectly cheap "lamb" kebabs on sidewalk grills—that what appears to be a bargain is often too good to be true.

But what can the average Zhou do? Man cannot live on bread alone. Food is the social fabric Chinese culture is woven around. These are the original foodies, where "Hello!" is replaced by "Have you eaten?" Food is more than mere substance here; it tells stories, gives blessings and cements relationships.

Unlike Americans, a communal 5 minute break to gobble down Power Bars may be seen as championing a hard work ethic, but in China a 10-course banquet gives one the opportunity to see if the guy sitting by the side should be viewed as friend or foe.

Will the fear of toxic food change the way we eat and shop? Are factory processed Power Bars the fuel of the future? One thing's for sure, if you're raising a chicken for the dinner table, forget about names like Buddy, Fluffy or Scooter. It'll look more delicious when it scurries over upon hearing its name—Gongbao Jiding.

(639 words, taken from *China Daily* 2012-06-19 by Dinah Chong Watkins)

17. ________ It took courage for the writer to eat toufu as her last meal.

18. ________ The majority of Chinese have no confidence in the safety of food.

19. ________ On receiving the preserved plums from the workers, the writer decided not to eat dried fruit again.

20. ________ Food in China is more than mere substance, because it tells stories, gives blessings and cements relationships.

Unit 8

Housing and Subprime Crisis

Part 1 Reading Skills

Section A Finding the Topic Sentence

Many paragraphs include a topic sentence that tells the main idea of the paragraph. The topic sentence is often, but not always, the first sentence in the paragraph. Sometimes, it is located in the last sentence, or in the middle of the paragraph. And in some cases, there are no topic sentences in the paragraph and you have to sum up yourself. Here are some examples:

1) ***Pollution spoils our environment in many ways.*** *The air we breathe, for instance, is constantly polluted by smoke and by chemicals such as carbon monoxide in the exhaust fumes of car and other kinds of motor vehicles. For wild life, however, there are even greater dangers in pollution of water—of rivers, for example, or lakes and seas. A good illustration of this is the oil released from tankers at sea. It kills all kinds of sea animals, including birds, whose feathers become covered with oil so they cannot fly, as well as fish and other forms of marine life. These are only a few examples; there are many more.*

In this paragraph, the first sentence "*Pollution spoils our environment in many ways.*" is the topic sentence. The remaining sentences try to explain how pollution damages our environment, including the air we breathe, the water (rivers, lakes and seas) the birds and fish rely on.

2) *In the United States during 1992, any family of four with an annual cash income of less than $14,335 (before taxes) was considered poor. The dollar amount was called the poverty line, an economic measuring rod devised in 1964. However,* ***the poverty line varies with location and social and political conditions.*** *While the poverty line in the United States was more than $14,000, the average annual per-person income in Bangladesh was $200, in Ethiopia $130, in Haiti $340, and in Mali $265. Anyone in those nations with an income of &14,000 would be considered wealthy.*

In the above paragraph the topic sentence "*The poverty line varies with location and social and political conditions.*" is put in the middle of the paragraph. Before and after this sentence, there are specific data showing the differences.

3) *The American basketball team announced that they would not yield first place to Russia, after a disputable end to their contest. The game had ended in disturbance. It was thought at first that the United States had won, by a single point, but it was announced that there were three seconds still to play. A Russian player popped it into the basket. It was the first time the USA had ever lost an Olympic basketball match. An appeal jury debated the matter for four and a half hours before announcing that the result would stand. The American players then voted not to receive the silver medals. Incidents of this kind will continue as long as sport is played competitively rather than for the love of the game. The suggestion that athletes should compete as individuals, or in non-national teams, might be too much to hope for.* ***But in the present organization of the Olympics there is too much encouragement of aggressive patriotism****.*

In the above paragraph, detailed description is offered about the dispute between American and Russian basketball teams and in the final sentence (acting as the topic sentence) the main idea is presented.

4) *"Disregard the last statement made by the witness," instructs the judge. Yet the clever lawyer knows that once her client has told the jury that her husband gave her a black eye during an argument, the client* ***cannot really "take it back."*** *This principle applies to all forms of communication. We may try to modify the meaning of a spoken message by saying something like, "Oh, I didn't really mean it." But in most cases, the damage has been done. Once created, communication has the physical property of matter;* ***it can't be uncreated****. Once interpersonal communication begins, it continues to be shaped by the events, experiences, and thoughts of the communication partners. A Russian proverb nicely summarizes the point:* ***"Once a word goes out of your mouth, you can never swallow it again."***

We can't find a topic sentence in the above paragraph. However we can conclude from the information conveyed repeatedly (in bold) that the main idea of this paragraph is "Interpersonal communication cannot be reversed."

Section B Practice

Directions: Read the following four paragraphs and underline the topic sentence or summarize the topic sentence in your own words.

Paragraph 1

If using sunscreen, apply it at least 30-45 minutes before exposure, then reapply it periodically, especially after you swim or sweat. It is especially important to protect children. One or more severe sunburns with blisters in childhood or adolescence can double the risk of skin cancer melanoma later in life. Additional protection can be provided by a wide-brimmed hat to protect your head and face, and opaque clothing to cover those body areas you wish to protect. Any fabric or material you can see through, including some beach umbrellas, does not give full protection. You should stay out of the sun between 10 a.m. and 2 p.m. when the rays are strongest.

Topic sentence: ____

____

Paragraph 2

Do you know that you could get sick from a pet reptile? Little turtles were very popular as pets in the United States. Doctors discovered that these turtles sometimes were sick with an infection called salmonella. People who touched the turtles could catch this infection and become seriously ill. Then the U.S. government banned these turtles as pets. Now doctors think that people, especially small children, can get the same infection from another kind of pet: the iguana. The iguana is a reptile like a turtle and has recently become a favorite pet in many American homes. The government may have to ban these animals, too. For now, doctors say that people should wash their hands very carefully after touching an iguana.

Topic sentence: ____

____

Paragraph 3

Obesity rates are likely to "grow even more in the next year due to the economic downturn," according to a report produced by the Trust for America's Health and the Robert Wood Johnson Foundation. Food prices are going up, and nutritious foods are often much more expensive than empty calories. And when folks are stressed and budgets are stretched, physical activity may be the first thing to go. Things are even worse for the Americans for whom poverty is a constant; poorer neighborhoods have fewer grocery stores and fewer areas for kids to play safely. The economy has a role.

Topic sentence: ____

____

Paragraph 4

In industrialized countries today, many elderly people suffer from depression. The main cause of this is loneliness. In the past, older people usually lived with other members of the family. They usually had some responsibilities around the home. For example, older women could help take care of the children or prepare meals. Older men could help their sons at work or around the house. These days, married children often prefer to live on their own, sometimes far away from their parents. Thus, older people may be cut off from family ties. They may feel cut off from the world around them. Life has changed so much so quickly that older people sometimes feel that they do not belong any more.

Topic sentence: ____

____

Part 2 Idioms, Proverbs and Sayings

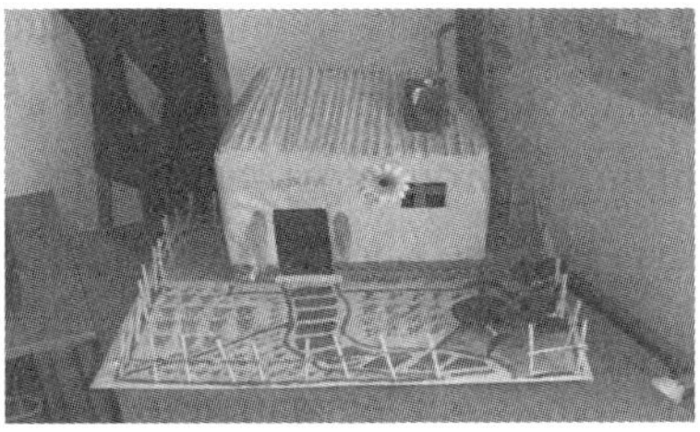

Directions: The following are idioms, proverbs or sayings about house and home. Choose what you think is correct and compare with the right ones.

1. A man's house is his ________.
   A. place　B. castle　C. palace　D. wall
2. Home is where the ________ is.
   A. hand　B. bosom　C. head　D. heart
3. I would rather be a poor man in a ________ with plenty of good books to read than a king who did not love reading. (John Lubbock)
   A. garret　B. corner　C. cellar　D. study
4. Home is home, be it never so ________.
   A. warm　B. plain　C. homely　D. ugly
5. Love your neighbour, yet pull not down your ________.
   A. wall　B. door　C. knob　D. hedge
6. Wash your dirty ________ at home.
   A. linen　B. dishes　C. clothes　D. floor
7. Two cats and a mouse, two ________ in one house, two dogs and a bone, never agree in

one.

A. sons B. wives C. husbands D. daughters

8. To marry a woman for her beauty is like buying a house for its ________.

A. paint B. furniture C. garden D. balcony

9. Three ________ are as bad as a fire.

A. movings B. decorations C. kitchens D. removes

10. There is a ________ in every house.

A. living room B. bedroom C. skeleton D. basement

Part 3 Reading Passages

Section A Obama Not Planning Another Big Housing Program

The Obama administration has no plans to introduce another large-scale program for relieving the troubled housing market, despite the president's recent admission that his past efforts have not solved the problem, according to a senior administration official.

The weak housing market has become one of Obama administration's chief burdens. But experts said the government's options are limited. There isn't likely to be the money or political will to push through any significant legislation to address the problem, they said.

Yet housing remains one of the biggest drags on the economic recovery and threatens to loom over the 2012 election. Millions of borrowers are facing foreclosure, while others are stuck in homes worth less than they owe, leaving them feeling cash-strapped at a time when consumer spending is needed to fuel economic growth.

"There is no money and, to some degree, we have run out of ideas. I have seen them all," said Mark Zandi, chief economist of Moody's Analytics. "I don't think there is something grand that could make a big difference."

Obama set off industry speculation about another large housing program earlier this month during a Twitter town hall when he said that dealing with the aftermath of the housing bubble had been one of his chief challenges. The administration had made progress, he said, but "it's not enough. And so we're going back to the drawing board."

The administration is keeping an eye on how the market is evolving and what is driving distress, said an administration official, who spoke on condition of anonymity to discuss internal deliberations. An inter-agency group that includes senior Department of Housing and Treasury officials continues to collect input from outside groups and members of Congress, the official said.

The administration is not preparing to launch a large new program, but is considering several options including expanding existing efforts, the official said.

The administration already has poured billions into programs to help homeowners avoid foreclosure, injected millions into teetering (move unsteadily) state housing finance agencies and made it easier for borrowers to refinance their loans even if they owe more than their homes are worth.

But most of those efforts have fallen short of expectations. Despite historically low interest rates, home prices remain near historic lows, sales are weak and a backlog of homes headed to foreclosure could prolong the crisis for years.

"I think the administration has put out quite a number of initiatives over the last couple of years to soften the blow of the housing crisis. Those measures did soften the blow," said Michael S. Barr, a former assistant Treasury secretary in the Obama administration.

But most foreclosures are now caused by economic factors like unemployment rather than subprime loans, said Barr, a law professor at the University of Michigan. "I don't think any housing specific answer is likely to make a significant difference right now. The larger macro issues are more important."

Still, the administration is being inundated with proposals from advocacy and industry groups for buoying the housing market, including a push to loosen strict lending standards and find ways to turn the foreclosed homes weighing on the market into rental properties. Many also want the administration to force banks to cut the principal balance for borrowers who owe more than their homes are worth, known as being underwater, according to industry officials and consumer advocates.

And not everyone has given up on finding a legislative solution. Sen. Barbara Boxer (D-Calif.) introduced legislation earlier this year that would require Fannie Mae and Freddie Mac, the mortgage financing giants, to allow borrowers who are underwater on their mortgage more flexibility to refinance into lower-interest rate loans without pricey upfront fees. Sen. Johnny Isakson (R-Ga.) recently signed on as a co-sponsor of the legislation, which the lawmakers say could keep 54,000 borrowers out of foreclosure.

The biggest opportunity for wide-ranging change may be a settlement being negotiated between a coalition of state attorneys general and large banks related to flawed foreclosure practices, industry officials and consumer advocates say. Those efforts are aimed at overhauling the industry's business practices and potentially creating funds that could be used to aid troubled homeowners facing foreclosure.

A provision could be added to the potential settlement requiring banks to write down the balances of underwater borrowers, according to consumer advocates.

Overall, the housing market is suffering from too much supply and not enough demand, said David Stevens, head of the Mortgage Bankers Association. It would take more than nine months to sell all of the homes on the market at the current sales rate, according to industry data. But there are also more than 4 million homeowners in trouble on their mortgage, with many somewhere in the foreclosure process.

But lending standards remain strict, particularly for investors, many of whom have a difficult time qualifying for the government-backed loans that make up a majority of the market, according to Stevens. "We clearly need an investor market to absorb the inventory," he said.

Some housing experts said that fixing the housing sector may be too big for a single plan. "New measures can make a difference at the margins and help in specific markets, but it will take more stakeholders working together to achieve the biggest scale" of changes, said Peter P. Swire, a law professor at Ohio State University.

(884 words, based on *http://www.washingtonpost.com* by Renae Merle)

I. Reading Comprehension

Directions: Choose the best answer to each question according to the passage.

1. At the beginning of the passage, the author indicates that ________.
   A. the president's past efforts have solved the problem of the troubled housing market
   B. the Obama administration has no plans to introduce another large-scale program for relieving the weak housing market
   C. the troubled housing market has become the biggest burden of the Obama administration
   D. the American government has political will to push through significant legislation to solve the problem
2. We can learn from the third paragraph that ________ remains one of the biggest resistance to the economic recovery.
   A. housing bubble B. 2012 election
   C. low consumption D. high expenditure
3. According to the sixth paragraph, an administration official ________ speaks that the government is keeping an eye on how the market is evolving and what is driving distress.
   A. without giving a name
   B. on behalf of the Obama administration
   C. who is a member of Congress
   D. from Department of Housing and Treasury
4. What is NOT mentioned as the problem borrowers are facing?
   A. foreclosure B. cash-strap
   C. homes flooded by heavy rains D. homes worth less than they owe
5. In the eighth paragraph, the underlined word "refinance" in the sentence "…and made it easier for borrowers to refinance their loans" refers to ________.
   A. pay off the remaining debt at former mortgage rates
   B. increase their monthly repayment obligations
   C. reduce their monthly repayment obligations
   D. replace an existing loan with a debt obligation under different terms.

6. In the opinion of Michael S. Barr, a law professor at the University of Michigan, most foreclosures are now caused by ________.
   A. an investor market
   B. subprime loans
   C. unemployment
   D. government-backed loans
7. According to the passage, the following experts have voiced their opinions EXCEPT ________.
   A. Mark Zandi, chief economist of Moody's Analytics
   B. Vivian S. Toy, a former assistant Treasury secretary in the Obama administration
   C. David Stevens, head of the Mortgage Bankers Association
   D. Peter P. Swire, a law professor at Ohio State University
8. Which of the following statements is INCORRECT?
   A. Most of the efforts done by the Obama administration have lived up to expectations.
   B. The administration is not preparing to launch a large new program, but is considering several options including expanding existing efforts.
   C. The administration already has poured billions into programs to help homeowners avoid foreclosure.
   D. Despite historically low interest rates, home prices remain near historic lows.
9. According to David Stevens, head of the Mortgage Bankers Association, what conclusion is drawn on the housing market?
   A. Demand exceeds supply.
   B. Supply exceeds demand.
   C. Sales are weak.
   D. A backlog of homes headed to foreclosure.
10. What is the tone of the passage?
   A. impatient
   B. serious
   C. ironic
   D. worried

II. Vocabulary

Directions: Fill in each blank with an appropriate word from the box below. Change the form where necessary. Each word can be used only once.

legislation	loom	aftermath	anonymity	teeter
backlog	inundate	buoy	underwater	coalition

1. According to a poll published on Wednesday, 94 percent of Norwegians have been satisfied with the prime minister's performance in the __________ of last week's massacre while only 2 percent have been dissatisfied.
2. Internet access will not be terminated, according to a statement from the industry partners __________ including groups representing movie studios, independent film makers and record labels.
3. The Chinese government made a public smoking ban one of its goals in its the Five-Year

Plan in March, and some Chinese cities have also been passing __________ to control second-hand smoke.

4. After her summer vacation, she has got a huge __________ of work to do.
5. Coral reefs are __________ structures made from calcium carbonate in the tropics and subtropics, which could help resist marine disasters and reduce damage.
6. China started the subsidy program in February 2009 to stimulate rural consumption and __________ the nation's economic growth during the global economic downturn.
7. One netizen said the money could be better spent on improving the drainage system to prevent the city from being __________ by rain water again.
8. Lonely and needy in their own individual ways, the three schoolmates are feeling themselves and each other out as they __________ on the brink of adulthood.
9. Local government debt accumulated over the past few years is relatively heavy, and some risks __________ as certain regions and industries are weak in repaying the debt.
10. The police official who spoke on condition of __________ said the bombing occurred at 3:26 p.m., and the camp shootings began one to two hours later.

III. Debate

Directions: Read the following short passage and have a debate over the topic "Affordable homes should never be used as a tool for profiteering by rich people."

China has witnessed escalating housing prices during recent years, while owning a subsidized affordable home has been a dream for many needy citizens. Netizens expressed the hope that the government will accelerate the supply of affordable homes to low-income groups and tighten measures to rein in rising property prices.

"Affordable homes should never be used as a tool for profiteering by rich people," said one online posting that stipulated subsidized homes should be strictly restricted to those requiring assistance.

On April 1, 2011,China issued new regulations to regulate real estate brokerage practices, released jointly by the Ministry of Housing and Urban-Rural Development, the National Development and Reform Commission, and the Ministry of Human Resources and Social Security, said the regulations will be put into effect. The move is part of the State Council's efforts to rein in China's sizzling property market.

According to officials, China plans to build 10 million affordable apartments and houses for the country's poorest citizens during 2011.

Section B Two Neediest Cases of Christina Natale and the Gatherses

by Abby Aguirre & Jennifer Mascia

Directions: Read the passage below and after it there are 10 questions followed by four choices marked A, B, C and D. Choose the ONE that best fits into the passage.

The Wrong Mortgage Derails a Mother's Plans

Christina Natale rehearses the details in Realtor shorthand, "Three bedrooms, one and a half baths, finished basement, washer-dryer, kitchen with island, granite tops—well, not granite tops, Formica tops—gas stove, stainless-steel appliances, side-by-side freezer and fridge with ice maker. ..."

She could go on, but cuts to the chase: What she mourns is not, in fact, material. "It made me feel good," she said.

When Ms. Natale, 37, bought the town house on Staten Island in 2006, it was important to her to feel good. She had divorced the father of her three children two years before, a distressing period followed by the death of her mother, and then of her grandfather, with whom she had been close.

It struck her as a new start, and perhaps a compensatory undertaking, she said: Her son, Victor, now 15, had been troubled since his father's move to Virginia. A nicer place might help the children, she thought, a hope she now dismisses in another kind of shorthand: "I wanted the white picket fence."

What she got was a mortgage she could not afford. Toward the $385,000 cost, Ms. Natale made a down payment of $185,000, a little less than what she took away from the sale of her grandfather's home. The loan that made up the difference, with closing costs, broker's fee, taxes and insurance, meant a monthly bill of $1,873.96, about $100 less than her monthly take-home pay as an administrative assistant.

It was a stretch, but the approval of her loan application encouraged her to attempt. The bank and the broker seemed unconcerned, so unconcerned that neither confirmed her income with the car dealership where she works. "They never called," she said. "I'm the one that answers the phones."

Ms. Natale found it a bit unsettling that the interest rate was adjustable but was assured by the broker that she could refinance. More heartening was her $20,000 in savings and sense that things were starting to look up. "I was hoping I would get a second job. I was hoping for a Prince Charming. I was just hoping things would get better," she said.

After she depleted her savings, she refinanced in June 2007, and again in July of this year, taking out another loan. It was then that her venture in optimism started to feel more like a venture in quicksand. She had not gotten a second job. Prince Charming had not turned up. And her ex-husband's small financial contributions had abruptly stopped. The breaking point came a few months later. "They wouldn't let me refinance again," she said.

After an intent-to-foreclose notice from the bank, in August, Ms. Natale decided to sell. With her lender's approval, she arranged a short sale that let her walk away solvent, if without her down payment.

The sale went through on a Friday in September; Ms. Natale had to be out the following Monday. She had no interim arrangements and no money for temporary shelter, let alone the security deposit on an apartment. It was at this point in the telling that Ms. Natale's youngest, Elayna, 6, chimed in for the first time: "I thought we were going to live in the bushes!"

The Children's Aid Society, one of the seven beneficiary agencies of The New York Times Neediest Cases Fund, drew on the fund to pay for a week's stay at a local hotel; for an apartment, including the first month's rent of $1,400, security deposit of $1,400 and broker's fee of $1,400; and moving and storage costs of $3,751.

The new apartment is not to Ms. Natale's taste—unremarkable cabinetry, limited counter space, stained blue carpet—but she has begun to decorate. Elayna and her sister, Diana, 16, share a room, and Ms. Natale has her own room, at least until Victor comes back from Lincoln Hall, a school upstate for adolescents with behavioral problems.

Ms. Natale works six days a week. She is determined to repair her credit, save for a house she can afford and resume studying the subject she abandoned when she married at 19: accounting. She has one indulgence. Every Sunday night, her only day off, she watches the TV show her children know she is not to miss, "Extreme Makeover: Home Edition."

Burned Out of Their Home in the Bronx, but Grateful to Be Together

Aug. 29, 2010 was supposed to be a night of celebration. But when Chaka and Carina Gathers returned from the hospital with their newborn son Cason, their third child, they found their Bronx apartment building in flames.

"She almost fainted," Mr. Gathers, 40, said of his wife.

"There was no running in to get nothing," Ms. Gathers, 25, said.

As the couple described it, the fire was the latest blow in a five-year battle that had been raging over the three-floor building in Van Nest, near Bronx Park. Sewage had been backing up in the bathroom for years; flooding from burst and backed-up pipes was common.

The building itself, on Holland Avenue, had landmark status, and an adjacent one was worth $750,000—leading the Gatherses to suspect that their landlord had allowed problems to accumulate in a bid to dislodge the small group of tenants.

The couple moved into a basement apartment in 2005, around Thanksgiving. It was quite an accomplishment for two people who had met in a shelter.

"There was not enough space at my mother's house," Ms. Gathers said. Her sister was also living there with her children, so Ms. Gathers relocated to HELP Bronx Crotona Park North, a short-term transitional housing facility for homeless families.

She was assigned to the same floor as her future husband.

They developed friends in common and started talking, "and after that, we wanted to spend time around each other," Ms. Gathers said.

Their first child, Jada, was born in 2004. After they moved to the building in Van Nest, the joy over having their own space faded when they saw that it lacked radiators, and they discovered that raw sewage frequently bubbled up from the toilets and drains and caused flooding. Repeated calls to the landlord went unanswered, they said, and eventually they began to believe that she had abandoned the property.

So the tenants, led by the Gatherses, started work on an adverse possession claim stating that the landlord had abandoned the property five years before. They banded together and took control of the building: instead of calling 311 with heat complaints, they fixed the problems themselves. Mr. Gathers became the acting superintendent, learning maintenance and demolition.

"Slowly but surely I learned everything I needed and got H.P.D. in there," he said, referring to the Department of Housing Preservation and Development.

In 2007, the couple had a son, whom they named All, for "a lot of love," Ms. Gathers said. She balanced child-rearing with the work of stripping and replacing the apartment's doors and floors, paying for materials out of her own pocket.

The landlord threatened to sue when she learned about the tenants' activities, but she skipped a housing court date, and the last anyone heard, she was in Africa. Ms. Gathers spoke to the State Division of Housing and Community Renewal and was trying to get the deed signed over to the tenants. An appointment was scheduled for the day after she brought baby Cason home from the hospital.

Then the fire came, gutting their urban experiment. It is being investigated as suspicious.

"I cried," Ms. Gather recalled. "I just came home from the hospital, I'm still weak, and my hormones...."

Her husband added, "I'm just hurt that we put so much into it."

After the fire, "we just had the clothes on our back," Mr. Gathers said. They were eventually placed in a transitional two-room Harlem apartment where they have mice, roaches and no privacy. Mr. Gathers is working for the Sanitation Department to qualify for public assistance; $555 in monthly food stamps keeps them fed.

"We're living on a shoestring budget," Mr. Gathers said.

They are moving up the waiting list for an apartment through the city's Housing Authority, and should be placed in a couple of months. At that time, Catholic Charities of the Archdiocese of New York, one of the seven charities supported by The New York Times Neediest Cases Fund, will apportion $500 from the fund to buy beds for the family.

"God is good," a thankful Ms. Gathers said.

Another thing she is grateful for?

"To have to go through the shelter system to find each other," she said, her eyes sparkling. "It was wonderful."

(1,432 words, based on *http://www.nytimes.com*)

1. According to the passage, when Ms. Natale bought the town house on Staten Island in 2006, ________.
   A. she had divorced her husband two years before
   B. her grandfather and then her mother passed away
   C. her father moved to Virginia
   D. her son Victor was only 15 years old
2. Toward the $385,000 house cost, Ms. Natale made a down payment of $185,000, so she got a mortgage loan of ________.
   A. $185,000 B. $195,000 C. $200,000 D. $385,000
3. We learn from the passage that Ms. Natale worked as ________.
   A. an administrative assistant B. a car dealer
   C. an accountant D. I was just hoping things would get better
4. Which of the following is NOT a reason why Ms. Natale's venture in optimism started to feel more like a venture in quicksand?
   A. She had not gotten a second job.
   B. Prince Charming didn't want to see her.
   C. Her ex-husband's small financial contributions had abruptly stopped.
   D. The bank wouldn't let her refinance again
5. After an intent-to-foreclose notice from the bank, Ms. Natale sold out her house on a Friday in September and ________.
   A. She had to be out the following Monday to stay at a cheap hotel
   B. She had no money for temporary shelter
   C. Fortunately she had the security deposit on an apartment
   D. She had to live in the bushes
6. According to the second case in the passage, what happened to Chaka and Carina Gathers on Aug. 29, 2010?
   A. They held a night of celebration for their newborn son Cason.
   B. Ms. Gathers fainted suddenly and was sent to the hospital.
   C. Their Bronx apartment building was in flames.
   D. Raw sewage suddenly bubbled up from the toilets and drains and caused flooding.
7. Which of the following is the reason why there was a five-year battle that had been raging over the three-floor building in Van Nest, near Bronx Park?
   A. Since the birth of their first child Jada in 2004, the couple started quarrelling.
   B. bubbled-up Sewage frequently caused flooding their landlord went unanswered
   C. Their abandoned allowed problems to accumulate in a bid to dislodge the small group of

tenants.

D. The pressure to pay for the debts each month was too great for them to bear.

8. After the fire, the Gathers were placed in a transitional two-room Harlem apartment and ________.

A. the landlord threatened to sue when she learned that her building was in flames

B. they spoke to the State Division of Housing and Community Renewal and was trying to get the deed signed over to the tenants

C. they worked for the Sanitation Department to qualify for public assistance of $555 monthly

D. they were funded $500 from Catholic Charities of the Archdiocese of New York to buy beds for the family

9. It can be concluded from the two cases in the passage that ________.

A. supported by The Neediest Cases Fund, both Ms. Natale and the Gatherses overcame their difficulties and gain new hope in life

B. The Children's Aid Society is an organization responsible for helping those who are unemployed

C. Catholic Charities of the Archdiocese of New York is one of the eight beneficiary agencies of The New York Times Neediest Cases Fund

D. Social welfare agencies serve people of all ages and backgrounds all over the world

10. Which of the following adjective can best describe how Ms. Natale and the Gatherses feel for the New York Times Neediest Cases Fund?

A. grateful B. excited C. wonderful D. suspicious

Part 4 Reading Comprehension Test

Directions: Read the following four passages. Choose the best answer to each question.

Passage 1

On Christmas day, 1911, Adolph S. Ochs, publisher of *The New York Times*, went out for a walk after a big turkey dinner and encountered a shabbily dressed man on the street. The man said he had just been given Christmas dinner at a Y.M.C.A. and had nowhere to sleep. The publisher looked him over, decided he looked respectable and gave him a few dollars and his card. "If you're looking for a job," he said, "come see me tomorrow."

The encounter left the publisher thinking about charity. Helping a stranger had given him a sense of satisfaction, and he wondered if one man's feeling might be the basis for a city's goodwill. The next year, he sent a reporter to several of the city's private welfare agencies to collect stories about the poor. He had a plan: to publish stories about the Hundred Neediest

Cases in New York. The appeal would be made not with a direct request for money but with the facts of their lives. These small chronicles, it turned out, sounded a powerful call.

The campaign began December 15, 1912. Soon other publishers in the United States and abroad adopted the idea that a newspaper could make a general appeal for the poor and thus help established welfare agencies solicit funds. Each year, more *New York Times* readers sent in more money. In 1912, 117 contributors sent in $3,630.88. In 2010-2011, 10,457 readers contributed over $6 million. All told, the Fund has raised over $256 Million in its 100 years.

The mechanics of the appeal have evolved over the years. In 1970, The Times stopped publishing the names of all the contributors. The campaign, no longer limited to a hundred specific cases, distributes its funds to seven participating social welfare agencies. They serve people of all ages and backgrounds in the metropolitan area.

The New York Times Company pays for all administrative costs so that every gift goes directly to serve the poor and the Company audits the work of the agencies accordingly. As a way to protect the next generation while serving this one, the fund invests unrestricted gifts of $100,000 or more from trusts or estates in an endowment. The income goes directly into the next year's campaign.

This year the Fund celebrates its Centennial anniversary. The 2011-2012 campaign begins Nov. 6, 2011, and will continue through Jan. 29, 2012. As always, The Times covers the campaign's costs. No money is taken from the Fund for administration. Cases of notable relieved distress are the subject of daily articles in the newspaper and on nytimes.com.

(437 words, based on *http://www.nytimes.com)*

1. The passage is mainly about ________.
   A. Adolph S. Ochs, publisher of The *New York Times*
   B. the work of The *New York Times* Company
   C. a brief history of *The New York Times* Neediest Cases Fund
   D. the centennial anniversary of *The New York Times* Neediest Cases Fund
2. What kind of experience did Adolph S. Ochs have on Christmas day 1911?
   A. He met a shabbily dressed man at a big turkey dinner.
   B. He went out for a walk after a Christmas dinner at a Y.M.C.A.
   C. He was taken in by a stranger who claimed to have nowhere to sleep.
   D. He helped a shabby man on the street with money and his name card.
3. The encounter left Adolph S. Ochs thinking about charity because ________.
   A. he had sent a reporter to several of the city's private welfare agencies to collect stories about the poor
   B. he had planned to publish stories about the Hundred Neediest Cases in New York
   C. helping a stranger had given him a sense of satisfaction
   D. a newspaper could make a general appeal for the poor
4. The underlined word "campaign" in the third paragraph refers to ________.
   A. helping established welfare agencies raise funds for the poor

B. each year, more New York Times readers sent in more money
C. in 1912, 117 contributors sent in $3,630.88
D. the Fund has raised over $256 Million in its 100 years

5. *The New York Times* Company pays for all administrative costs so that ________.
A. the Company audits the work of the agencies accordingly
B. every gift goes directly to serve the needy
C. the Times covers the campaign's costs
D. cases of notable relieved distress are the subject of daily articles in the newspaper and on nytimes.com.

Passage 2

Chinese banks will not run a great risk of bad loans should a property bubble burst because only a small part of bank lending went to homebuyers, said China's top banking regulator.

Liu Mingkang, chairman of the China Banking Regulatory Commission (CBRC), said on Monday that China's banking system won't run considerable risks on bad home loans because the mortgages are backed by sufficient downpayments and the total lending volume is limited. Instead, Liu warns about the risk of local government financing vehicles, saying that the regulator is investigating and cleaning up these lending platforms.

Last year, the Chinese government began launching a series of measures to tame surging real estate prices, including raising interest rates and asking commercial banks to suspend mortgage loans for buyers of more than two homes.

Many analysts have expressed concern that the measures will lead to a Chinese version of the "subprime mortgage crisis" that may strain developers' finances and cause homebuyers to default on their mortgages. According to Richard Fox, a London-based analyst at Fitch Ratings Ltd, China faces a 60 percent risk of a banking crisis by mid-2013 in the wake of record lending and surging property prices, Bloomberg reported. The US rating firm was quoted as saying that a property bubble burst can punch "holes in banks' balance sheets" in China.

In August, the CBRC demanded that lenders test the possible effect of up to a 50 percent fall in housing prices in key cities. The watchdog said earlier that most banks can withstand up to a 30 percent drop.

Dong Wenbiao, chairman of Minsheng Banking Corp, told media during the weekend that he thinks most Chinese banks can weather a 40 percent plunge in real estate prices. He said only 10 percent of lending at Minsheng Banking goes to homebuyers.

Liu from CBRC said on Monday that China's top banking watchdog will keep a close eye on the possible risk brought about by local government financing vehicles, which help local government to borrow money from banks. He said the risk of the financial platforms is under control, but the CBRC will keep tracking the risks during the next three to five years.

Data released by the People's Bank of China, the central bank, showed new yuan-denominated loans stood at 535.6 billion yuan ($81.5 billion) last month, lower than what many economists had estimated. M2, the broadest measure of money supply, climbed 15.7 percent, the smallest amount in more than two years, perhaps a result of several increases in bank interest rates and reserve ratio requirements.

(420 words, The text is based on *http://www.chinadaily.com.cn*)

6. According to the passage, China's banking system won't run considerable risks on bad home loans if a property bubble bursts because ________.
   A. only a small part of bank lending goes to homebuyers
   B. the mortgages are backed by downpayments
   C. the total lending volume is unlimited.
   D. bank interest rates are increased several times
7. The underlined word "downpayment" in the second paragraph is closest in meaning to ________.
   A. the risk of local government financing vehicles
   B. a certain percent fall in housing prices in key cities
   C. cleaning up the lending platforms
   D. the initial upfront portion of the total amount due
8. Last year, the Chinese government began launching a series of measures to ________.
   A. raise interest rates
   B. reduce bad home loans
   C. ask commercial banks to suspend mortgage loans for buyers
   D. regulate surging real estate prices
9. In the opinion of Dong Wenbiao, chairman of Minsheng Banking Corp, ________.
   A. most Chinese banks can weather a 30 percent plunge in real estate prices
   B. China's top banking watchdog will keep a close eye on the possible risk of the financial platforms
   C. only 10 percent of lending at Minsheng Banking goes to homebuyers
   D. China faces a 60 percent risk of a banking crisis by mid-2013 in the wake of record lending and surging property prices
10. Which of the following might be the best title for this passage?
    A. China's Banking Watchdog Is at Work
    B. Subprime Mortgage Crisis? Not Here
    C. A 50 Percent Fall in Housing Prices
    D. Financial Platforms Is Under Control

Passage 3

The White House is exploring new proposals to boost the struggling economy, including tax cuts to spur hiring and programs that could provide a lift to the housing market, as

President Obama shifts his focus from the debate over the debt, said people familiar with the efforts. Obama, who is planning a three-day bus tour of the Midwest this month to discuss the economy, has been searching for ways to generate economic growth that could attract broad public support.

White House officials are weighing a proposal to offer tax cuts to employers in return for hiring new workers. The administration considered this idea last year, but it gave way to a broader payroll tax deduction for workers in a bipartisan deal in December. In addition, administration officials are considering proposing new investments in domestic clean energy as well as renewing tax breaks for companies using renewable energy—particularly wind power—that are to expire this year. Also on the table is an initiative designed to help the ailing housing market without the need for more public spending. Under that proposal, the government-controlled mortgage giants Fannie Mae and Freddie Mac would rent out foreclosed properties that they own rather than try to sell them at depressed prices. That approach could relieve pressure on the housing market, one of the main drags on the economy.

The search for new ideas comes as the economic recovery is running out of steam, dashing hopes that the unemployment rate will come down significantly in the near term. But as they discuss new ideas, White House officials are lowering expectations that any new policy could make a massive difference in the economy. "The president will continue to promote and put forward ideas for things we can do to create jobs and grow the economy," White House press secretary Jay Carney said. "The fact is that there is no magic bullet that lowers our unemployment rate to where it would be ideally."

A top goal for Obama and congressional Democrats is to extend both unemployment insurance and a payroll tax break. These measures were enacted at the beginning of the year. Obama could not achieve those extensions in the budget deal with Congress.

In addition to the payroll tax cut and unemployment insurance, Obama has talked publicly about several other ideas for bolstering the economy. They include passing free trade agreements with Korea, Colombia and Panama; patent reform; and an "infrastructure bank" that would help fund spending by companies and localities.

(410 words, based on *http://www.washingtonpost.com*)

11. What is the passage mainly about?
    A. Payroll tax cut
    B. Unemployment insurance
    C. White House pursues ways to boost economy
    D. The economic recovery is running out of steam

12. According to the passage, to boost the struggling economy the White House is exploring new proposals EXCEPT ________.
    A. tax cuts to spur hiring and programs that could provide a lift to the housing market
    B. a broader payroll tax deduction for workers
    C. searching for ways to generate economic growth that could attract broad public support

D. proposing new investments in clean energy abroad

13. We learn from the passage that the government-controlled mortgage giants Fannie Mae and Freddie Mac would ________.

A. relieve pressure on the housing market, one of the main drags on the economy

B. rent out foreclosed properties that they own rather than try to sell them at depressed prices

C. eliminate unnecessary regulations prevent new tax increases

D. fund highway construction and help veterans get jobs

14. The underlined word "enacted" in the last paragraph but one is closest in meaning to ________.

A. passed B. portrayed C. represented D. enabled

15. The president will continue to promote and put forward ideas for things in order to ________.

A. lower expectations that any new policy could make a massive difference in the economy

B. create jobs and grow the economy

C. help the depressed housing market without the need for more public spending

D. pursue programs that would require new federal spending

Passage 4

Your house may be a threat to your figure. Experts say the way you design and maintain your home could play a role in whether you pack on the pounds or keep them off. "You can make your environment work for you instead of against you," says Dawn Jackson Blatner, dietitian and author of *The Flexitarian Diet*. "There are ways to use your house to successfully watch your weight, rather than relying solely on willpower."

1. Turn down the thermostat

Keeping your home too warm could be making you fat, suggests a recent study published in *Obesity Reviews*. Perhaps it's no coincidence that the prevalence of central heating has increased in step with obesity rates: Exposure to cold causes people to generate their own heat, often by shivering—and that, in turn, helps burn calories. There's no need for your home to feel like an igloo, but lower the thermostat a tad and your waistline could benefit. Most living rooms in the United States, for example, are heated to about 70 degrees Fahrenheit in the winter. Dropping the temperature to 60 degrees could increase energy expenditure by 100 or 200 calories a day—enough to shed a pound or so over a few weeks.

2. Downsize those dishes

"Big serving bowls and plates can easily make us fat," says food psychologist Brian

Wansink, author of *Mindless Eating: Why We Eat More Than We Think*. Wansink's research paints a compelling argument: We eat about 22 percent more when using a 12-inch plate instead of a 10-inch plate. When we choose a large spoon over a smaller one, total intake jumps by 14 percent. And we'll pour about 30 percent more into a short, wide glass than a tall, skinny glass that can hold the same amount of liquid. Jackson Blatner suggests giving smaller dishes a 7-day trial run: "If you don't think it helps you, stop doing it. But almost everybody I know agrees that it works like magic," she says. "It's kind of shocking how simple it can be."

3. Store food strategically

You're nearly three times more likely to eat healthy food if it's in your line of sight, a Cornell University study reports. That means keeping fruit, vegetables, and other nutritious options on eye-level shelves in the fridge, and relegating chocolate fudge and chip dip to the crispers. What's out of sight is out of mind, Jackson Blatner says: "Proximity is a big thing. If you're looking directly at beer and cheese, that's what you're going to eat. You're more likely to forget those things if they're hidden away."

4. Spray the smartest scents

Research suggests that certain aromas can make your waistline as happy as your nose. Jasmine, for example, increases alertness, which in turn ups the likelihood of exercising. Lavender helps you snooze more soundly—no small matter, since sleep deprivation can cause weight gain. And consider lighting green apple or peppermint candles; those scents are thought to suppress appetite. One study, for example, found that people who got a whiff of peppermint every two hours ate 2,700 fewer calories each week than they typically did.

(520 words, based on *http://health.usnews.com*)

16. According to dietitian Dawn Jackson Blatner the way you design and maintain your home could play a role in ________.
    A. eating more or les
    B. dark environment or light environment
    C. gaining weight or losing weight
    D. feeling relaxed or uneasy
17. We learn from the passage that if you want to consume more calories to keep fit in winter you'd better ________.
    A. keep your house as warm as 70 degrees Fahrenheit
    B. keep your home heated to about 60 degrees Fahrenheit
    C. keep your home so cold that you shiver
    D. keep your home cold to feel like an igloo
18. Research suggests that certain aromas can successfully watch your weight. For example, ________ helps you sleep peacefully since lack of sleep can cause weight gain.
    A. peppermint B. lavender

C. jasmine D. lighting green apple

19. Which of the following way is NOT used in the passage to turn your house into part of your diet plan?

A. Open the curtains and turn up the lights C. Turn down the thermostat

B. Use smaller dishes rather than bigger ones D. Store food strategically

20. Which of the following can best serve as the title of the passage?

A. No Meat in Your House B. Small Serving Bowls and Plates

C. A Whiff of Peppermint Every Day D. Is Your House Making You Fat?

Unit 9

Health and Medicine

Part 1 Reading Skills

Section A Patterns of Details I

Once a topic is offered, a writer needs to explain, discuss or argue for it and put forward his point of view, thus forming the main idea. In this course he will use specific information or details to support, explain or prove his idea. All the details will center around the topic and lead to the main idea. In English there are certain patterns to follow while developing the topic sentence, for example, listing, exemplification, cause and effect, comparison and contrast, which will be introduced in the following units.

Grasping the patterns of details contributes to your understanding of the thread of thoughts of the writer, thus leads to a full comprehension of what you are reading.

1. Listing

Listing is a frequently-used pattern of details in writing. Listing is to make a list of a series of things, facts or steps etc. For example,

1) *Finding the main idea involves a three-step process. Ask yourself the following three questions to find the main idea: (1) "What is the topic?" (2) "What is the point the author is trying to make about the topic? (3) and "How is the passage organized?" The way that the passage is organized can help with forming the main idea statement and deciding how that statement should be phrased.*

In the paragraph three questions are listed one by one. By following the suggestions, it's not difficult for you to find the main idea.

2) *People with disabilities have specific rules to follow when taking the airliner.* ***The first*** *and the simplest thing to do is to tell the airline company and explain to them. You* ***also*** *need to know the screening process in the airport.* ***Besides****, you have to provide the proper medical identification and prescription if you have to bring that medication in your carryon luggage. Keeping these reminders in mind will help you travel easily.*

The above paragraph is also an example of listing. Several rules for disabilities to take the airliner are enumerated one after another.

Usually, listing is used to describe a process or explain something step by step, point by point. When listing employed, there are certain connectors indicating this kind of pattern, for example, *first, second, third, firstly, next, also, besides, then, finally*, *one, another,* etc. and sometimes just numerals as used in the first example.

2. Exemplification

Giving examples to support one's idea is not only convincing but also vivid, so it's a very popular skill for writers. For example,

On April fourth of 1989, Joyce Palsa told a House Panel in Washington how her heart had been damaged as a result of cosmetic surgery on her abdomen. Mrs. Palsa, however, called herself "lucky" to be alive. According to her testimony, a woman who had had similar surgery had not survived the same complications. During that same hearing, Joyce Brown testified that a cosmetic procedure called liposuction, designed to remove excess fat, had left her unable to walk properly. A group of medical officials also pointed out that not all doctors who practice cosmetic surgery have the same qualifications. They testified that any medical school graduate with a license can perform cosmetic surgery, and they agreed that there was a need to toughen the regulations governing cosmetic surgery.

In the above paragraph the writer begins with several examples of the harm that cosmetic surgery has done to several women, leaving us a deep impression, thus the main idea he tries to convey "*There was a need to toughen the regulations governing cosmetic surgery*" is convincing and impressive.

Section B Practice

Exercise 1

Directions: Supply a topic sentence according to the details provided below.

Topic sentence: ____.

1. Examine the title page:
2. Examine the preface or introduction:
3. Examine the table of contents:
4. Examine index, glossary, other material at the back of the book:
5. Examine study questions, guides, and other helps:
6. Examine chapter headings, sectional headings, and margin guides:
7. Examine maps, pictures, charts, diagrams, and tables.

Exercise 2

Directions: A topic sentence is provided below. Please support the main idea by giving two examples in complete sentences.

Topic sentence: Nowadays people are not so honest as before.

Example 1: ____

____.

Example 2: ____

____.

Exercise 3

Directions: In the following paragraph, there is one sentence irrelevant to the main idea. Please pick it out and write it down.

Smiling makes us look good. No one likes to look at a person who is frowning. Such people make us want to turn and walk away. Frowns are ugly. Smiles make us look our very best. If we wear a happy face, then the world will be more cheerful. If you can keep a smiling face, the world will be yours. So frowning is nothing good, indeed.

____.

Part 2 Idioms, Proverbs and Sayings

Directions: The following are idioms, proverbs or sayings about health and medicine. Choose what you think is correct and compare with the right ones.

1. Early to bed and early to rise makes a man ________, wealthy and wise.
   A. healthy B. strong C. vigorous D. energetic
2. Exercise, temperance, fresh air, and needful rest are the best of all ________.
   A. cures B. doctors C. medicines D. physicians
3. Wealth is ________ without health.
   A. useless B. worthless C. nothing D. everything
4. A good medicine tastes ________.
   A. sweet B. bitter C. sour D. salty
5. Health is not ________ till sickness comes.
   A. mentioned B. valued C. respected D. esteemed
6. He who has health has hope, and he who has hope has ________.
   A. something B. nothing C. everything D. wealth
7. If doctors fail thee, be these ________ thy doctors; rest, cheerfulness, and moderate diet.
   A. one B. two C. three D. four
8. Many dishes make ________ diseases.
   A. many B. some C. more D. no
9. Without health, life is not life, life is ________.
   A. hopeless B. in vain C. nothing D. lifeless
10. A good healthy body is worth more a crown in ________.
    A. gold B. silver C. bronze D. diamond

Part 3 Reading Passages

Section A Medicine's Bright Future

The Internet and social media are capturing the public's attention, but some of the most significant advances today are happening in medicine. Technology and medicine are converging in new ways to make possible the types of innovations that could be seen on "Star Trek." Consider this: We spend the majority of our health-care dollars on treating chronic diseases. Technological advances will enable us to shift those investments into improving our health and preventing disease.

My colleague Daniel Kraft is a physician who chairs the medicine track and heads the FutureMed Program for Singularity University. The Silicon Valley-based university teaches business executives, technologists and government leaders about "exponential technologies." These are inventions in fields that experience faster growth than average—such as robotics, nanotechnology and artificial intelligence. Singularity University's founders believe that these technologies, when combined in new ways, could solve some of the world's major problems, such as poverty, hunger, energy shortages and disease.

Here are the three major trends Kraft sees in health and medicine:

Trend 1 ________________

Many aspects of health care and disease management will become cheaper and more effective as our mobile phones and other, similar technology platforms become smaller, Web-enabled and interconnected. In essence, these smartphones will become health platforms. They already contain a wide array of sensors, including an accelerometer that can serve as a pedometer, a camera that can photograph external ailments and transmit them for analysis, and a global positioning system (GPS) that can track our locations.

Developers are also looking beyond the smartphone when it comes to developing these new technologies. For example, Fitbit is a clip-on, Web-integrated device that helps track how many calories you burn during the day; Zeo is a wireless headband that helps you track the quality and duration of your sleep. Other devices, such as the Basis monitor, which is still in development, can keep track of heart rates and movement. Meanwhile, an array of devices, including scales, blood pressure monitors and blood glucose monitors, are becoming Wi-Fi-enabled. These technologies, when they are connected to electronic and personal health records and to social networks, can create powerful feedback loops with friends, and provide clinicians with better information for helping their patients.

Expect to see products that keep track of your health by connecting to global health-care systems similar to the in-car assistance program OnStar. These will incorporate ubiquitous sensors embedded in toothbrushes and clothes, for example. They may even analyze our bathroom visits and food intake. They will likely use artificial-intelligence to constantly monitor our health data, predict disease and summon help in the event we fall ill.

Trend 2 ________________

We learned how to sequence the genome a decade ago, and doing it cost billions of dollars. Companies like 23andMe are now offering partial DNA genotyping for as low as $99 (with a one-year subscription to their information service). Expect prices to continue to rapidly decline to that of a regular blood test.

This means that it is now becoming more affordable to compare one person's DNA with another's, learn what diseases those with similar genetics have had and discover how effective different medications or other interventions were in treating them. Imagine doing a Google search on specific genes to find others like you and learn their abilities, allergies, likes and dislikes and what diseases they are predisposed to. That future is closer than you may think.

This opens up an era of crowd-sourced, data-driven, participatory, genomics-based medicine. Today, medicines are prescribed on a "one size fits all" basis. When a particular medication causes a significant negative reaction with a small part of the population, it is prevented from being available to anyone. In the future, expect to see doctors prescribing and selecting the most patient-appropriate medicines based on a person's DNA (the field of "pharmacogenomics").

Trend 3 ________________

Physicians have been conducting adult stem-cell therapy for more than 40 years in the field of bone-marrow transplantation, which involves transplanting stem cells that become red blood cells. Adult stem cells are now being applied in a variety of arenas, from orthopedics to cardiovascular therapy. The first trials using cells derived from embryonic stem cells were for acute spinal cord injury and started within the last year. But embryonic stem cells have raised ethical and moral controversy even though the research remains critical for future progress.

The good news is a new type of cell, induced pluripotent stem cells, which will enable the generation of personalized stem cell lines for use in diagnostics, prognosis or potentially for therapy in the same patient. IPS cells can replace embryonic stem cells for some applications and are, for example, being used to develop neurons from patients with ALS/Lou Gehrig's disease in order to better understand the disease and develop new therapies.

Tissue engineering and 3-D printing technologies are also beginning to merge. The combination of the two technologies could lead to an era of personalized organ generation. Indeed, earlier this month, surgeons in Sweden carried out the world's first synthetic organ transplant—a synthetic trachea/windpipestructure created and seeded with the patient's own progenitor cells.

These developments are just the beginning. There will undoubtedly be regulatory, reimbursement and other challenges. And there will be heated debates about ethics and morals. But it won't be long before we are using devices similar to the "Star Trek" tricorder and synthesizing our medications.

(900 words, based on *http://www.washingtonpost.com* by Vivek Wadhwa)

I. Reading Comprehension

Questions 1-3

Directions: Do the following statements agree with the information in the reading passage? Mark:

Y for Yes	if the statement is true according to the passage
N for No	if the statement contradicts the passage
NG for Not Given	if there is no information about this in the passage

1. ________ Technology and medicine make possible the types of innovations that could be seen on "Star Trek."
2. ________ In the future, we expect to see doctors prescribing medicines based on a person's DNA on a "one size fits all" basis.
3. ________ Physician Daniel Kraft from Singularity University carried out the world's first synthetic organ transplant created and seeded with the patient's own progenitor cells.

Questions 4-7

Directions: The list below gives some of the names of the devices. According to the passage, which FOUR of these devices are mentioned by the writer? Match the names of the devices with their functions. Write the appropriate letters.

NB: There are more functions than devices, so you will not use all of them.

List of Functions
A. a wireless headband that helps you track the quality and duration of your sleep
B. a new type of cell, which will enable the generation of personalized stem cell lines for use in diagnostics
C. a clip-on, Web-integrated device that helps track how many calories you burn during the day
D. a monitor still in development, which can keep track of heart rates and movement
E. a camera that can photograph external ailments and transmit them for analysis, and a global positioning system (GPS) that can track our locations

4. pedometer ________
5. Fitbit ________
6. Zeo ________
7. Basis ________

Questions 8-10

Directions: According to the passage, there are three major trends Daniel Kraft, a physician who chairs the medicine track and heads the FutureMed Program for Singularity University, sees in health and medicine. Choose the most suitable heading for each trend from the list of headings below. Write the appropriate letters.

NB: There are more headings for the three trends, so you will not use all of them.

List of Headings
A. Personalization: From genomics to proteomics
B. The Internet and social media
C. Medicine goes mobile and goes home
D. Tissue engineering
E. Regenerative medicine

8. Trend 1 ________ 9. Trend 2 ________ 10. Trend 3 ________

II. Vocabulary

Directions: Fill in each blank with an appropriate word from the box below. Change the form where necessary. Each word can be used only once.

converge	chronic	exponential	loop	ubiquitous
medication	therapy	acute	embryonic	reimbursement

1. The luxury giants' confidence in the market has been boosted by sales in China. The Sweden-based tax __________ agent Global Refund Group recently released a report, showing that the total amount of tax-free products bought by Chinese tourists in France in 2010 totaled 650 million euros.
2. But as more and more friends joined weibo, I became addicted and plugged in to the constant feedback __________ created by the posts, replies, and comments to follow up and share with friends whatever happens around you.
3. The Prince of Wales Hospital has set up a committee to investigate the death of a 73-year-old woman, who suffered kidney failure after receiving __________ intended for another patient.
4. When he stood up, trying to stretch his legs a bit after a long spell on the lower bunk, he suddenly fell over and __________ pain raced through his back.
5. According to Chinese medical theory, in the hottest days of summer, cupping and plaster __________, applied to strategic points on the body, can help combat common winter ailments.
6. Twenty-two chairpersons of international film festivals will __________ in the capital city of Beijing.
7. The US had, under the George W. Bush administration, banned the use of federal funding for new lines of __________ stem cell research but President Barack Obama reversed that

decision.

8. Shanghai is emerging quickly as a new financial center in Asia with an annual GDP of 1.69 trillion yuan, and its financial services are expanding at an __________ rate.
9. The life-expectancy disparity, which begins around the age of 50, stems from higher levels of middle-age obesity and obesity-related __________ diseases, such as hypertension and diabetes.
10. People in Seoul, where smartphones are ____________, posted dozens of photos on Twitter showing inundated streets and mud-covered cars.

III. Debate

Directions: Read the following short passage and have a debate over the topic "China is facing a severe challenge in terms of psychological health of children."

BEIJING—Nearly one in ten young Chinese under the age of 17 have some sort of mental disorders, a recent survey suggests.

The Beijing Anding Hospital and the Chinese Medical Association hosted an international conference about the mental health of young people on Sunday. At the meeting, Chinese scholars said that at least 30 million minors in China are plagued with mental disorders or behavior problems. By the year 2007, China had 341 million minors, accounting for 26 percent of the country's total population.

"The number 30 million is based on regional researches in recent years. Since the mental health of children must have worsened over time, the real number could be even higher," said Cui Yonghua, a child psychiatrist with the Beijing Anding Hospital.

"China is facing a severe challenge in terms of psychological health of children, which embodies in phenomenon such as unreasonable usage of Internet and mental issues of children who lag behind," said Chen Zhu, head of the Ministry of Health.

According to a recent survey in Heilongjiang province, 96 percent primary school students don't get enough sleep as they are overburdened with schoolwork and are said to start having love affairs as early as 12 years old. Mental disorder covers a wide range of symptoms such as emotional instability, obsession, and depression. And behavior problems include Internet addiction, smoking, destructiveness and early pregnancy. The survey also said that mental health of young people needs more public attention.

"Change in environment change, growing pressure and sharper competition all play a part in the problem," Cui said.

(Based on *Chinadaily*)

Section B It Takes Courage

by Bill Sanders

Directions: Read the following passage and choose the best answer.

You gain strength; experience and confidence by experience where you really stop look fear in your face... You must do thing you cannot do.

Eleanor Roosevelt

Her name is Nikki. She lives just down the road from me. I have been inspired by this young lady for a number of years. Her story has touched my heart and when times get tough, I reflect on her courage.

It started when she was in seventh grade, with the doctor's report. Everything that her family had feared was true. The diagnosis: leukemia. The next few months was filled with regular visits to the hospital. She was poked and jabbed and tested hundreds and thousands times. Then came the chemotherapy. Along with it, and a chance to possibly save her life, she lost her hair. Losing your hair as a seventh grader is a devastating thing. The hair didn't grow back. The family started to worry.

The summer before the eighth grade she bought a wig. It felt uncomfortable, it was scratchy, but she wore it. She was very popular and loved by so many students. She was a cheerleader and always had other kids around her, but things seemed to change. She looked strange and you know how kids are. I guess maybe like the rest of us. Sometimes we go after laughter and do things even though it causes great pain in someone else. The wig was pulled off from behind about a half a dozen times in the first two weeks of the eighth grade. She would stop, bent down, shake from fear and embarrassment, put her wig back on, wipe away the tear and walk to class, always wondering why no one stood up for her.

This went on for two agonizing, hellish weeks. She told her parents she couldn't take it any more. They said: "you can stay home if you wish." You see, if your daughter is dying in the eighth grade; you don't care if she makes it to ninth. Having her happy and giving her a chance at peace is all the matter. Nikki told me to lose her hair is nothing. She said, "I can handle that." She even said that losing her life is of little concern. "I can handle that, too," she said, "but do you know what it's like to lose your friends? To walk down the hall and have them part like the red sea because you are coming, to go into the cafeteria one pizza day, our best meal, and have them leave with half-eaten plates?" They say that they are not hungry but you know they're leaving because you are sitting there. Do you know what it's like to have no one want to sit next to you in math class and the kids in the locker in the left and right of you have pulled out? They're putting books in with someone else, all because they might have to stand next to the girl wearing the wig, the one with the weird disease. It's not even catching. They can't get it from me. Don't they know that I need my friends most of all? Oh, yes," she said, "losing your life is nothing when you know that because of you belief in God you know exactly where you are going to spend eternity. Losing your hair is nothing either, but losing your friends is so devastating."

She had planned to stay home from school, but something happened that weekend. She heard two boys, one in sixth grade, one in seventh, and their stories gave the courage to go on. The seventh grade is from Arkansas and even it wasn't popular, he took his New Testament Bible in his shirt to school. As the story goes, three boys approached him, grabbed the Bible and said, "You sissy. Religion is for sissies. Prayer is for sissies. Don't ever again bring this Bible to school." He reportedly handed the Bible back to the biggest one of the three and said, "Here see if you've got enough courage to carry this around school just one day." They said that he made their friends.

The next story that inspired Nikki was a sixth grader from Ohio named Jimmy Masterdino. He was jealous of California because California has a motto, "Eureka!" Ohio didn't have any. He came up with six-changing words. He single handedly got enough signatures. With his petitions full, he took it before the State Legislature. Today, because of a brave sixth grader, the official state motto for Ohio is "All is possible with God."

With Nikki's new-found courage and inspiration, she put her wig on that next Monday morning. She got dressed as pretty and as fancy as she could. She told her mom and dad, "I'm going back to school today. There's something I've got to do. There's something I've got to find out." They didn't know what she meant and they were worried, fearing the worst, but they drove her to school. Every day for the last several weeks, Nikki would hug and kiss her mom and dad before she got out. As unpopular as this was and even though many kids sneered and jeered at her, she never let it stop her. Today was different. She hugged and kissed them, but as she got out of the car, she turned quickly and said, "Mom and dad, guess what I'm going to do today?" Her eyes were filling with tears, but they were tears of joy and strength. Oh, yes, there was fear of unknown, but she had a cause. They said, "What, baby?" She said, "Today I'm going to find out who my best friend is. Today I'm going to find out who my real friends are." And with that she grabbed the wig off her head and she set it on the seat beside her. She said, "They take me for who I am, Daddy, or they don't take me at all. I don't have much time left. I've got to find out who they are today." She started to walk, took two steps, then turned and said, "Pray for me." They said, "We are, baby." And as she walked toward 600 kids, she could hear her dad say, "That's my girl."

A miracle happened that day. She walked through the playground, into that school, and not one loud-mouth or bully, no one, made fun of the little girl with all the courage.

Nikki has taught thousands of people that to be yourself, to use your own God-given talent, and to stand up for what is right even in the midst of uncertainty, pain, fear and persecution is the only true way to live.

Nikki has since graduated from high school. The marriage was never supposed to take place happened a few years later, and Nikki is the proud mother of a little girl that she named after my little girl, Emily. Every time something that seems impossible comes before me, I think of Nikki and I gain strength.

(1,180 words)

1. According to the story, the writer has been impressed for years by Nikki's ________.
   A. leukemia B. chemotherapy C. courage D. agony
2. Nikki was diagnosed as leukemia when she was in seventh grade and she had to receive chemotherapy. As a result of it, she suffered from the side effect of ________.
   A. feeling sick B. hair loss C. pain D. infection
3. What happened to Nikki when she wore a wig to school in the first two weeks of the eighth grade?
   A. She looked so strange that many kids followed her everywhere at school.
   B. She became a cheerleader and loved by so many students.
   C. Her wig was pulled off from behind about a half a dozen times.
   D. She felt so scratchy and uncomfortable that she pulled the wig off by herself.
4. Nikki had planned to stay home from school, but she changed her mind and returned to school because ________.
   A. many kids got used to her wig and stopped sneering and jeering at her
   B. two boys' stories, one in sixth grade and the other in seventh, gave the courage to go on
   C. she was afraid of losing her friends if she stayed at home for a long time
   D. losing her life is nothing when she knows that
5. Nikki has taught thousands of people ________.
   A. to be yourself for what is right even in the midst of pain, fear and persecution
   B. that suddenly tears and chemotherapy overtook her life in one day
   C. a miracle happened that day as she walked toward 600 kids at school
   D. all is possible with God who knows exactly where you are going to spend eternity

Part 4 Reading Comprehension Test

Passage 1

Directions: Read the following passage. Choose the best answer to each question.

The more years a mother works during her children's growing-up years, the more likely the children's weight is to rise, according to a new study. The findings echo some previous findings but also extend them, according to researcher Taryn Morrissey, Ph D, assistant professor in public administration and policy at American University.

Whereas many previous studies have examined intensity of maternal employment in terms of her work hours, we extend this line of work by showing an association between intensity of maternal employment over the child's lifetime—that is, cumulative exposure to maternal employment as the child grows older—and her child's BMI [body mass index] ," Morrissey writes.

Bottom line: The longer a mom's employment—whether she's toiling at a regular 9-to-5 job or works irregular hours—the more likely her child is to gain more weight than is healthy.

"This is not a reason for moms to feel guilty," Morrissey tells WebMD. "It's not maternal employment per se that's the issue. It's an underlying environmental factor that leads to this association." What that factor (or factors) is has yet to be uncovered, she says.

Morrissey and her team evaluated data on 990 children who were enrolled in the Study of Early Child Care and Youth Development, sponsored by the Eunice Kennedy Shriver National Institute of Child Health and Human Development. The children lived in 10 different cities across the country. The researchers checked data about mothers' employment and kids' BMI when the children were in grades three, five, and six. The researchers looked at whether the mothers worked, whether they worked traditional schedules or not, and the length of the employment. They didn't look at how many hours were worked, Morrissey says, so there's no way to give a threshold of how many hours is linked to increasing weight in kids.

What they did find it that the total number of years that the mothers were working had a small but cumulative effect on the child's BMI. How small? For every 5.3-month period the mother was employed, the child had a slight increase in BMI over and above what would be expected with normal weight gain with age.

"For a child of average height," Morrissey writes, "this is equivalent to a gain in weight of nearly 1 pound every five months above and beyond what would typically be gained as a child ages."

The association was strongest when the children were in fifth and six grade compared to third grade, perhaps because at that age children may make more food choices on their own. Over time, the slight increases can tip the child into being overweight.

(440 words, based on *http://children.webmd.com*)

1. According to researcher Taryn Morrissey, the findings of a new study show ________.

   A. factors affecting why the kids gain weight

   B. working mothers feel guilty for having little time to grocery shop and to prepare healthy food

   C. the link between changes in physical activity, the time spent in supervised activity

   D. The longer a mom's employment, the more likely her child is to gain more weight than is healthy

2. Many previous studies have examined ________.

   A. children of working mothers tend to skip breakfast

   B. intensity of working mothers' employment in terms of her work hours

   C. Fast food doesn't necessarily have to be higher calorie

   D. feeding children breakfast before work and school may help reduce weight gain

3. Which of the following is NOT done by Morrissey and her team?
   A. They evaluated data on 990 children living in 10 different cities across the country.
   B. They checked data about mothers' employment and kids' BMI when the children were in grades three, five, and six.
   C. They looked at whether the mothers worked and how many hours were worked.
   D. They looked at whether the mothers worked traditional schedules or not, and the length of the employment.
4. The association between mothers' employment and kids' BMI was strongest when the children were in 5th & 6th grade compared to 3rd grade because ________.
   A. parents could try to ensure that the child in fifth and six grade get more chances for physical activity
   B. children in fifth and six grade understand a family meal at home once a week is linked with lower obesity
   C. a child in third grade may gain in weight of nearly 1 pound every five months
   D. children in fifth and six grade may make more food choices on their own
5. Which of the following might be the best title of this passage?
   A. Working Mothers and Weight Gain in Kids
   B. Food and kids' BMI
   C. Little Time to Prepare Dinner
   D. The More Moms Work, the Less Kids Gain Weight

Passage 2

Directions: Read the passage below and decide whether the following statements are true or false according to the passage. Write T for True and F for False.

The promise of those "golden years" may be losing some luster for many baby boomers deeply worried about the financial pressures that come with age—even more of a concern for them than facing a major disease like cancer.

Among the top worries for the nation's 77 million boomers: being able to pay medical bills and losing their financial independence, a new poll finds. With the economy struggling, a longer life expectancy, ever-increasing health care costs, deflated housing prices and challenges facing Social Security, it is not hard to understand why many people born between 1946 and 1964 might feel uneasy. According to the Associated Press-LifeGoesStrong.com poll, 43 percent of boomers polled said they were "very" or "extremely" worried about being able to pay for their medical costs, including long-term care. Almost the same number, 41 percent, said losing their financial independence was a big concern.

Krall, 50, a manager of an orthopedic office, has an 18-year-old son whom she and her husband are helping put through college. She said she's worried about paying for health-care costs down the road and isn't banking on Social Security. The oldest boomers are turning 65 this year, but it's the younger ones like Krall who might be feeling more apprehension.

"Boomers are not all created equal," says Olivia Mitchell, professor at the Wharton School of the University of Pennsylvania and executive director of the Pension Research Council. Many in the older group still have a defined benefit pension plan, probably some decent retiree medical insurance and Social Security, said Mitchell, a boomer herself who has studied pensions and retirement extensively.

"The youngest boomers—the people who were born in the 60s—face more uncertainty about their pensions, their Social Security, their housing and their medical care," Mitchell said.

Her advice: Don't retire.

"Push your retirement back two or three or five years if you can. As long as you are still working then you're not drawing down on your nest egg," Mitchell said in an AP interview. "What most people don't realize is how expensive it is to live in retirement."

Many people in their late 60s, and some into their 70s, are still among the ranks of the employed. According to the Bureau of Labor Statistics, 29.1 percent of people aged 65 to 69 worked at least part-time last year. And almost 7 percent of people aged 75 or older were employed in 2010.

(400 words, based on *http://www.washingtonpost.com*)

6. ________ Many boomers concerned about paying for their short-term medical costs with the economy struggling, a longer life expectancy, and deflated housing prices.
7. ________ According to Olivia Mitchell, professor at the Wharton School of the University of Pennsylvania, what most people don't realize is how expensive it is to live in retirement.
8. ________ Krall, who belongs to the younger group of the 65 million boomers in the US, has an 18-year-old son whom she and her husband are helping put through college.
9. ________ Many boomers push back their retirement for several years: 29.1 percent of people aged 65 to 69 worked at least part-time last year. And almost 7 percent of people aged 75 or older were employed in 2010.
10. ________ According to the Associated Press-LifeGoesStrong.com poll, 43 percent of boomers polled said losing their financial independence was a big concern.

Passage 3

Directions: Read the following passage and decide whether the statements that follow are true or false. Write T for True and F for False.

Many aspects of our health are genetically linked. According to researchers from the Institute of Cancer Research at the University of London, there's a 57 percent chance that a girl will start menstruating within three months of the date that her mother began.

There's a 70-80 percent chance that you'll suffer from migraines if your mother did. Researchers believe that a flawed gene may cause severe headaches and can be passed on. If this gene is defective, outside factors, like light, are more liable to trigger pain centers in the brain that cause headaches. Other triggers include sensitive foods like chocolate, coffee, cheese, citrus fruit and red wine and should be avoided.

Women who carry the mutated gene BRCA1 or BRCA2 are more at risk to develop breast cancer. Most women who have the defective gene will develop cancer at a very young age, says cancer geneticist, Dr. Elizabeth Rapley. As a preventative measure, it's extremely important for women to get mammograms after age 40.

We can inherit up to 50 percent of our fitness levels genetically. Even though we all need to exercise to build muscle, it is true that people require far less physical activity to achieve the same amount of tone and fitness level. Unfair, we know. Louise Sutton, the head of Carnegie Centre for Sports Performance at Leeds Metropolitan University, says, "You need to do 30-45 minutes of moderate to high-intensity aerobic activity, such as running, swimming or cycling, preferably with bursts of speed, on at least three days a week." Adding resistance and stretching will also help.

People who carry two copies of the fat FTO gene have a 70 percent higher chance of being obese than those with none. Another study found that 4 percent of girls with normal-weight mothers were obese, while 41 percent with overweight mothers became obese. According to Sutton, apple-shaped bodies are more genetically linked than pear-shapes and thin figures. Interestingly enough, a 2009 study discovered strong ties between mother-daughter obesity and father-son obesity, but no links between genders. Of course, there may be a nurture as well as a nature connection to obesity. Did your overweight mom encourage you to eat more as you were growing up? She may have established a pattern you find hard to break. While you can't control genetics, watching your calorie and fat intake will help you maintain a healthy weight, as will exercising and living an active lifestyle.

(400 words, based on *http://www. ThirdAge.com*)

11. ________ There are some women's health conditions that experts say we may have inherited from our mothers.
12. ________ There's a 57 percent chance that a girl will get breast cancer if you have a family history.
13. ________ Rheumatoid arthritis is more often seen in people who smoke and consume large quantities of red meat and caffeine.
14. ________ You're up to 70 to 80 percent more likely to develop migraines if your mother had it.
15. ________ According to the passage, there's a chance that you'll suffer from migraines, breast cancer, fitness level and obesity if your mother did.

Passage 4

Directions: Read the following passage. Choose the best answer to each question.

Fathers-to-be should stop smoking to protect their unborn child from the risk of stillbirth or birth defects, scientists say. University of Nottingham researchers found that pregnant women exposed to smoke at work or home increased their risk of stillbirth by 23% and of having a baby with defects by 13%. They looked at 19 previous studies from around the world. A UK expert said it was "vital" women knew the risks of second-hand smoke. The studies used to pull this research together were carried out in North America, South America, Asia and Europe. All the studies focused on pregnant women who did not smoke themselves but were passive smokers due to their proximity to a partner who smoked or work colleagues who smoked. The combined data from the studies suggests that being exposed to more than 10 cigarettes a day is enough for the risks to be increased. However, the University of Nottingham study did not find an increased risk of miscarriage or newborn death from second-hand smoke—only an increased risk of still birth and birth defects.

The researchers say fathers who smoke should be more aware of the danger they pose to their unborn child. Previous research has shown that women who smoke during their pregnancy create serious health risks for their unborn baby, including low birth weight, premature birth and a range of serious birth defects such as cleft palate, club foot and heart problems.

Andrew Shennan, professor of obstetrics at St. Thomas' Hospital in London and spokesperson for baby charity Tommy's, said: "It is vital that women are made aware of the possible risks associated with second-hand smoke and alert those around them of the impact it could potentially have on the health of their unborn baby. The chemicals in cigarettes are known to significantly increase the risk of serious pregnancy complications."

(300 words, based on *http://www.bbc.co.uk*)

16. Which of the following is not the finding of the University of Nottingham researchers?
    A. An increased risk of miscarriage or newborn death from second-hand smoke
    B. pregnant women exposed to smoke at work or home increased their risk of stillbirth by 23% and of having a baby with defects by 13%.
    C. it was "vital" women knew the risks of second-hand smoke.
    D. being exposed to more than 10 cigarettes a day is enough for the risks to be increased
17. All the studies focused on pregnant women who did not smoke themselves but were passive smokers are carried out ________.
    A. at the University of Nottingham
    B. in North America, South America, Asia and Europe
    C. at St. Thomas' Hospital in London
    D. at Baby Charity Tommy's
18. According to the passage, previous research has shown that ________.
    A. fathers who smoke should be more aware of the danger they pose to their unborn child
    B. Fathers-to-be should stop smoking to protect their unborn child from the risk of stillbirth or birth defects
    C. Mothers-to-be should stop smoking to protect their unborn child from the risk of

miscarriage

D. women who smoke during their pregnancy create serious health risks for their unborn baby

19. According to Andrew Shennan, professor at St. Thomas' Hospital, ________.

A. the risks are related to the amount of cigarettes that are smoked

B. women should be aware when the effects of the second-hand smoke begin

C. women should be aware of the possible risks associated with second-hand smoke

D. it is very important for men to cut down smoking

20. An appropriate title for the passage might be ________.

A. Impact on child development

B. Passive Smoking Increases Still Birth Risk

C. Birth Defects

D. What Should Fathers-to-be Do

Unit 10

Trade and Economy

Part 1 Reading Skills

Section A Pattern of Details II

3) Comparison

Comparison is a writing skill that writers often appeal to when they are trying to emphasize the resemblances or similarities between two things. And there are some signifying words to show the relationship of comparison, for example, *similarly, likewise, so, both...and, similar to* etc. For example,

Chinese Mid-Autumn Festival is somewhat similar to American Thanksgiving Day. ***Both*** *of them have a long history. Chinese Mid-Autumn Festival is a day to celebrate the autumn.* ***So*** *is American Thanksgiving Day. On Mid-Autumn Festival Chinese families will get together to enjoy themselves.* ***Likewise****, American families will reunite on Thanksgiving Day to have a good time.*

4) Contrast

Contrast is also often used by writers in their writing. Contrary to comparison, contrast is to emphasize the differences. There are also words and phrases functioning as connectors to make a contrast between two things, like *different from, contrary to, however, but, on the contrary,* etc. Here is an example of contrast about the differences between two kinds of foods:

Fresh foods are quite different from canned food. The most notable ***difference*** *between them is their flavor. Fresh foods have great flavor and taste because they keep all their natural conditions. Canned foods,* ***however****, lack a lot of its flavor characteristics because there are some other chemical products added to the natural foods.* ***Another difference*** *lies in the health factor. Canned foods lose some of the original fresh food nutrients when stored, and also it has to be tinned with many conservatives and chemical factors that prolong the shelf life and apparent freshness of the food but could also become toxic if consumed too often. Fresh foods are relatively cheap.* ***On the contrary****, canned foods are much more expensive.*

Actually in our daily life, we are faced with many tasks to use comparison and contrast at the same time, like deciding which university to attend, even which dress to wear. Writers, too, tend to employ both of them. Look at the following example:

Country music and alternative music seem like very different entities, but they have a few similarities as well. The two types of music use different vocalization, volume, and rhythm styles. Alternative music has a tendency to be more discordant, noisy, and rhythmic, whereas country music is usually more harmonious and uses softer sounds. Country music and alternative music use many of the same instruments such as the lead and bass guitars, drums, and keyboards, but country music also uses steel slide guitars. Country and alternative music both often use the lyrics of songs to tell stories and often express angst although the subjects of the sorrowful stories in country music usually deal with passionate relationships and in alternative music the anguish is related to many areas of life.

Section B Practice

Exercise 1

Directions: In the following paragraph, there is one sentence irrelevant to the main idea. Please pick it out.

My hometown and my college town have several things in common. First, both are small rural communities. For example, my hometown has a population of only about 10,000 people. Similarly, my college town consists of about 11,000 local residents. But the people in my hometown are much more warm-hearted. A second way in which these two towns are similar is that they are both located in rural areas. My hometown is surrounded by many acres of farmland which is devoted mainly to growing corn and soybeans. In the same way, my college town lies in the center of farmland which is used to raise hogs and cattle.

Exercise 2

Directions: A topic sentence is given below. First decide what kind of pattern of details is required to develop the topic sentence and offer at lest two differences.

Topic sentence: Hangzhou and Shanghai are strikingly different.

Exercise 3

Directions: Read the following paragraph and answer the questions below.

Abraham Lincoln was elected president in 1860. Exactly one hundred years later in 1960, John Kennedy was elected president. The first name of Lincoln's private secretary was John, and the last name of Kennedy's private secretary was Lincoln. Both men were succeeded by vice-presidents named Johnson who were southern democrats and former senators. Andrew Johnson was born in 1808. Lyndon Johnson was born in 1908, exactly one hundred years later. Lyndon Johnson and Andrew Johnson each contain thirteen letters. Lincoln was killed in Ford's theater. Kennedy met his death while riding in a Lincoln convertible made by the Ford motor company. Both assassins were southerners who held extremist views. Both assassins were murdered before they could be brought to trial. John Wilkes Booth was born in 1839. Lee Harvey Oswald was born one hundred years later in 1939. Lee Harvey Oswald and John Wilkes Booth each contain 15 letters. Booth shot Lincoln in a theater and fled to a barn. Oswald shot Kennedy from a warehouse and fled to a theater.

1. What's the main idea of this paragraph?

____

2. What kind of pattern of details is used in this paragraph?

____

Part 2 Idioms, Proverbs and Sayings

Directions: The following are idioms, proverbs or sayings about trade and economy. Choose what you think is correct and compare with the right ones.

1. Jack of all trades, ________ of none. (Proverb)
   A. merchant B. economist C. expert D. master
2. The knowledge of a trade is worth a handful of ________. (Proverb)
   A. dollars B. salt C. gold D. silver
3. There are ________ in all trades. (Proverb)
   A. tricks B. traps C. regulations D. standards
4. Two of a trade can never ________. (Proverb)
   A. quarrel B. agree C. dispute D. disagree
5. There are no foolish trades, there are only ________ people. (Proverb)
   A. foolish B. clever C. honest D. dishonest
6. Economy is the basis of society. When the economy is stable, society develops. The ideal economy combines the spiritual and the material, and the best commodities to trade in are ________. (Morihei Ueshiba)
   A. honesty and modesty B. sincerity and love
   C. peace and stability D. harmony and development
7. This is the moment when we must build on the wealth that open markets have created, and share its benefits more equitably. Trade has been a ________ of our growth and global development. But we will not be able to sustain this growth if it favors the few, and not the many. (Barack Obama)
   A. foundation B. milestone C. cornerstone D. landmark
8. Globalization and ________ trade do spur economic growth, and they lead to lower prices on many goods. (Robert Reich)
   A. market B. international C. foreign D. free
9. Advertising is the art of ________ people to spend money they don't have for something they don't need." (Will Rogers)
   A. imposing B. preventing C. convincing D. hijacking
10. Things aren't right. If a burglar breaks into your home and you shoot him, he can sue you. For what? ________ of trade. (Bill Maher)
    A. Restraint B. Encourage C. Promote D. Discourage

Part 3 Reading Passages

Section A The Right Approach

Although many professionals and business entities appear to have developed a knack for cross-cultural communication, the truth is that successful communication is the result of a well thought-out strategy. For example, it is not unusual for international Japanese companies to require their overseas representatives to spend considerable time in the designated foreign country before the representative's input or recommendations are requested by the company's top executives. The light speed of globalization, as well as the continuing trend toward cultural diversity, has inspired a wide variety of books, videos, audio tapes and seminars on the "nuts and bolts" of cross-cultural negotiation. Communication difficulties have been discussed in numerous publications, such as *Beyond Borders*. The majority of advice recommends that the expat become familiar with each country and learn what is acceptable and what isn't acceptable in each culture.

Professionals with a successful track record of negotiating in a different cultural environment consistently strive to understand the etiquette of the culture they're dealing with. It is in their best interest to avoid any preconceived notions of the culture or to be tempted to assume that the foreign country mirrors their homeland. Successful overseas professionals become cultural specialists in a sense. For example, they study the target culture carefully to determine appropriate behavior in a variety of situations. They look for clues by asking such pertinent questions as:

Is the culture rooted in tradition or is it liberal minded? For example, would bringing an unmarried partner be accepted?

Does the culture hold the belief that some individuals are superior by virtue of their bloodline or do they accept general equality?

Does the culture believe that events are predetermined or do they consider events to be determined by individual behavior?

Once some of these questions are answered, a clearer picture of the cultural landscape is visible. The next step is to consider other cultural factors that influence behavior and attitudes within the country. In terms of getting a clearer picture of the culture itself, take a close look at its historical background. A country whose military capabilities have prevented the occupation by any foreign military forces ultimately has a much different perspective on life than a country that has been invaded. Other factors that have ultimately made an impact on a culture's perspectives and attitudes include: geography, climate, ethnic heritage, and natural resources. Inevitably, these regional factors often determine not only how your prospective business partners perceive their own culture, but they also serve to influence their perceptions and attitudes in dealing with foreigners, such as yourself. Also keep in mind that no country can pretend to be an "ivory tower" that is isolated from the social influences of other cultures, even though these influences may go against the grain of the culture's own set of values. Remember, cross-cultural communication invariably flows in both directions. Their interaction with you is likely to be influenced by what they have been led to believe about the behavior of American culture, and vice versa.

The successful expat will take the trouble to determine the new culture's operating code of etiquette for business relationships. Just as in the US (whether you are conscious of them or not) there are certain "ground rules" that need to be observed, and this will be so in your overseas assignment. The tricky part is that these rules vary from culture to culture. Let's consider some of the primary issues that will need to be addressed:

How should people of various rank be addressed? When is it acceptable to use first names? Should you address them by their official business title? Should attention be paid to birth names, married names, or clan names? How should business cards be exchanged? Are there designated physical greeting gestures? What about gifts? Are they a necessity? If so, who should be on the receiving end? Also, what gift is appropriate, and when should it be presented?

How important is punctuality? Is the appointment scheduled at a time (and season) that is acceptable? What should be the length of the visit? Should conversation be focused strictly on business or should it also be social in nature? If dining is involved, what is appropriate as far as food and beverages?

What is acceptable regarding the pace of negotiations? What is the status of the individuals with whom you are negotiating? Are final decisions actually final? In the end, is "no" an acceptable answer?

What about entertaining? Should business be discussed? Should the setting be at a restaurant or at one's private residence? If entertaining is done at a restaurant, who is responsible for picking up the tab? Should alcohol be consumed? Are there specific table manners that need to be observed? Are there limitations as to how much food should be consumed?

How does body language in this culture differ from yours? Do people tend to stand closer or farther apart from each other in conversation? When is direct eye contact appropriate? How appropriate is it to touch another person during conversation? What kinds of gender differences in body language need to be respected? How are gestures or facial expressions used differently?

Ideally, expats should have some command of the country's language and be somewhat familiar with issues involving the country's political agenda, the state of its economy as well as the social culture. In terms of the assignment itself, the expat needs to adopt a certain flexibility in work habits without compromising personal standards of excellence. According to one human resource director of an East Coast manufacturing company with employees around the world, one of the biggest mistakes professionals commit on foreign assignments is attempting to invoke the same approach towards business that proved to be successful in the United States. In any given situation, it is unrealistic for Americans to expect people from other cultures to react in a manner comparable to people from the United States.

Keep in mind that advance preparation in cultural communication does not necessarily guarantee a successful impression. And by the same token, committing the occasional faux pas will not ruin your career. Some of the most "seasoned" multi-cultural professionals commit cultural gaffes and it is inevitable that you will too. Do not become overwhelmed by this challenge. The willingness to observe carefully and learn, combined with flexibility and a healthy sense of humor, are likely to disarm most anyone you might do business with and will get you past all but the most heinous of offenses.

Does this mean that it is necessary for a multiculturalist executive to jump from one cultural extreme to another? Not necessarily. Consider that every culture has certain "common denominators" of values and beliefs which in turn enable them to interpret variations in philosophy that exist from country to country—even if it means negotiating with strange foreign characters, such as the person you see in the mirror each morning. Most experts agree that if there is such a thing as a universal trait, it is that all customers want to be on the receiving end of a "good deal." All customers, regardless of their culture, want to know specifically why it is in their best interest to agree to a proposed deal. Starting from this common ground, much can be accomplished.

(1,205 words)

I. Reading Comprehension

Directions: Choose the best answer to complete each statement according to the passage.

1. The following statements are all false EXCEPT ________ according to Paragraph 1.
   A. Many professionals and business entities are very good at cross-cultural communication.
   B. Many top executives in Japanese companies attach great importance to cross-culture communication.
   C. Many books, videos, audio tapes and seminars deal with the similarities and differences in cross-cultural negotiation.
   D. Most people are familiar with the rules of other countries.
2. The expat most probably refer to ________.
   A. experts B. professionals and business entities
   C. overseas representatives D. company's top executives
3. The successful negotiators will do all of the following EXCEPT ________.
   A. manage to understand the etiquette of the culture they're dealing with
   B. avoid forming false ideas of other cultures
   C. assume that the foreign country mirrors their homeland
   D. study the target culture carefully to determine appropriate behavior
4. The expat will consider all of the following questions of another culture EXCEPT ________.
   A. individual behavior B. operating code of etiquette
   C. body language D. beliefs and traditions
5. The final goal of doing business according to the passage is to ________.
   A. know about values and beliefs B. know about universal traits
   C. to interpret variations in philosophy D. maximize their interest

II. Vocabulary

Directions: Fill in each blank with an appropriate word from the box below. Each word can be used only once.

knack	designated	diversity	strive	preconceived
pertinent	heritage	agenda	invoke	compromising
gaffe	disarm	heinous	token	

1. In many villages, men had to work all year long, leaving home to __________ for a better life.
2. The down-to-earth approach the Chinese government has so far adopted to push ahead with the pursuit of sustainable development is __________ to the country's economic and environmental realities.
3. According to the old measures, owners could __________ two types of reasons to hold unused land—enterprise reasons and government reasons, with the latter exempt of all penalizations.
4. Issues on the __________ include measures to boost trade, tourism, education and cultural ties.
5. The company not only employs software to help Chinese students train for the SAT, but uses nontraditional methods to help them develop a __________ for critical thinking.
6. This diplomatic __________ pushed the two countries' relations to the verge of tension, and caused the president to cancel his trip.
7. Ms. Zhang felt angry or enraged, threatening to drag the websites, circulating the __________ photos, to court.
8. Nowadays in many universities an experienced teacher is often __________ as a master to each young teacher.
9. The Chinese government advocates mutual trust, mutual benefits, equality, respect for cultural __________ and common development.
10. To the US elites who are still critical of China, the Olympics is a gold opportunity to cast away their __________ opinions and lend a listening ear to the voices of the general public in China.
11. The college student, after hitting the victim, did not try to help her but instead resorted to murder to silence her. That split-second decision made his crime ______________ and eliminated a possibility of receiving a lesser punishment.
12. The resolution calls for a UN force monitor a ceasefire and help to __________, demobilize the fighters.
13. The Great Wall has been a World Cultural ______________ site for more than two decades, but the Grand Canal failed to gain significant public attention until 2005.
14. The gifts are just a ______________ of friendship or a symbol of respect for the typical Chinese society.

III. Debate

Directions: Sending gifts during Spring Festival has been a big burden for young people and so many of them are reluctant to go back to their hometown to spend the festival with the parents and relatives. Debate over the topic:

Sending gifts should be got rid of during Spring Festival.

Section B Colors and Their Associations

Directions: Read the following passage and the statements after it. Mark

Y for Yes	if the statement agrees with the passage
N for No	if the statement does not agree with the passage
NG for NOT GIVEN	if it is not given in the passage

Different colors have different associations. The following passage is of help to manufacturers in designing and packing their products.

In all cultures, different colors have different associations. Here are the associations that different colors have for British and American people.

RED: Red warns of danger. The expression red alert is used to warn of a sudden and very dangerous situation. People imagine that the DEVIL is red.

Red heart shapes and red roses are used to represent romantic love. Red clothes, and lips and fingernails that are painted red are often associated with sexual desire. Red is thought to be an exciting color; the expression paint the town red means to go out at night to bars, clubs etc and have a very good time.

In politics, red is used to represent COMMUNISM and SOCIALISM. In the UK the LABOUR PARTY is represented by a red rose.

If someone is red in the face, they are very embarrassed.

It is traditional to welcome a king, queen, or president to a place by having a red carpet for them to walk on.

GREEN: British and American people think of green as the color that represents nature. If you describe a place as green, you mean that it is covered with grass or trees: green fields. The green belt is an area of land around a city where building is not allowed, in order to protect fields and woods. Green is the national color of Ireland, also known as the EMERALD ISLE because of its many green fields.

Green also means "connected with the environment". Green issues are ideas about the environment that are discussed in parliament, newspapers etc. Products that are described as green are thought to cause less harm to the environment than other products.

Green is used to describe someone who is young and lacks experience in a job.

Green represents jealousy. If you are green with envy, you are very jealous of someone who has something that you want. The expression green-eyed monster is used to mean sexual jealousy.

If someone's face is green, they look pale and unhealthy, especially because they are about to OMIT.

PURPLE: Purple is associated with kings and queens and Roman EMPERORS, and in the past, these were the only people who were allowed to wear purple clothes. It is also connected with the POPE.

Purple prose is a piece of writing that has a grand style.

If someone is purple with rage or purple in the face, they are extremely angry.

BLUE: In the US and UK it is very common for clothes to be blue. NAVY BLUE (=very dark blue) is a common color for UNIFORMS such as those worn by sailors and the police, and formal clothes worn for work: a navy blue suit.

In the UK, blue is the color of the CONSERVATIVE PARTY. There is a joke that old ladies who support this party have a blue rinse, which means that they have their white or gray hair dyed a pale blue color.

In the US, the expression blue-collar is used to talk about social class. A blue-collar worker works in a factory, repairs machines etc.

Blue is connected with coldness. If you say that someone is blue with cold, you mean that they are very cold.

Pale blue is associated with baby boys, who are traditionally dressed in this color. Today many parents avoid dressing their boys in blue because they think that it strengthens sexual STEREOTYPES.

People who belong to royal families are said to be blue-blooded (=to have blue blood).

PINK: In the UK and US, pink is thought of as a pretty color that is worn by women and girls. Pale pink is associated with baby girls, who are traditionally dressed in this color. Today many parents avoid dressing their girls in pink because they think that it strengthens sexual STEREOTYPES.

Pink is also connected with HOMOSEXUAL men, and is used in expressions such as the pink pound (=the money that homosexual men have available to spend).

GREY BrE, **GRAY** AmE: In the US and UK, gray is connected with being dull and boring. It is, however, also a common color for (both men and women's clothes.

A gray day is an unpleasant one because the sky is full of gray clouds.

Grey is connected with old people, and is used in expressions such as the gray vote (=the support of old people in an election).

BLACK: In the US and UK, black is a very popular color or clothes of all types, and especially "formal clothes. It is typically worn at funerals to show respect and sadness. Black clothes are often worn social occasions in the evening, when women sometimes wear a little black dress (=a simple, short, black dress with no SLEEVES, that is acceptable at most social occasions that happen in the evening or at night) and men sometimes wear a lack DINNER

JACKET.

Black is associated with death and evil. WITCHES (=women thought to have magic powers that they use to do bad things) are thought to wear black and to have black cats. Black magic is believed to be magic that uses the power of the EVIL for evil purposes.

The black sheep of a family is a member of a family who chooses to live their life in a way that is different from the other members, and that they disapprove of.

WHITE: In the UK and US, white is associated with purity and VIRGINITY (=the condition of never having had sex). Traditionally women wear long white dresses when they get married.

White is also associated with moral goodness. People imagine that the Christian god and his ANGELS (=spirits that live with god and have white wings) wear white, and that HEAVEN (=believed by Christians to be the home of god, where good Christians go when they die) is a place where there are many white clouds.

If someone's face looks as white as a sheet, they are pale because they are ill or very frightened.

A white flag is traditionally used by people fighting in a battle, to show they SURRENDER (=accept that they have been defeated).

In the US, the expression white-collar is used to talk about social class. A white-collar worker works in an office, bank etc.

(1,053 words)

1. Red has both positive and negative connotations in western countries. ________
2. Red means a rise in stock market in China but a drop in America. ________
3. Green is associated with environmental protection. ________
4. If one's face is green, it means that person is healthy. ________
5. Purple is a color indicating dignity, power and unique position. ________
6. In the US blue is a common color for clothes. But it's not the case in the UK. ________
7. Pink is connected with homosexual women. ________
8. In both the US and UK, gray is associated with being dull and boring. ________
9. A black horse indicates someone who succeeds unexpectedly. ________
10. White is a color to symbolize purity and moral goodness. ________

Part 4 Reading Comprehension Test

Passage 1 The Language of Color Is Not International

Directions: Read the following passage and decide whether the statements are true or false according to it. Write T for true and F for false.

"Black is the color of mourning." "Red stands for danger or radicalism." "Green is the symbol for envy" "When you are sad, you're blue." "If you are afraid, you are yellow."

Not at all. At least, not outside the English-speaking world. In China and Korea, white not black, is the color of mourning. In Russia, red stands for beauty and life. White is the color of the frozen Siberian wastes and holds the meaning of death. In France, "to be green" to Germany, you're yellow with envy, not with fear.

What different colors symbolize to different people is anything but universal. A few do have some wide usage since languages borrow from one another. But in general, what a color symbolizes to one culture will be different in another. For example, the Italian expression for "to be in the red" is "to be in the green". They see the color green as hope,. not of envy. And hope remains when all else is lost. "Blue Monday' means going back to work in the office in the United States. In Germany, it means a long weekend.

Disagreement on color appears to be the case even for concrete objects. What is "red cabbage" to us is "blue cabbage" to the Germans and "black cabbage" to the Italians. What is a "black eye" to us is a "blue eye" to the Germans. And they call the kings of spades not the "black king" but "the green king".

Much color symbolism has a partly historical meaning. For example, "white elephant" comes to us from Siam. The white elephant of Thailand is a rare and delicate animal. And it is very expensive to support. The kings of Siam made presents of white elephants to those of their subjects whom they wished to ruin financially. One could not, of course, sell or otherwise dispose of a royal gift without encouraging the charge of treason.

Many studies have been done on color and how colors are used in various languages. In many languages, certain color words are lacking. They are often taken care of by using a figure of speech. For example, Spanish and Italian have no words for "tan". Tan-colored objects are usually described as "cinnamon-colored" or "milk-and-coffee". Japanese uses "peach-colored" for pink, "tea-colored" for brown, "mouse-colored" for gray and "wasp-colored" for yellow.

Where we may see one color, other groups may see many different ones. Italian and French have two words for brown and two for gray. Lithuanian uses different words for "gray" as applied to wool, horses, cows, or human hair.

Do you still think the language of color is international?

(437 words)

1. Black stands for mourning and red for danger or radicalism in America. ________
2. White stands for cold and death in Russia. ________
3. What different colors symbolize to different people is universal. ________
4. Green symbolizes hope in Britain but envy in Italy. ________
5. The king in Thailand would only send a white elephant to whoever he liked. ________
6. Some countries use different words for the same color. ________

Passage 2

Directions: Read the following passage. Choose the best answer to finish each incomplete statement.

One of the most authoritative voices speaking to us today is, of course, the voice of the advertisers. Its shrilling clamor dominates our lives. It shouts at us from the television screens and the radio loudspeakers; waves to us from every page of the newspaper, plucks at our sleeves on the escalator, signals to us from the road-side billboards all day and flashes messages to us in colored lights at night. It has forced on us a whole new conception of the successful man as a man no less than 20% of whose mail consists of announcements of giant carpet sales.

Advertising has been among England's biggest growing industries since the war, in terms of the ratio of money earnings to demonstrate achievement. Why all this fantastic expenditure?

Perhaps the answer is that advertising saves the manufacturers from having to think about the customer. At the stage of designing and developing a product, there is quite enough to think about without worrying over whether anybody will want to buy it. The designer is busy enough without adding customer-appeal to all his other problems of man-hours and machine tolerances and stress factors. So they just go ahead and make the thing and leave it to the advertiser to find eleven ways of making it appeal to purchasers after they finished it, by pretending that it gives status, or attracts love, or signifies manliness. If the advertising agency can do this authoritatively enough, the manufacturer is in clover.

Other manufacturers find advertising saves them from changing their product. And manufacturers hate changes. The ideal product is one or another, some alteration seems called for - how much better to change the image, the packet or the pitch made by the product, rather than go to all the inconvenience of changing the product itself.

(313 words)

7. According to the passage the reason for the authority of modern advertising lies in the fact that ________.
   A. it disturbs us wherever we go.
   B. it continually persuades us into buying commodities.
   C. it exerts too much influence on our private home life.
   D. it sets up for us an image of a successful man.
8. The successful form of advertising makes the most use of ________ which can show the personal position of an individual.
   A. television screens　　B. the postal service
   C. radio loudspeakers　　D. colored lights
9. Manufacturers appreciate advertisers very much in that they ________.
   A. give them advice on the promotion of products
   B. take the responsibility for giving a product customer-appeal

C. give them advice on the best time to produce products

D. consult them during the design and development stages

10. According to the passage a product attracts customers in that it seems to ________.

A. have an attractive design

B. provide good service

C. satisfy the manufacturer's needs

D. satisfy their personal needs

Passage 3 Naming a Brand

Directions: Read the following passage. Choose the best answer to each question.

Naming a brand should not go wrong. Just as a child can be burdened with a terrible name, so too can a product or service suffer under poor judgment in naming. Still everything from registering the trademark to picking the right sound or meaning is an area for pitfalls. Well-known brands from Corona to Ford have faced the hurdles of naming and ended up compromising to preserve decorum or accept a previous trademark.

In branding, a name means business. If we get it wrong from the start, we are doomed to face many different problems that will affect the way we do business.

Unfortunately sometimes you have the perfect name, only to find that someone already trademarked it. Corona, the Mexican beer producer, had its share of problems when it had to negotiate in different countries to secure its name, which means crown in Spanish.

In Spain negotiations proved to be tough; Corona eventually adapted its name to Coronita as a compromise. "We fall into the same category as the wine Corona," explains José Pares, spokesman of the beer maker. "This is why we had to negotiate with the company Vinos Torres. After some talks with them, they allowed us to use the name of Coronita, which is the one we use in Spain for 11 plus years."

For Corona it was a good compromise, allowing the company to retain association with its global name. "After all there wasn't a great disparity with the brand name we use around the world," continues Pares. "In fact, the smaller version of the beer in Mexico is called Coronita."

Obviously finding an open trademark is not the only reason to be unique and differentiated; in the pharmaceutical industry naming a product is literally a matter of life and death. According to the US Food and Drug Administration (FDA), 13 percent of medication errors stem from communication errors and 13 percent stem from name confusion (May 2002).

Naming companies generally develop a "name safe" test to make sure that an anti-depressive does not sound too similar to a strong tranquilizer, or that the name does not get lost in the doctor's handwriting.

In addition to making sure that the product name does not sound similar to other brands, organizations such as the FDA, make sure that the name is not misleading or too similar to other pharmaceutical products.

It's not always successful however. The list of names that sound similar in medicine (not to mention look similar in packaging) is long and causes concern among medical practitioners who may prescribe or administer a drug that sounds similar but is completely inappropriate for the symptoms. For example Endocet, a narcotic analgesic, is similar in sound to Indocid, which is a non-steroidal anti-inflammatory; Kaletra, an antiretroviral, can be mistaken for Levitra, a genitourinary; Lexapro, an antidepressant, should not be prescribed in place of Loxapine, an antipsychotic, and so on.

Another potential landmine is translation or association issues across countries or regions.

Ford faced its share of culture clash when it had to change the name Pinto to Corcel in Brazil. The word literally means dick in Portuguese, which could result in giggles at best and off-putting to potential drivers at worse. "The concept of the car was very offending here in Brazil, and we were forced to change its name," says a company spokeswoman.

Losing a name though doesn't necessarily mean that all of the brand equity is lost. It just takes more effort to make the association. In Belgium, telecommunications brand Orange lost its trademark to competitor Mobistar in a mismanagement maneuver. The company took months to re-brand itself with a different name (BASE), and with lots of advertising, managed to persuade its customers that it was running business as usual.

"There is no magic formula for names," says Paul Norman, Director of Nomen, a European naming company. "There are success factors: distinctive, flexible enough to allow the company to expand in other businesses, and it has to be legally robust."

Although the market of naming companies is not yet saturated, naming companies say that their main competitors lie within the company itself, which tries to name brands internally. After failing, they often approach a naming company.

"At the moment in the UK, there is often a distress purchase which is similar to buying a washing machine," Norman explains, "Generally one buys a new washing machine because the other one has broken or is damaged. People often come to a brand naming company after they try to generate it internally and failed."

(757 words, from *http://www.brandchannel.com/features_effect*)

11. Which of the following doesn't need to be considered in naming a brand?
    A. registering the trade mark　　B. the sound of the brand
    C. the form of the brand　　D. the meaning of the brand
12. Why did the Mexican company change its brand Corona into Coronita in Spain?
    A. Because it was not a good trademark.
    B. Because the trademark had negative connotations in Spanish.
    C. Because they wanted to be unique and different.
    D. Because the trademark had been registered by others.
13. Which of the following is NOT true about naming a product in the pharmaceutical industry?
    A. It is sometimes a matter of life and death.
    B. It should be unique and different.
    C. Medication errors mainly come from name confusion.
    D. Doctors sometimes make mistakes in writing their prescriptions.

14. Why did Ford change its name Pinto to Corcel in Brazil?
   A. Because "Pinto" had negative connotations in the Brazilian language.
   B. Because "Pinto" had negative connotations in Portuguese which the majority of the population in Brail speak.
   C. Because "Pinto" would make the Portuguese laugh.
   D. Because "Pinto" would prevent Brazilians from buying their cars.
15. Which of the following is NOT a factor for a successful brand?
   A. stability B. typicality C. flexibility D. legal robustness

Passage 4 Lost In Translation: Language Blunders Can Sully Ad Efforts

Directions: Read the following text and mark

Y (for Yes) if the statement agrees with the information given in the text;
N (for NO) if the statement contradicts the information given in the text;
NG (for Not Given) if the information is not given in the text.

Even small mistakes can cost marketers sales and confidence. Want fries with that underwear? Message to marketers: One man's pizza may be another man's pants.

That is a lesson at least one U.S. advertiser would like to have known before trying to market his folded-over pizza, called a calzone, to Spanish speakers. To them, calzone means underwear. The poor translation was one example on a list of botched advertising and branding efforts cited in a recent national survey of people who speak English as a second language.

Even as grand a brand as Rolls Royce can make mistakes. The Rolls-Royce Silver Mist never sold well in Germany perhaps because in German, mist means "human waste."

When Parker Pens marketed a ballpoint pen in Mexico, its ads were supposed to have read: "it won't leak in your pocket and embarrass you". Unfortunately, the company thought that the word "embarazar" (to impregnate) meant to embarrass, so the ads read: "It won't leak in your pocket and make you pregnant."

When American Airlines wanted to advertise its new leather first class seats in the Mexican market, it translated its "Fly In Leather" campaign literally. Unfortunately, 'vuela en cuero' translated as 'fly naked'.

Sometimes you can still get it wrong even when words aren't involved. When Gerber started selling baby food in Africa, they used the same packaging as in the US, with the beautiful baby on the label. Later they learned that in Africa, companies routinely put pictures on the label of what's inside, since most people can't read English.

Finally, here's one just to show how marketers can get it wrong even when dealing with the (supposedly) same language. Following great success with a tagline in the UK, Scandinavian vacuum manufacturer Electrolux decided to use it in America, not realizing the alternative meaning there of a key word: 'Nothing sucks like an Electrolux.'

Of the 513 people surveyed, 57% said they had spotted advertising that was incorrectly translated from English into other languages. Though the blunders are often humorous, they can cost the advertiser sales, suggested the survey, conducted by New York based translation service TransPerfect Translations Inc. Close to 50% of respondents said they simply tune out the message if an ad is poorly translated, and about 65% interpret bad translations as evidence that the advertiser doesn't care about the consumer. Even small mistakes, such as advertising a store where everything costs a dollar as "Un Dollar," rather than the correct Spanish "Un Dolar," was enough to put off potential customers, the survey found.

"It makes a lot of people feel negatively about a product," says Liz Elting, cofounder of TransPerfect Translations. Respondents were actually offended by some advertising slip-ups, like the translation of "point" into Spanish as "puta," which means prostitute.

The continuing globalization of corporate brands makes correct translations all the more important nowadays for U.S. companies, as does the fast-growing Hispanic market in the U.S. itself.

When U.S. milk processors decided to take their successful "Got Milk" campaign to a Spanish-speaking audience, they managed to avoid the pit-falls that Coke had encountered decades earlier. Quickly realizing the catchy slogan wouldn't go down so well in Spanish—the literal translation means something like "Are you lactating?"—the Milk Processor Education Program tapped Siboney USA, a Spanish-language advertising agency, to do an adaptation of the campaign.

"In order to succeed, translated ad copy must be crafted as if it were originally written in the target language," says Ms. Elting of TransPerfect Translations. She recommends using native speakers, who know the culture, particularly idiomatic expressions, in order to get across the meaning of the message rather than just a literal rendering of it.

The message the milk processors and Siboney eventually settled on was "Mas Leche, Mas Logro." The slogan, which means, "More Milk, More Achievement," was specifically crafted to appeal to "Hispanic moms," says Victor Zaborsky, spokesman for the Milk Processor Education Group in Washington, D.C.

But clearly the degree of precision shown by the milk processors isn't yet the rule. "Companies still are not putting the money into foreign-language copy that they should be," Ms. Elting says. "They might allocate a year and spend millions on a campaign in the U.S., and maybe a week or two weeks and thousands of dollars on a foreign campaign."

Of the respondents to the June survey, 35% thought advertisements for food products were the worst translation offenders, while 20% pointed to ads for pharmaceuticals, 13% ads for baby products and 12% ads for soda and other beverages. About 35% of respondents said that newspaper advertisements were the most likely to have translation errors, while 31% pointed to television ads. Magazines were cited by 27%, billboards by 15% and radio by 12%.

(809 words, adapted from *The Wall Street Journal Europe* - September 19, 2003)

16. ________ World-famous companies like Parker Pens would not make mistakes in translating ads.

17. ________ When advertising in backward countries, you have to take the literacy of the citizens into consideration.
18. ________ Even a small mistake in the translation of an ad would discourage customers from buying the product.
19. ________ Ads for baby products were translated the worst.
20. ________ There are too many mistranslations of brands or advertisements in Chinese market.

Unit 11

Festivals and Holidays

Part 1 Reading Skills

Section A Pattern of Details III

Writers often use cause and effect pattern of details to develop the topic sentence. It is a common method of organizing and discussing ideas.

5) Cause

Usually, if the topic sentence presents the result (effects) of something, then details will be provided to explain why this happens or what causes it to happen. As a reader, you need to examine the relationships between how certain events bring about or lead to other events. Sometimes, many causes contribute to a single effect.

Some transition words and phrases are used to indicate the cause relationship like *because*, *due to, one cause (reason) is, another is, since, for,* etc. For example,

Fireworks should be banned during the Spring Festival. ***One reason is*** *that they are a source of danger. Each year many serious fires and human deaths and injuries are caused by*

fireworks during the Spring Festival. And we also should keep the environmental protection in mind ***for*** *fireworks will lead to air pollution as well as noise pollution which will do great harm to our environment and health. So it's time to stop fireworks now.*

6) Effect

Effect is a method of paragraph writing to develop the topic sentence in which a writer analyzes the consequences of an action, event, or decision. There are also many connectors used in conveying this kind of relationship, for example, *accordingly, as a consequence, as a result, consequently, hence, so that, then, therefore, thereupon, thus, so, as such, one result is, another is, result in*. Now look at the following paragraph:

As *the Chinese New Year's Eve is a time where the family gathers, the typical situation involves a large 3-generation family gathered in front of their TV set while making dumplings for the first New Year's meal. The Spring Gala adds a mood of celebration in the house as people laugh, discuss and enjoy the performance. It has become an ingrained tradition on Mainland China to watch the New Year's Gala on New Year's Eve, and the estimated audience numbers over 700 million people.* ***So*** *the CCTV New Year's Gala is currently the most watched annual Arts and Performance event anywhere in the world, and* **as such**, *its importance has reached over to political, economic, and ethical territory.* (Based on http://en.wikipedia.org)

Actually these two approaches are closely related and sometimes not easily distinguished. And for the same topic sentence we can use either cause or effect to develop it. Look at the following topic sentence:

The water in the river has been seriously polluted.

1) ***One reason is*** *that there is a paper factory along the river which pours wastes in it every day.* ***Another reason is*** *that the inhabitants nearby dump their rubbish directly into the river.*

2) ***As a result,*** *many fish in the river die.* ***Besides,*** *the animals become ill because they drink the water in the river.* ***The most serious result is*** *that some people living nearby get a strange disease.*

In the first paragraph, cause is used to explain the reason why the water in the river has been seriously polluted. And connectors "one reason is…", "another reason is" are used. In the second paragraph, however, it is obvious that the effects are introduced because it begins with the phrase "as a result" which indicates the effect relationship.

Section B Practice

Exercise 1

Directions: A topic sentence is given below. Write two paragraphs, applying cause and effect separately.

Topic sentence: Nowadays it's not easy for young people to find jobs.

1. offering reasons:

____

____

____

2. providing results:

____

____

____

Exercise 2

Directions: Read the following paragraphs from "Why We Crave Horror Movies" by Stephen King and finish the exercises below.

When we pay our four or five bucks and seat ourselves at tenth-row center in a theater showing a horror movie, we are daring the nightmare.

Why? Some of the reasons are simple and obvious. To show that we can, that we are not afraid, that we can ride this roller coaster. Which is not to say that a really good horror movie may not surprise a scream out of us at some point, the way we may scream when the roller coaster twists through a complete 360 or plows through a lake at the bottom of the drop. And horror movies, like roller coasters, have always been the special province of the young; by the time one turns 40 or 50, one's appetite for double twists or 360-degree loops may be considerably depleted.

We also go to reestablish our feelings of essential normality; the horror movie is innately conservative, even reactionary. Freda Jackson as the horrible melting woman in *Die, Monster, Die!* confirms for us that no matter how far we may be removed from the beauty of a Robert Redford or a Diana Ross, we are still light-years from true ugliness.

And we go to have fun.

Ah, but this is where the ground starts to slope away, isn't it? Because this is a very peculiar sort of fun, indeed. The fun comes from seeing others menaced—sometimes killed. One critic has suggested that if pro football has become the voyeur's version of combat, then the horror film has become the modern version of the public lynching.

1. What's the topic of the paragraphs?

____

2. What's the main idea of the paragraphs?

____

3. What are the details to support the writer's idea?

____

____

____

____

____

Part 2 Idioms, Proverbs and Sayings

Directions: The following are idioms, proverbs or sayings by famous people about festivals and holidays. Choose what you think is correct and compare with the right ones.

1. You are invited to the festival of this world and your life is ________. (Rabindranath Tagore)
   A. doomed B. blessed C. destined D. preconceived
2. There is nothing funny about ________. This sarcastic festival reflects, rather, an infernal demand for revenge by children on the adult world. (Jean Baudrillar)
   A. Halloween B. April Fool's Day
   C. Christmas D. Thanksgiving Day
3. Life is a festival only to ________. (Ralph Waldo Emerson)
   A. the stupid B. the rich C. the wise D. the poor
4. The festivals are like a ________ charting our spiritual progress in God. (Proverb)
   A. guide B. compass C. GPS D. map
5. A good holiday is one spent among people whose notions of time are ________ than yours. (John B. Priestly)
   A. vaguer B. more valuable C. less valuable D. clearer
6. Working hours are never long enough. Each day is a holiday, and ________ holidays are grudged as enforced interruptions in an absorbing vocation. (Winston Churchill)
   A. interesting B. ordinary C. dull D. long
7. Christmas is the antithesis of ________. Christmas is pretty much a man-made holiday.

(John Clayton)

A. Valentine's Day B. Thanksgiving
C. Halloween D. Lincoln Memorial Day

8. The holiest of holidays are those kept by ourselves in silence and apart; The secret anniversaries of the ________. (Henry Wadsworth Longfellow)

A. brain B. hand C. heart D. mind

9. This is my wish for you: peace of mind, ________ through the year, happiness that multiplies, health for you and yours, fun around every corner, energy to chase your dreams, joy to fill your holidays! (D.M. Dellinger)

A. happiness B. good luck C. fortune D. prosperity

10. Our hearts grow tender with childhood memories and love of kindred, and we are better throughout the year for having, in spirit, become a ________ again at Christmas-time. (Laura Ingalls Wilder)

A. child B. teenager C. youth D. mother

Part 3 Reading Passages

Section A Public Holidays in the United States

The United States does not have national holidays in the sense of days on which all employees in the U.S. receive mandatory a day free from work and all business is halted by law. The U.S. federal government only recognizes national holidays that pertain to its own employees; it is at the discretion of each state or local jurisdiction to determine official holiday schedules. There are eleven such federal holidays, ten annual and one quadrennial holiday (Inauguration Day).

The annual federal holidays are widely observed by state and local governments; however, they may alter the dates of observance or add or subtract holidays according to local custom. Pursuant to the Uniform Monday Holiday Act of 1968 (taking effect in 1971), official holidays are observed on a Monday, except for New Year's Day, Independence Day, Veterans Day, Thanksgiving, and Christmas. There are also U.S. state holidays particular to individual U.S. states, such as Good Friday observed by 12 states.

Malls, shopping centers and most retail stores close only on Easter, Thanksgiving and Christmas Day, but remain open on all other holidays (early closing on Christmas Eve and New Year's Eve, and sometimes on other major holidays). Virtually all companies observe and close on the "major" holidays (New Year's Day, Easter, Memorial Day, Independence Day, Labor Day, Thanksgiving, and Christmas). Some also add the day after Thanksgiving (Black

Friday), most businesses also add religious holiday of Good Friday, and sometimes one or more of the other federal/state holidays.

Federal holidays are designated by Congress in Title V of the United States Code. Federal holiday is a day off for federal employees, which also means that banks and postal offices are closed. Most private companies and certain other businesses observe federal holidays as well, or the big holidays. If a holiday falls on a Saturday it is celebrated the preceding Friday; if a holiday falls on a Sunday it is celebrated the following Monday. Most, but not all, states and most private businesses also observe a Sunday holiday on the following Monday.

There is no generally accepted policy, however, on whether to observe a Saturday holiday on the preceding Friday or the following Monday. Most states and private businesses may observe on the preceding Friday, some may observe it on the following Monday, and some may not observe the holiday at all in those years. In particular, banks that close on Saturdays do not observe a holiday when it falls on Saturday.

New Year's Day

New Year's Day is observed on January 1, the first day of the year. It is often celebrated with fireworks at the stroke of midnight as the New Year starts. It's a federal holiday.

Martin Luther King, Jr. Day

Martin Luther King, Jr. Day is a United States federal holiday marking the birthday of Dr. Martin Luther King, Jr. It is observed on the third Monday of January each year, which is around the time of King's birthday, January 15. The floating holiday is similar to holidays set under the Uniform Monday Holiday Act, though the act predated the establishment of Martin Luther King, Jr. Day by 15 years.

King was the chief spokesman for nonviolent activism in the civil rights movement, which successfully protested racial discrimination in federal and state law. The campaign for a federal holiday in King's honor began soon after his assassination in 1968. Ronald Reagan signed the holiday into law in 1983, and it was first observed on January 20, 1986. At first, some states resisted observing the holiday as such, giving it alternative names or combining it with other holidays. It was officially observed in all 50 states for the first time in 2000.

United States presidential inauguration

The inauguration of the president of the United States takes place during the commencement of a new term of a president of the United States, which is every four years on January 20. Prior to the Twentieth Amendment, the date was March 4, the day of the year on which the Constitution of the United States first took effect in 1789; the last inauguration to take place on the older date was Franklin D. Roosevelt's first one on March 4, 1933. The day a presidential inauguration occurs is known as "Inauguration Day".

The only inauguration element mandated by the United States Constitution is that the president make an oath or affirmation before that person can "enter on the Execution" of the office of the presidency. However, over the years, various traditions have arisen that have expanded the inauguration from a simple oath-taking ceremony to a day-long event, including parades, speeches, and balls.

Washington's Birthday

Washington's Birthday is a United States federal holiday celebrated on the third Monday of February in honor of George Washington, the first President of the United States. The holiday is also commonly referred to as Presidents Day (sometimes spelled Presidents' Day or President's Day). As Washington's Birthday or Presidents Day, it is also the official name of a concurrent state holiday celebrated on the same day in a number of states.

Memorial Day

Memorial Day is an American federal holiday observed annually on the last Monday of May. Memorial Day is a day of remembering the men and women who died while serving in the United States Armed Forces. Formerly known as Decoration Day, it originated after the American Civil War to commemorate the Union and Confederate soldiers who died in the Civil War. By the 20th century Memorial Day had been extended to honor all Americans who have died in all wars. It typically marks the start of the summer vacation season, while Labor Day marks its end.

Many people visit cemeteries and memorials, particularly to honor those who have died in military service. Many volunteers place an American flag on each grave in national cemeteries.

By the early 20th century, Memorial Day was an occasion for more general expressions of memory, as people visited the graves of their deceased relatives in church cemeteries, whether they had served in the military or not. It also became a long weekend increasingly devoted to shopping, family gatherings, fireworks, trips to the beach, and national media events.

Memorial Day is not to be confused with Veterans Day; Memorial Day is a day of remembering the men and women who died while serving, while Veterans Day celebrates the service of all U.S. military veterans, living or dead.

Independence Day

Independence Day, commonly known as the Fourth of July, is a federal holiday in the United States commemorating the adoption of the Declaration of Independence on July 4, 1776, declaring independence from the Kingdom of Great Britain. Independence Day is commonly associated with fireworks, parades, barbecues, carnivals, fairs, picnics, concerts, baseball games, family reunions, and political speeches and ceremonies, in addition to various other public and private events celebrating the history, government, and traditions of the United States. Independence Day is the national day of the United States.

Labor Day

Labor Day is an American federal holiday celebrated in September (September 3, in 2012) that celebrates the economic and social contributions of workers.

Columbus Day

Many countries in the New World and elsewhere celebrate the anniversary of Christopher Columbus's arrival in the Americas, which occurred on October 12, 1492, as an official holiday. The event is celebrated as Columbus Day in the United States and it was celebrated unofficially since the late 18th century, and officially in various areas since the early 20th century.

Veterans Day

Veterans Day, formerly Armistice Day, is an annual United States holiday honoring armed service veterans. It is a federal holiday that is observed on November 11. It coincides with other holidays such as Armistice Day or Remembrance Day, which are celebrated in other parts of the world and also mark the anniversary of the signing of the Armistice that ended World War I.

Veterans Day is not to be confused with Memorial Day; Veterans Day celebrates the service of all U.S. military veterans, while Memorial Day is a day of remembering the men and women who died while serving.

Thanksgiving Day

Thanksgiving Day, is a holiday celebrated in the United States on the fourth Thursday in November. It has officially been an annual tradition since 1863, when, during the Civil War, President Abraham Lincoln proclaimed a national day of "Thanksgiving and Praise to our beneficent Father who dwelleth in the Heavens," to be celebrated on Thursday, November 26. As a federal and popular holiday in the U.S., Thanksgiving is one of the major holidays of the year to celebrate the giving of thanks for the autumn harvest. Together with Christmas and the New Year, Thanksgiving is a part of the broader holiday season.

Christmas

Christmas is an annual commemoration of the birth of Jesus Christ, celebrated generally on December 25 as a religious and cultural holiday by billions of people around the world. Christmas is a civil holiday in many of the world's nations, is celebrated by an increasing number of non-Christians, and is an integral part of the Christmas and holiday season.

(1498 words, based on *Wikipedia*)

I. Reading Comprehension

Questions 1-8

Directions: Fill in the table with the missing information according to the passage.

Name	Celebration Date	To Honor
New Year's Day	Jan, 1st	the start of a new year
Martin Luther King, Jr. Day	1. __________	Martin Luther King, Jr
Inauguration Day	Jan, 20th	inauguration of the president
Washington's Birthday	2. __________	George Washington
Memorial Day	3. __________	the dead soldiers
Independence Day	July, 4th	the independence of USA
Labor Day	4. __________	the workers
Columbus Day	5. __________	Christopher Columbus
Veterans Day	6. __________	armed service veterans
Thanksgiving Day	7. __________	the autumn harvest
Christmas	Dec, 25th	8. __________

Questions 9-15

Directions: Decide whether the following statements are true or false according to the passage. Write T for true and F for false.

9. ________ American national holidays are observed all around the country.
10. ________ According to the Uniform Monday Holiday Act of 1968, all American official holidays are observed on a Monday.
11. ________ Malls, shopping centers and most retail stores close only on Easter, Thanksgiving and Christmas Day.
12. ________ It is not easy for Martin Luther King, Jr. Day to be established as a national holiday.
13. ________ Franklin D. Roosevelt was the president whose inaugurations took place on both March 4 and January 20.
14. ________ Independence Day is a national holiday to celebrate the history by having public events only.
15. ________ Thanksgiving Day was proclaimed a national holiday by Abraham Lincoln in 1863.

II. Vocabulary

Directions: Fill in each blank with an appropriate word from the box below. Each word can be used only once.

discretion	pursuant	predate	discrimination	assassination	inauguration
mandate	deceased	coincide	concurrent	commencement	commemorate

1. Across the country, millions of migrant workers are struggling to secure a better life in cities, despite the __________ they endure because of their rural identity.
2. Hundreds of fans are expected at Forest Lawn on Friday to __________ Jackson's death.
3. Beijing began offering free services to residents who wished to bury their __________ relatives at sea, as the capital's cemetery space is inadequate.
4. To prevent these tragedies, lawmakers should __________ qualifications for school buses and drivers.
5. It is a pity that the __________ complaints about the short supply of qualified talents and over-supply of college graduates are yet to make the authorities seriously reflect on the status quo.
6. The sisters, both art degree holders, have seen their company grow three to four-fold since its __________.
7. Obama was to deliver the __________ speech at the University of Notre Dame in South Bend, Indiana, founded in 1842.
8. It is my belief that diligence and __________, combined with a mastery of the principles and techniques, would help us win the battle for wealth.
9. __________ to the law, we protect the rights of all members of society to equal participation and development.
10. During a royal visit in 1868, Queen Victoria's son, Prince Alfred, was shot in an __________ attempt as he picnicked on Bondi Beach.
11. On either side of the paved walkway stand two ornamental pillars that __________ the university by a couple of hundred years.
12. It's very interesting that this year Valentine's Day is to __________ with the Chinese New Year.

III. Debate

Directions: Nowadays more and more western festivals are observed among young people in China, first Christmas day, followed by Valentine Day. Debate over the topic: ***Western festivals should be banned in China.***

Section B A Moving Story

Directions: Read the following passage carefully and complete the summary with ***no more than three words*** *for each blank.*

For many of us, one Christmas stands out from all the others, the one when the meaning of the day shone clearest. My own "truest" Christmas began on a rainy spring day in the bleakest year of my life.

Recently divorced, I was in my 20s, had no job and was on my way downtown to go the rounds of the employment offices. I had no umbrella, for my old one had fallen apart, and I could not afford another one.

I sat down in the streetcar—and there against the seat was a beautiful silk umbrella with a silver handle inlaid with gold and necks of bright enamel. I had never seen anything so lovely.

I examined the handle and saw a name engraved among the golden scrolls. The usual procedure would have been to turn in the umbrella to the conductor, but on impulse I decided to take it with me and find the owner myself.

I got off the streetcar in a downpour and thankfully opened the umbrella to protect myself. Then I searched a telephone book for the name on the umbrella and found it. I called and a lady answered.

Yes, she said in surprise that was her umbrella, which her parents, now dead, had given her for a birthday present. But, she added, it had been stolen from her locker at school (she was a teacher) more than a year before.

She was so excited that I forgot I was looking for a job and went directly to her small house. She took the umbrella, and her eyes filled with tears.

The teacher wanted to give me a reward, but—though twenty dollars was all I had in the world—her happiness at retrieving this special possession was such that to have accepted money would have spoiled something. We talked for a while, and I must have given her my address. I don't remember.

The next six months were wretched. I was able to obtain only temporary employment here and there, for a small salary. But I put aside twenty-five or fifty cents when I could afford it for my little girl's Christmas presents.

My last job ended the day before Christmas, my thirty-dollar rent was soon due, and I had fifteen dollars to my name—which Peggy and I would need for food.

She was home from convent boarding school and was excitedly looking forward to her gifts next day, which I had already purchased. I had bought her a small tree, and we were going to decorate it that night.

The air was full of the sound of Christmas merriment as I walked from the streetcar to my small apartment. Bells rang and children shouted in the bitter dusk of the evening, and windows were lighted and everyone was running and laughing. But there should be no Christmas for me; I knew, no gifts, no remembrance whatsoever.

As I struggled through the snowdrifts, I had just about reached the lowest point in my life. Unless a miracle happened, I would be homeless in January, foodless, jobless. I had prayed steadily for weeks, and there had been no answer but this coldness and darkness, this harsh air, this abandonment.

God and men had completely forgotten me. I felt so helpless and so lonely. What was to become of us?

I looked in my mail box. There were only bills in it, a sheaf of them, and two white envelopes which I was sure contained more bills. I went up three dusty flights of stairs and I cried, shivering in my thin coat.

But I made myself smile so I could greet my little daughter with a pretense of happiness. She opened the door for me and threw herself in my arms, screaming joyously and demanding that we decorate the tree immediately.

Peggy had proudly set our kitchen table for our evening meal and put pans out and three cans of food which would be our dinner. For some reason, when I looked at those pans and cans, I felt brokenhearted. We would have only hamburgers for our Christmas dinner tomorrow.

I stood in the cold little kitchen, misery overwhelmed me. For the first time in my life, I doubted the existence and his mercy, and the coldness in my heart was colder than ice.

The doorbell rang and Peggy ran fleetly to answer it, calling that it must be Santa Claus. Then I heard a man talking heartily to her and went to the door. He was a delivery man, and his arms were full of parcels. "This is a mistake," I said, but he read the name on the parcels and there were for me.

When he had gone I could only stare at the boxes. Peggy and I sat on the floor and opened them. A huge doll, three times the size of the one I had bought for her. Gloves. Candy. A beautiful leather purse. Incredible! I looked for the name of the sender. It was the teacher; the address was simply "California", where she had moved.

Our dinner the night was the most delicious I had ever eaten. I forgot I had no money for the rent and only fifteen dollars in my purse and no job. My child and I ate and laughed together in happiness.

Then we decorated the little tree and marveled at it. I put Peggy to bed and set up her gifts around the tree and a sweet peace flooded me like a benediction. I had some hope again. I could even examine the sheaf of bills without cringing.

(935 words)

The story happened on a 1. ________________ when the writer, a single mother, had just lost her job and was in great difficulty. On her way home, she found 2. ________________ on the streetcar and decided to send it back to the owner by herself. The owner was surprised and moved to see it again because it was 3. ________________ from her parents who had been dead and it had been stolen one year before. She would give the writer 4. ________________ but was refused. The next months were wretched for the writer. Soon Christmas came. The writer felt depressed as she was jobless again. She hardly had enough money to pay her bills and buy gifts for her little daughter. Just as she felt brokenhearted and helpless and lonely, a delivery man came, his arms were 5. ________________ which were sent by the owner of the umbrella.

Part 4 Reading Comprehension Test

Passage 1 May Day

Directions: Read the following passage and mark

Y (for Yes) if the statement agrees with the information given in the text;

N (for NO) if the statement contradicts the information given in the text;

NG (for Not Given) if the information is not given in the text.

May Day occurs on May 1 and refers to several public holidays. In many countries, May Day is synonymous with International Workers' Day, or Labour Day, a day of political demonstrations and celebrations organised by the unions, communists, anarchists, and socialist groups. May Day is also a traditional holiday in many cultures.

International Workers' Day

May Day can refer to various labour celebrations conducted on May 1 that commemorate the fight for the eight hour day. May Day in this regard is called International Workers' Day, or Labour Day. The idea for a "workers holiday" began in Australia in 1856; after a Stonemason's victory, April 22nd was "Eight-Hour Day", a public holiday. With the idea having spread around the world, the choice of May 1st became a commemoration by the Second International for the people involved in the 1886 Haymarket affair.

The Haymarket affair occurred during the course of a three-day general strike in Chicago, Illinois, United States that involved common laborers, artisans, merchants, and immigrants. Following an incident in which police opened fire and killed four strikers at the McCormick Harvesting Machine Co. plant, a rally was called for the following day at Haymarket Square. Towards the end of the rally, as police moved in to disperse the event and opened fire on the unarmed crowd on the plea that an unknown assailant threw a bomb into the crowd of police. The bomb and resulting police riot left at least a dozen people dead, including one policeman. A sensational show trial ensued in which eight defendants were openly tried for their political beliefs, and not necessarily for any involvement in the bombing. The trial led to the eventual public hanging of four anarchists. The Haymarket incident was a source of outrage from people around the globe. In the following years, memory of the "Haymarket martyrs" was remembered with various May Day job actions and demonstrations.

Now May Day has become an international celebration of the social and economic achievements of the labour movement.

Traditional May Day Celebrations

Traditional May Day is related to the Celtic festival of Beltane. The earliest May Day celebrations appeared in pre-Christian times, with the festival of Flora, the Roman Goddess of flowers, and the Walpurgis Night celebrations of the Germanic countries. A more secular version of May Day continues to be observed in Europe and America.

May Day falls exactly half of a year from November 1 and marks the end of the unfarmable winter, half of the year in the Northern hemisphere, and it has traditionally been an occasion for popular and often raucous celebrations.

May Day may be best known for its tradition of dancing the Maypole and crowning of the Queen of the May. Various Neopagan groups celebrate reconstructed versions of these customs on May the 1st. The day was a traditional summer holiday in many pre-Christian European pagan cultures. While February 1 was the first day of Spring, May 1 was the first day of summer; hence, the summer solstice on June 25 (now June 21) was Midsummer.

Children in England celebrate the end of winter and the arrival of spring on May 1 each year. The festivities center around a huge striped maypole that's decorated with flowers and streamers. Children hold the streamers as they dance around the pole, weaving intricate patterns as they pass each other. Men also join in on the fun. A group of six or eight Morris dancers arrange themselves in two lines and wave handkerchiefs or sticks as they dance by each other. A May Queen is crowned each year to preside over the celebration.

(601 words)

1. ________ May Day has different connotations for different countries.
2. ________ The idea for a workers' holiday originated from Chicago, United States.
3. ________ The Haymarket affair led to the death of 20 people altogether.
4. ________ During the traditional May Day, dancing the maypole and crowning the Queen of the May are the most popular events.
5. ________ Old people will also join in the May Day dancing in England.

Passage 2 Labor Day in America

Directions: Read the following passage. Choose the best answer to each question.

History

Although the commemoration of May Day as International Workers' Day received its inspiration from the United States, the U.S. Congress designated May 1 as Loyalty Day in 1958 due to the day's perceived appropriation by the Soviet Union. Alternatively, Labor Day traditionally occurs on the first Monday in September in the United States. People often use May Day as a day for political protest, such as the million people who demonstrated against far-right candidate Jean-Marie Le Pen in France, or as a day for protest against government actions, such as rallies in support of illegal alliens across the United States.

In 1882, Matthew Maguire, a machinist, first proposed the holiday while serving as secretary of the CLU (Central Labor Union) of New York. Others argue that it was first proposed by Peter J. McGuire of the American Federation of Labor in May 1882, after witnessing the annual labor festival held in Toronto, Canada.

Oregon was the first state to make it a holiday in 1887. By the time it became a federal holiday in 1894, thirty states officially celebrated Labor Day. Following the deaths of a number of workers at the hands of the U.S. military and U.S. Marshals during the Pullman Strike, the United States Congress unanimously voted to approve rush legislation that made Labor Day a national holiday; President Grover Cleveland signed it into law a mere six days after the end of the strike. The September date originally chosen by the CLU of New York and observed by many of the nation's trade unions for the past several years was selected rather than the more widespread International Workers' Day because Cleveland was concerned that observance of the latter would be associated with the nascent Communist, Syndicalist and Anarchist movements that, though distinct from one another, had rallied to commemorate the Haymarket Affair in International Workers' Day. All U.S. states, the District of Columbia, and the territories have made it a statutory holiday.

Pattern of celebration

The form for the celebration of Labor Day was outlined in the first proposal of the holiday: A street parade to exhibit to the public "the strength and esprit de corps of the trade and labor organizations", followed by a festival for the workers and their families. This became the pattern for Labor Day celebrations. Speeches by prominent men and women were introduced later, as more emphasis was placed upon the civil significance of the holiday. Still later, by a resolution of the American Federation of Labor convention of 1909, the Sunday preceding Labor Day was adopted as Labor Sunday and dedicated to the spiritual and educational aspects of the labor movement.

Retail Sale Day

To take advantage of large numbers of potential customers free to shop, Labor Day has become an important sale weekend for many retailers in the United States. Some retailers claim it is one of the largest sale dates of the year, second only to the Christmas season's Black Friday.

Paradoxically, because of the importance of the sale weekend, some of those who are employed in the retail sector not only work on Labor Day, but work longer hours. More Americans work in the retail industry than any other, with retail employment making up 24% of all jobs in the United States. The Bureau of Labor Statistics reports that of those employed in the retail sector, only 3% are members of a Labor Union.

End of summer

Labor Day has come to be celebrated by most Americans as the symbolic end of the summer. In high society, Labor Day is (or was) considered the last day of the year when it is fashionable to wear white or seersucker.

In the U.S., most school districts that started summer vacation in early June will resume school the day after this day, while schools that had summer vacation begin on the Saturday before Memorial Day in late May will have already been in session since late August. However this tradition is changing as many school districts end in early June and begin mid-August.

(673 words)

6. Which of the following is false about American May Day?
   A. May Day was not chosen as the Labor Day due to the day's perceived appropriation by the Soviet Union.
   B. May Day is used as a day to protest politically.
   C. May Day can also be used as a day to protest against government actions.
   D. May Day is used to support illegal actions.
7. Which of the following is true about the history of American Labor Day?
   A. It is certain that it's Matthew Maguire who first proposed the holiday.
   B. Labor Day was first made a holiday in 30 states.
   C. Labor Day was not adopted as a national holiday until 1894.
   D. The date of Labor Day was originally chosen by President Grover Cleveland due to political considerations.
8. Which of the following activities is not included in the Labor Day celebrations?
   A. a street parade
   B. a festival for workers and their families
   C. a resolution offered by the American Federation of Labor
   D. speeches by prominent men and women
9. What is ironic about American Labor Day?
   A. The merchants take advantage of this day and attract large numbers of free workers to shop
   B. It has become one of the largest sale dates of the year.
   C. Many workers in the retail sector have to work overtime instead of having a good rest.
   D. The majority of workers employed in the retail sector are not members of the Labor Union.
10. When is the summer vacation for American schools?
   A. From early June to the day after Labor Day
   B. From the Saturday before Memorial Day in late May to late August
   C. From early June to mid-August
   D. Not definite

Passage 3 Good Friday

Directions: Fill in each blank with the missing information from the passage and write with no more than three words for each blank.

Good Friday is a religious holiday observed primarily by Christians commemorating the crucifixion of Jesus Christ and his death at Calvary. It is also known as Holy Friday, Great Friday, Black Friday, or Easter Friday, though the latter properly refers to the Friday in Easter week.

According to the accounts in the Gospels, the Temple Guards, guided by Jesus' disciple Judas Iscariot, arrested Jesus in the Garden of Gethsemane. Judas received money (30 pieces of silver) for betraying Jesus and told the guards that whomever he kisses is the one they are to arrest. Following his arrest, Jesus was brought to the house of Annas. There he was interrogated with little result.

Conflicting testimony against Jesus was brought forth by many witnesses, to which Jesus answered nothing. Finally the high priest adjured Jesus to respond under solemn oath, saying "I adjure you, by the Living God, to tell us, are you the Anointed One, the Son of God?" Jesus testified ambiguously, "You have said it, and in time you will see the Son of Man seated at the right hand of the Almighty, coming on the clouds of Heaven." The high priest condemned Jesus for blasphemy, and the Sanhedrin concurred with a sentence of death.

Later he was crucified along with two criminals. Jesus agonized on the cross for six hours. During his last 3 hours on the cross, from noon to 3 p.m., darkness fell over the whole land. With a loud cry, Jesus gave up his spirit. There was an earthquake, tombs broke open, and the curtain in the Temple was torn from top to bottom. The centurion on guard at the site of crucifixion declared, "Truly this was God's Son!"

Joseph of Arimathea took Jesus' body, wrapped it in a clean linen shroud, and placed it in his own new tomb that had been carved in the rock in a garden near the site of crucifixion. Nicodemus also brought 75 pounds of myrrh and aloes, and placed them in the linen with the body, in keeping with Jewish burial customs. They rolled a large rock over the entrance of the tomb. Then they returned home and rested, because Shabbat had begun at sunset. On the third day, Sunday, which is now known as Easter Sunday, Jesus rose from the dead.

(385 words)

11. Good Friday is a religious holiday to commemorate the ________________ of Jesus Christ.
12. Jesus was betrayed by his disciple ________________ Judas Iscariot, who told the guards that whomever he kissed was the one they were to arrest.
13. Faced with ________________ provided by the witnesses, Jesus kept silent.
14. Jesus agonized on the cross for ________________ when he was crucified.
15. Jesus came to life again ________________ after his death.

Passage 4 Bank Day

Directions: Read the following passage and decide whether the following statements are true or false. Write T for true and F for false.

A bank holiday is a public holiday in the United Kingdom or a colloquialism for public holiday in Ireland. There is no automatic right to time off on these days, although banks close and the majority of the population is granted time off work or extra pay for working on these days, depending on their contract. The first official bank holidays were the four days named in the Bank Holidays Act 1871, but today the term is colloquially (albeit incorrectly) used for public holidays which are not officially bank holidays, for example Good Friday and Christmas Day. Many large shops open on bank holidays, when most people have a day off for shopping, heavily advertising sales and bargains.

Prior to 1834, the Bank of England observed about thirty-three saints' days and religious festivals as holidays, but in 1834 this was reduced to four: 1 May (May Day), 1 November (All Saints Day), Good Friday, and Christmas Day. In 1871, the first legislation relating to bank holidays was passed when Liberal politician and banker Sir John Lubbock introduced the Bank Holidays Act 1871. The English people were so thankful that they called the first Bank Holidays *St Lubbock's Days* for a while. Scotland was treated separately because of its separate traditions; for example, New Year is a more important holiday there.

The act did not specify Good Friday and Christmas Day as bank holidays in England, Wales, and Ireland because they were already recognised as common law holidays, and because of common observance, they became customary holidays before records began.

In 1903, the Bank Holiday (Ireland) Act added 17 March, Saint Patrick's Day, as a bank holiday for Ireland only. New Year's Day did not become a bank holiday in England until 1 January 1974.

Banking and Financial Dealings Act 1971

A century after the 1871 Act, the Banking and Financial Dealings Act 1971, which currently regulates bank holidays in the UK, was passed. The majority of the current bank holidays were specified in the 1971 Act, but New Year's Day and May Day were introduced after 1971.

From 1965, the date of the August bank holiday was changed to the end of the month.

Curiously, there were a few years (e.g., 1968) when this holiday fell in September, but this no longer occurs—presumably reflecting a change in the way of defining the relevant day. The Whitsun bank holiday (Whit Monday) was replaced by the Late Spring Bank Holiday—fixed as the last Monday in May—in 1971. In 1978 the first Monday in May in the UK, and the final Monday of May in Scotland, were designated as bank holidays.

In January 2007, the St Andrew's Day Bank Holiday (Scotland) Act 2007 was given royal assent, making 30 November (or the nearest Monday if a weekend) a bank holiday in Scotland.

Royal proclamation

Under the Banking and Financial Dealings Act 1971, bank holidays are proclaimed each year by the legal device of a royal proclamation. Royal proclamation is also used to move bank holidays that would otherwise fall on a weekend. In this way, public holidays are not 'lost' in years when they coincide with weekends. These deferred bank holiday days are termed a 'bank holiday in lieu' of the typical anniversary date. In the legislation they are known as 'substitute days'. The movement of the St Andrew's Day Scottish holiday to the nearest Monday when 30 November is a weekend day is statutory and does not require a proclamation.

Campaigns for extra bank holidays

The number of holidays in the UK is relatively small compared to that in many other European countries. However, direct comparison is inaccurate since the 'substitute day' scheme of deferment does not apply in most European countries, where holidays that coincide with a weekend (29% of fixed-date holidays) are 'lost'. In fact, the average number of non-weekend holidays in such countries is only marginally higher (and in some cases lower) than the UK.

There have been calls for an increase in the number of bank holidays. Among the most notably absent dates from the existing list are the feast days of patron saints; 23 April (St George's Day and the birthday of William Shakespeare) in England and 1 March (St David's Day) in Wales are not currently recognised. 17 March (St Patrick's Day) is a public holiday in Northern Ireland and, since 2008, 30 November (St Andrew's Day) is a bank holiday in Scotland. St Piran's Day (patron saint of Cornwall) on 5 March is already given as an unofficial day off to many government and other workers in the county, and there are renewed calls for the government to recognise this as an official bank holiday in the region.

Proposed move of May Day Bank Holiday (England and Wales)

After the election of the Coalition Government in May 2010, the Department of Culture Media and Sport launched a pre-Consultation in 2011 which included the suggestion of moving the May Day Bank Holiday to a date in October, to be a "UK Day" or to "Trafalgar Day" (21 October) or move the holiday to St David's day and St George's day.

It is suggested that a move from the May Day bank holiday to a St Piran's day bank holiday in Cornwall, on 5 March, would benefit the Cornish economy by £20-35 million.

16. ________ Bank holidays were and are still used for officially public holidays only.
17. ________ The English people thanked Sir John Lubbock so much that they have been calling the first Bank Holiday *St Lubbock's Day*.
18. ________ Though New Year's Day is a more important holiday, it has not been accepted as a bank day.
19. ________ Bank holidays have been changing all the time.
20. ________ In 1978 the first Monday in May in Scotland, and the final Monday of May in the UK, were designated as bank holidays.
21. ________ Since 1971, all bank holidays are proclaimed each year by the legal device of a royal proclamation, including the St Andrew's Day.
22. ________ A 'bank holiday in lieu' refers to a public holiday which coincides with a weekend and is postponed to Monday by royal proclamation. It is also called 'substitute days' legally.
23. ________ It's improper to compare the number of holidays of the UK with those in other European countries directly because different from the UK, the holidays on weekends will not be substituted in those countries.
24. ________ People in UK are calling for more bank holidays and in some places unofficial bank holidays arise.
25. ________ May Day has been called for to be cancelled because it has political connotations with communism.

Unit 12

Music and Movies

Part 1 Reading Skills

Section A Outlining

To be the best reader you must be active and systematic. An important challenge is to choose the skills that will help you be most successful. Outlining is one of those skills.

Why is an outline a good active reading skill?

An outline can be valuable in two ways. First, to make an outline you must read carefully. You must identify main ideas and supporting details. You must also decide if some ideas are not so important. To make these decisions you must read actively and carefully.

Second, an outline is a picture of how ideas relate to each other. You can often answer many questions just by reading a good outline. Outlines are great for reviewing. You can test your understanding and memory of what you have read by using an outline. So, outlining is a way to organize and relate ideas.

How do you make an outline?

Begin by reading systematically with pen and paper. After you prepare, write the main points in your outline as you read. Under main points, write details. The purpose of an outline is to identify all the important information and condense it in small space. An outline also shows how ideas relate to each other.

What does an outline look like?

You can see examples of outlines in most textbooks by looking at the table of contents or the beginning of chapters. These outlines are very general and include only the most important topics. A good outline of these topics would be much longer.

Outlines follow a simple rule—the most general information is briefly written on the left margin. Supporting information for any item is then written somewhat to the right and underneath the main point. It is not necessary to write sentences. Below is an example of the form of an outline without any topics.

From this outline we can tell there are two supporting topics for the Main Topic. The title indicates the main topic, and Roman I and II indicate the two supporting topics. Similarly, we can tell that Topic II has three subtopics, and that each is supported by at least two details. Now, look at the same outline with topics filled in.

Elements of United States Government

I. Basic Structure
   A. Politics
   B. Federal System
   C. Constitution
II. Branches of Government
   A. Legislative
      1. Congress
      2. Powers and Duties
      3. The Work of Congress
   B. Executive
      1. Presidency
      2. Leadership
      3. The Bureaucracy
   C. Judicial
      1. Federal Courts
      2. Supreme Court

You can learn much from an outline. In this outline, for example, you can learn that there are three branches of government (II, A, B, C) and two types of courts (II, C, 1, 2).

An outline may contain many or few levels of detail; each grouping to the right is a level of detail. The outline presented above has three levels. You must decide how much detail your outlines should have.

Section B Practice

Directions: Read the following passage carefully and finish the outline of the passage by filling in the blanks.

Michael Joseph Jackson (August 29, 1958 – June 25, 2009) was an American recording artist, dancer, singer-songwriter, musician, and philanthropist. Referred to as the King of Pop, Jackson is recognized as the most successful entertainer of all time by Guinness World Records. His contribution to music, dance, and fashion, along with a much-publicized personal life, made him a global figure in popular culture for over four decades.

The seventh child of the Jackson family, he debuted on the professional music scene along with his brothers as a member of The Jackson 5, then the Jacksons in 1964, and began his solo career in 1971. In the early 1980s, Jackson became a dominant figure in popular music. The music videos for his songs, including those of "Beat It", "Billie Jean", and "Thriller", were credited with transforming the medium into an art form and a promotional tool, and the popularity of these videos helped to bring the relatively new television channel MTV to fame. Videos such as "Black or White" and "Scream" made him a staple on MTV in the 1990s. Through stage performances and music videos, Jackson popularized a number of dance techniques, such as the robot and the moonwalk, to which he gave the name. His distinctive musical sound and vocal style have influenced numerous hip hop, pop, contemporary R&B, and rock artists.

Jackson's 1982 album Thriller is the best-selling album of all time. His other records, including Off the Wall (1979), Bad (1987), Dangerous (1991), and History (1995), also rank among the world's best-selling. Jackson is one of the few artists to have been inducted into the Rock and Roll Hall of Fame twice. He was also inducted into the Dance Hall of Fame as the first (and currently only) dancer from the world of pop and rock 'n' roll. Some of his other achievements include multiple Guinness World Records; 13 Grammy Awards (as well as the Grammy Legend Award and the Grammy Lifetime Achievement Award); 26 American Music Awards (more than any other artist, including the "Artist of the Century"); 13 number-one singles in the United States in his solo career (more than any other male artist in the Hot 100 era); and the estimated sale of over 750 million records worldwide. Jackson won hundreds of awards, which have made him the most-awarded recording artists in the history of music. He was also a notable humanitarian and philanthropist, donating and raising hundreds of millions of dollars for beneficial causes and supporting more than 39 charities. According to David Winters, Jackson also donated tens of millions of dollars to many children's charities anonymously, and spent a lot of his time visiting seriously ill children tirelessly going from hospital to hospital meeting these children just to brighten up their lives. When Jackson finished the visits he would ask the hospital nurses and the doctors what was needed at the hospital in terms of equipment for the children and would then make anonymous donations to the hospital to purchase expensive equipment or whatever else was needed.

Aspects of Jackson's personal life, including his changing appearance, personal relationships, and behavior, have generated controversy. In 1993, he was accused of child sexual abuse, but the case was settled out of court and no formal charges were brought. In 2005, he was tried and acquitted of further sexual abuse allegations and several other charges after the jury ruled him not guilty on all counts. While preparing for his concert series This Is It, Jackson died of acute propofol intoxication on June 25, 2009, after suffering from cardiac arrest. Before his death, Jackson had been administered drugs including propofol and lorazepam. The Los Angeles County Coroner declared his death a homicide, and his personal physician pleaded not guilty to charges of involuntary manslaughter. Jackson's death triggered a global outpouring of grief, and as many as one billion people around the world reportedly watched his public memorial service on live television. In March 2010, Sony Music Entertainment signed a $250 million deal with Jackson's estate to retain distribution rights to his recordings until 2017, and to release seven posthumous albums over the decade following his death.

(Adapted from *http://en.wikipedia.org/wiki/Michael_Jackson*)

Outline

I. General introduction

II. Life and career

A. He entered the professional music career as a member of 1 ____________________.

B. In the early 1980s, Jackson became 2 ____________________.

1. "Beat It",
2. "Billie Jean",
3. "Thriller"

C. 3 ____________________ on MTV in the 1990s

1. "Black or White"
2. "Scream"

III. Awards and influences

A. 4 ____________________

1. multiple Guinness World Records

2. 13 Grammy Awards
3. 26 American Music Awards
……

B. He was also a notable 5 ____________________

1. He donated and raised hundreds of millions of dollars for beneficial causes and supported more than 39 charities.
2. He also donated tens of millions of dollars to many children's charities anonymously.

IV. Controversy and death aftermath

A. Aspects of Jackson's personal life have generated 6 ____________________.

1. In 1993, he was accused of 7 ____________________.
2. In 2005, he was tried and acquitted of further sexual abuse allegations and several other charges.

B. Jackson died of acute propofol intoxication on June 25, 2009, after suffering from cardiac arrest.

1. Jackson's death triggered 8 ____________________.
2. In March 2010, Sony Music Entertainment signed a $250 million deal with Jackson's estate.

Part 2 Idioms, Proverbs and Sayings

Directions: The following are idioms, proverbs or sayings by famous people about music and movies. Choose what you think is correct and compare with the right ones.

1. In music one must think with the heart and feel with the ________. (Victor Hugo)
   A. minds B. souls C. brains D. hands
2. ________ tickles your muscles, symphonies stretch your soul. (Paul Whiteman)
   A. Jazz B. Hip-hop C. Country music D. Blues
3. Music has charms to soothe a savage breast, to ________ rocks or bend a knotted oak. (William Congreve)
   A. widen B. soften C. shorten D. harden
4. I think music in itself is healing. It's an explosive expression of humanity. It's something we are all touched by. No matter what ________ we're from, everyone loves music. (Billy Joel)
   A. custom B. country C. nation D. culture
5. Without music, life would be a(n) ________. The German imagines even God singing songs. (Friedrich Nietzsche)
   A. problem B. error C. trouble D. fault
6. Love is like a ________. The music may stop now and then, but the strings remain forever.

(June Masters Bacher)

A. violin B. piano C. saxophone D. horn

7. Of all the music that reached farthest into heaven, it is the ________ of a loving heart. (Henry Ward Beecher)

A. hitting B. smashing C. beating D. crashing

8. Music washes away from the soul the ________ of everyday life. (Red Auerbach)

A. stain B. dust C. garbage D. rubbish

9. Without music, life is a journey through a ________. (Pat Conroy)

A. mountain B. river C. land D. desert

10. The movie is going over ________ everywhere in China.

A. huge B. large C. big D. vast

Part 3 Reading Passages

Section A Hollywood and Los Angeles

Hollywood is a district in Los Angeles, California, U.S.A., situated west-northwest of Downtown. Due to its fame and cultural identity as the historical center of movie studios and stars, the word "Hollywood" is often used as a metonym for the American film and television industry. Today much of the movie industry has dispersed into surrounding areas such as Burbank and the Westside, but significant ancillary industries (such as editing, effects, props, post-production, and lighting companies) remain in Hollywood. Many historic Hollywood theaters are used as venues to premiere major theatrical releases, and host the Academy Awards. It is a popular destination for nightlife and tourism, and home to the Walk of Fame.

Hollywood is the land of stars to its visitors, you can visit your favorite Celebrity Grave or drive past Celebrity Homes and Famous Hollywood Houses. Whilst driving you will also recognize many famous Hollywood Film Locations, from films which the stars appeared in. The world famous Beverly Hills, Sunset Boulevard and Sunset Strip are just a few minutes away, as is the Hollywood Bowl, and opposite is the historic "Barn" where the worlds first full length movie was made. The grave and last home of Hollywood icon Marilyn Monroe are both within easy reach and visited daily by her admirers. The world famous Rodeo Drive and Wilshire Boulevard shopping districts can be found not far away, as can the "Hard Rock Cafe" and the unique "Tail of the Pup" hotdog stand which has appeared in numerous films. Visitors to the area will be unable to miss the famous Hollywood Sign set in the Hollywood Hills. Hollywood Boulevard is also a destination most tourists won't want to miss. The Hollywood Walk of Fame comprises of 18 blocks of Hollywood stars embedded in the sidewalk that honor Hollywood stars of the past and present. Grauman's Chinese Theatre is a must see attraction along Hollywood Boulevard. Here, you can match your foot and handprints with the Hollywood stars in this famous landmark's courtyard. The theatre itself opened in 1927, the same year movie idols began leaving their hand and footprints outside the building. Today over 200 prints of Hollywood legends exist for tourists to see. Hollywood is brimming with the faces of the stars, and murals can be found in all kinds of places. A short walk past Grauman's Chinese Theatre is the Hollywood Entertainment Museum where you can see how movies and TV shows are made or sit in Captain Kirk's chair on the Starship Enterprise or Norm's at the Cheers set. If you don't catch a glimpse of a real-life Hollywood celebrity, stare as long as you want to at the life like figures in the Hollywood Wax Museum. Or, feel the excitement of movie-making on one of the famous Hollywood Studio Tours.

Hollywood became part of greater Los Angeles in 1910, and just one year later the first motion picture studio was established. Today, Hollywood is synonymous with the film industry, portraying visions of glamour and nostalgia unmatched anywhere else in the world. Since 1911 Hollywood has been known as the movie capital of the world and is now visited by over 10 million people a year. Many of these visitors come to Hollywood, to visit the fabled places where their legendary idols lived, worked and played. Since the Golden Age of Hollywood, many historic buildings and landmarks have been demolished and lost forever in the name of progress.

Los Angeles, known as "L.A." or the "City of Angels", is the largest city in the state of California and the second-largest in the United States. Los Angeles has year round sunshine, palm trees & fabulous golden beaches making Los Angeles one of god's paradises on earth. "Los Angeles" covers over 1000 sq. miles and consists of 88 incorporated cities & dozens of individual neighborhoods many of which have their own city halls, police forces & fire brigades. Los Angeles was incorporated as a municipality on April 4, 1850, five months before California achieved statehood and is the county seat of Los Angeles County. As of the 2005 U.S. Census estimate, the city had a population of 3.8 million and is the core cultural and economic center of the Los Angeles—Long Beach—Santa Ana metropolitan area, with a population of 12.9 million. Los Angeles is one of the world's most important centers of culture, science, technology, international trade, and higher education. It has also hosted two Olympic Games—in 1932 and 1984 and is home to numerous world-renowned institutions of a broad range of professional and cultural fields. In addition, the city is arguably the world's leading producer of popular entertainment such as motion pictures, television, and recorded music which forms the base of its international fame and global status. Los Angeles is also one of the most cosmopolitan places in the world. People have long been attracted to the world-class city for its balmy weather, unique and vibrant lifestyle, laid-back energy, Pacific Rim Gateway status, and the hope of realizing the "Hollywood Dream."

(839 words)

I. Reading comprehension

Directions: Choose the best answer to each question according to the above passage.

1. The word "metonym" (in Line 3, Paragraph 1) most probably means ________.
   A. antonym B. synonym C. pun D. sarcasm
2. If you want to go shopping in Hollywood, you can go to ________.
   A. the Hollywood Wax Museum B. the Hollywood Bowl
   C. the Hollywood Walk of Fame D. Rodeo Drive and Wilshire Boulevard
3. In LA, you can see how movies and TV shows are made in ________.
   A. Grauman's Chinese Theatre B. the Hollywood Entertainment Museum
   C. the Hollywood Hills D. Hollywood Boulevard
4. Which is not true about Hollywood?
   A. It is a popular destination for nightlife and tourism.
   B. Grauman's Chinese Theatre is a must see attraction along Hollywood Boulevard.
   C. Hollywood is brimming with the faces of the stars, and murals can be found here and there.
   D. Since the Golden Age of Hollywood, many historic buildings and landmarks have been protected and restored in the name of progress.
5. Which is not true about Los Angeles?
   A. Los Angeles was incorporated as a municipality on April 4, 1850, shortly after California achieved statehood.
   B. the city is the world's leading producer of popular entertainment such as motion pictures, television, and recorded music.
   C. Los Angeles is one of the world's most important centers of culture, science, technology, international trade, and higher education.
   D. People have long been attracted there for its fine weather, unique and vibrant lifestyle, laid-back energy, and the hope of realizing the "Hollywood Dream."

II. Vocabulary

Directions: Fill in each blank with an appropriate word from the box below. Each word can be used only once.

legendary	celebrity	releases	glamour	embed
synonymous	vibrant	disperse	brimming	icon

1. Yaoming, the 2.26-meter Houston Rockets star, with the combination of strength, height, skills, as well as his global celebrity, is the perfect sport __________ to represent the growth and global status of an emerging China.

2. China will search for a new "diving queen" at the World Championships after the retirement of __________ medal-machine Guo Jingjing.
3. Police use tear gas to try to __________ demonstrators on the streets of the Chilean capital, Santiago, after anti-government march turns violent.
4. The latest "Transformers" added \$39 million overseas, bringing its international haul to \$460 million and worldwide total to \$762.8 million. Among this year's __________, that's second only to "Pirates of the Caribbean: On Stranger Tides" at \$1.03 billion.
5. Technology is not the most important thing. The critical thing is how to __________ it into the business and a find a viable model. Then the community can benefit from more jobs and income—while the business can also earn money."
6. The Beckhams' sons are Brooklyn Joseph, Romeo James and Cruz David, but for their first daughter, the __________ couple have decided to hold back on her first name and go freestyle for her second.
7. Despite the concerns around cost, London is regarded by European travelers as a __________ and accessible destination."
8. Even with the emphasis on work and business, wherever they went William and Kate brought a royal __________ that even Hollywood couldn't emulate.
9. Critics have so far praised the last Harry Potter film, with The Sun newspaper saying "the final instalment is still __________ with the old Potter magic".
10. "Made in China" used to be __________ with cheap consumer goods, but China's Shanghai Zhenhua Heavy Industry Co Ltd (ZPMC), wants to change the image by taking part in the world's most challenging infrastructure projects.

III. Discussion

Directions: Read the following news and debate over the topic "Should celebrities donate to society?"

Jolie and Pitt donate to Pakistan

Hollywood stars Angelina Jolie and Brad Pitt have donated \$1 million to help Pakistanis displaced by fighting, the UN refugee agency says. More than two million people have been uprooted since the army began fighting Taliban militants in Pakistan's Swat region earlier this year, the UN says.

Ms Jolie has visited Pakistan three times since becoming a goodwill ambassador for the agency in 2001. The two actors made the donation through their charitable foundation.

Ms Jolie and Mr Pitt—who are partners—have set up the foundation to help counter humanitarian crises.

(*http://news.bbc.co.uk/2/hi/south_asia/8108543.stm*)

Section B How about China's Hollywood?

Directions: Read the following passage and the statements after it, mark

Y (for Yes) if the statement agrees with the information given in the text;

N (for No) if the statement contradicts the information given in the text;

NG (for Not Given) if the information is not given in the text.

Like in the past several years, imported blockbusters, or called "dapian" in Chinese, are destined to dominate China's cinemas this year, again.

The past Spring Festival season saw the success of the first blockbuster in 2002, Harry Potter and the Sorcerer's Stone, which drove millions of audiences crazy in China as it had done in other regions. In the first week after its China premier in late January, the Warner Brothers production had earned about 18 million yuan (US.2 million) out of Chinese audiences' wallets. So far, the film has reaped a national ticket-office receipt of about 56.8 million yuan (US.6 million), according to Zhou Tiedong, the manager of import department of China Films groups Corporation.

Following the footsteps of Harry Porter is the Lord of the Rings, which will be shown nationwide soon. There are signs that the film will also stage a perfect performance.

Although it is only April, it is definitely sure that imported blockbusters will play the leading role on Chinese markets this year.

Hollywood's influence is seemingly remarkable, and omnipresent. "I love watching Hollywood blockbusters. They gave me audio and visual enjoyment which domestic films can not provide," said 26-year-old Chen Qiang who work at a Beijing-based joint venture. The devoted Hollywood fan had watched "Harry Porter and the Sorcerer's Stone" for twice. In 1995, he watched Titanic for three times. And now he is waiting eagerly for the screening of "The Lord of Rings".

Besides going to cinemas, Chen also buy film magazines regularly every month. His favorite magazine is *Movie View Biweekly* which is published in Southwest China's Sichuan Province. The magazine, which introduce the latest Hollywood films and stars, boasts itself as "the mouthpiece of China's Hollywood fans" There are many other film publications with a similar market orientation on newsstands now, most of which are selling well. Each issue of these magazines comes with a full color poster of a recent American film or star. Chen put up such posters on the wall of his bedroom.

History of blockbusters

China began to import blockbusters in 1994. In principle, the word blockbuster does not indicate producing area itself. However, since most blockbusters shown in China are imported from the United States, blockbuster is the synonym to "Hollywood movie" in China.

Since 1994, there were 10 blockbusters introduced to China each year, most of which had a handsome market performance. That was the beginning of Hollywood's domination of China. Before then, there were also foreign movies shown at cinemas. But most of them were low cost productions of low quality, which had been shown 10 years earlier in other countries.

In 1994, partly because of the drastic slump in cinema revenues, Chinese film authority finally began its market-oriented reform discreetly, with the introduction of revenue-sharing films. In November that year, the first imported revenue-sharing film "The Fugitive" was shown in six major cities including Beijing, Shanghai, Tianjin and Guangzhou. Among the first batch of imported revenue-sharing movies, there were three Jackie Chan works and seven others from Hollywood, including "The Fugitive", "The Lion King", "Speed", "Forrest Gump" and "True Lies" These were real blockbusters "Oscar winners and best-sellers in the United States, thus they attracted a great deal of movie fans. Combined together, the ten films occupied 70 per cent of the market that year, leaving the remaining 30 per cent for the 100 or so domestic movies.

During the following years, though there were ups and downs for Hollywood movies in Chinese market, they had absolute advantages over domestic movies. In terms of box-office, Hollywood's greatest success in China was Titanic, which garnered 370 million yuan (US million) in 1998, or one fourth of the country's total box-office revenue that year.

Hollywood's success has been reflected by surveys on audience preferences. In a survey held in Beijing, Shanghai and Guangzhou by a consulting company, as much as 35 per cent of the 1,500 18-year-old interviewees said their favorite film was Titanic.

The popularity of Hollywood blockbusters has brought an upgrade of cinemas. Since most Hollywood films require top grade audio and visual facilities, big cinemas have been generous in upgrading themselves while vying for expanding their market share. Smaller cinemas which failed to do so, however, were ruled out of the market.

In the early 1990s, there were about 15,000 cinemas in China. In 2000, only less than 4,000 of them were still running business.

While Hollywood is getting increasingly popular and influential in China, critics and industry insiders are falling apart in their attitudes towards Hollywood blockbusters.

Confrontation of thoughts has begun, though not directly currently, and such debates will provide food for thought and have influence on the future development of Chinese film industry for sure.

Impact on Chinese film industry

Parallel to the success of Hollywood films was the failure of Made-in-China. For many years, local film industry of China has been struggling on the verge of life and death.

In 2001, the total national ticket office was 800 million yuan (US million), 20 per cent less than that in 2000. Only 10 per cent of the about 100 domestic films had profit, another 10 per cent barely kept balance, while the remaining 80 per cent were losing money. Examples of domestic films' handsome performance in market are rare, with the exception of "The Painted Woman", "In the Heat of the Sun", "The Red Cherry", "Shanghai Triad" in 1995, and renowned director Feng Xiaogang's happy-new-year comic series. This year, Feng's "Big Shot's Funeral" made a great hit again, with a ticket-office receipt of 25 million yuan (US million). But ironically, "Big Shot" is invested by Columbia Pictures. "The reality is that the domestic film industry is shrinking into non-existence," said Dai Jinhua, professor of Chinese Literature and Culture at Beijing University. Dai attributed this to the "invasion" of Hollywood blockbusters.

While Warner Brothers, Touch Stone and other Hollywood entertainment giants are far from being satisfied with their limited access to Chinese market, Dai argued that the door of Chinese market had opened too wide. According to Dai, in 1995, in order to give way to Hollywood movies, more than 70 domestic Chinese films were shelved, without a chance to be exhibited in theaters. Hollywood movies have given Chinese film industry a destructive blow," Dai said anxiously. Dai's view sounds going to extremes, and is not shared by many people.

In many countries where Hollywood dominate the screens, the local productions have almost ceased to exist. That is one of the reasons that in these countries, such as Korea and France, Hollywood movies run across severe reject from industry insiders.

But in the China, experts, critics and other insiders are much more positive and optimistic. Du Qingchun, a teacher from the Beijing Film Academy, while admitting that some protection measures were necessary, said it was unnecessary to make fuss about Hollywood. "Competition is a good thing, it is for the benefit for local film industry in the long run," said Du, Chinese film industry has never been beat down by Hollywood. The 1930s, when Hollywood movies flooded China, was also the golden period of Chinese film industry" "Anyway, moviegoers did not blindly follow blockbusters. Wheather to watch Hollywood or not was based on their voluntary choice," said Du. "Even if we have not imported any blockbusters, it is highly possible that the local industry will not get any better now," Said Du, arguing that the real obstacles did not come from competition. What Du and many other insiders believe to be the real hurdles for Chinese films, lie in the highly planned industry itself. "Strictly speaking, there is no film business currently in China," Said Li Xiaofeng, a film free-lancer who is currently studying films in Belgium. In Li's view, there remains a great deal of things to learn for China's "film industry" to become "real business" from distribution to advertising and cinema administration. To take distribution for example, for years, the China Filmsgroups (CFG) had a monopoly in film distribution.

The good news is that Chinese film authorities are setting out to establish a new company to distribute foreign films. However, CFG will remain its monopoly on importing films. People also call film authorities for taking more flexible standards while handing out financial support. According to Du Qingchun, each year the central government allocates about 100 million yuan to aid film production. The absolute majority of the money are used to shoot "main melody" movies, while the works of talented directors which might as not politically important, are neglected.

Another reason that Dai Jinhua opposes Hollywood blockbusters was based on cultural observation. "Films are not only industrial products and goods, they are also cultural products," Said Dai, "Only when being diversified can a culture demonstrate its glamour and bear significance." Dai Jinhua is worried that Hollywood films, which are considered as mere commodities instead of artworks, might kill people's imagination. "We should be more aware of Hollywood's "Cultural invasion" Zhu Jingjiang, a director at China Central Television's movie channel, put it in a more ardent way. Zhu compared Hollywood megaproductions with fast food, "Which has no nutrition at all".

More people, who do not have a liking for Hollywood movies either, scoffed off such an attitude. "Chinese people do not have a tradition of entertaining themselves. They always act too seriously," said Li Xun, a fellow researcher at the Beijing-based China film study centre, "Although Hollywood films are inferior to European productions in terms of art, we can not rob film-goers of the right of entertaining themselves." Li Xun's view was shared by Li Xiaofeng. "Audiences are the source of box-office, and the market is the result of audiences' choice," said Li Xiaofeng.

(1,614 words)

1. ________ Many Hollywood blockbusters achieved great success and reaped high box office receipts in China.
2. ________ The main reason that Chinese film authority began its market-oriented reform was the drastic slump in cinema revenues.
3. ________ Dai Jinhua believed that the "invasion" of Hollywood blockbusters had negative influence on the domestic film industry.
4. ________ The money that the central government allocated to aid film production mainly went to "main melody" movies as well as the works of talented directors.
5. ________ The majority of people are aware of the Hollywood's "Cultural invasion" and compare them to "fast food".

Part 4 Reading Comprehension Test

Passage 1

Directions: Read the passage and choose the best answer to each question.

I live in the land of Disney, Hollywood and year-round sun. You may think people in such a glamorous, fun-filled place are happier than others. If so, you have some mistaken ideas about the nature of happiness.

Many intelligent people still equate happiness with fun. The truth is that fun and happiness have little or nothing in common. Fun is what we experience during an act. Happiness is what we experience after an act. It is a deeper, more abiding emotion.

Going to an amusement park or ball game, watching a movie or television, are fun activities that help us relax, temporarily forget our problems and maybe even laugh. But they do not bring happiness, because their positive effects end when the fun ends.

I have often thought that if Hollywood stars have a role to play, it is to teach us that happiness has nothing to do with fun. These rich, beautiful individuals have constant access to glamorous parties, fancy cars, expensive homes, everything that spells "happiness". But in memoir after memoir, celebrities reveal the unhappiness hidden beneath all their fun: depression, alcoholism, drug addiction, broken marriages, troubled children and profound loneliness.

Ask a bachelor why he resists marriage even though he finds dating to be less and less satisfying. If he's honest, he will tell you that he is afraid of making a commitment. For commitment is in fact quite painful. The single life is filled with fun, adventure and excitement. Marriage has such moments, but they are not its most distinguishing features.

Similarly, couples that choose not to have children are deciding in favor of painless fun over painful happiness. They can dine out ever they want and sleep as late as they want. Couples with infant children are lucky to get a whole night's sleep or a three-day vacation. I don't know any parent who would choose the word fun to describe raising children.

Understanding and accepting that true happiness has nothing to do with fun is one of the most liberating realizations we can ever come to. It liberates time: now we can devote more hours to activities that can genuinely increase our happiness. It liberates money: buying that new car or those fancy clothes that will do nothing to increase our happiness now seems pointless. And it liberates us from envy: we now understand that all those rich and glamorous people we were so sure are happy because they are always having so much fun actually may not be happy at all.

1. Which of the following is true?
   A. Fun creates long-lasting satisfaction.
   B. Fun provides enjoyment while pain leads to happiness.
   C. Happiness is enduring whereas fun is short-lived.
   D. Fun that is long-standing may lead to happiness.
2. To the author, Hollywood stars all have an important role to play that is to ________.
   A. write memoir after memoir about their happiness
   B. tell the public that happiness has nothing to do with fun
   C. teach people how to enjoy their lives
   D. bring happiness to the public instead of going to glamorous parties
3. In the author's opinion, marriage ________.
   A. affords greater fun
   B. leads to raising children
   C. indicates commitment
   D. ends in pain
4. Couples having infant children ________.
   A. are lucky since they can have a whole night's sleep
   B. find fun in tucking them into bed at night
   C. find more time to play and joke with them
   D. derive happiness from their endeavor
5. If one gets the meaning of the true sense of happiness, he will ________.
   A. stop playing games and joking with others
   B. make the best use of his time increasing happiness
   C. give a free hand to money
   D. keep himself with his family

Passage 2

Directions: Choose the best answer to each of the following questions.

There are good reasons to be troubled by the violence that spreads throughout the media. Movies, television and video games are full of gunplay and bloodshed, and one might reasonably ask what's wrong with a society that presents videos of domestic violence as entertainment. Most researchers agree that the causes of real-world violence are complex. A 1993 study by the U.S. National Academy of Sciences listed "biological, individual, family, peer, school, and community factors" as all playing their parts. Viewing abnormally large amounts of violent television and video games may well contribute to violent behavior in certain individuals.

The trouble comes when researchers downplay uncertainties in their studies or overstate the case for causality. Skeptics were dismayed several years ago when a group of societies including the American Medical Association tried to end the debate by issuing a joint statement: "At this time, well over 1,000 studies point overwhelmingly to a causal connection between media violence and aggressive behavior in some children."

Freedom-of-speech advocates accused the societies of catering to politicians, and even disputed the number of studies (most were review articles and essays, they said). When Jonathan Freedman, a social psychologist at the University of Toronto, reviewed the literature, he found only 200 or so studies of television-watching and aggression. And when he weeded out "the most doubtful measures of aggression", only 28% supported a connection.

The critical point here is causality. The alarmists say they have proved that violent media cause aggression. But the assumptions behind their observations need to be examined. When labeling games as violent or non-violent, should a hero eating a ghost really be counted as a violent event? And when experimenters record the time it takes game players to read 'aggressive' or 'non-aggressive' words from a list, can we be sure what they are actually measuring? The intent of the new Harvard Center on Media and Child Health to collect and standardize studies of media violence in order to compare their methodologies, assumptions and conclusions is an important step in the right direction.

Another appropriate ster would be to tone down the criticism until we know more. Several researchers write, speak and testify quite a lot on the threat posed by violence in the media. That is, of course, their privilege. But when doing so, they often come out with statements that the matter has now been settled, drawing criticism from colleagues. In response, the alarmists accuse critics and news reporters of being deceived by the entertainment industry. Such clashes help neither science nor society.

(427 words)

6. Why is there so much violence shown in movies, TV and video games?
   A. There is a lot of violence in the real world today.
   B. Something has gone wrong with today's society.
   C. Many people are fond of gunplay and bloodshed.
   D. Showing violence is thought to be entertaining.
7. What is the skeptic's (Line 2. Para.2) view of media violence?
   A. Violence on television is a fairly accurate reflection of real-world life.
   B. Most studies exaggerate the effect of media violence on the viewers.
   C. A causal relationship exists between media and real-world violence.
   D. The influence of media violence on children has been underestimated.
8. The author uses the term "alarmists" (Line 1. Para.4) to refer to those who ________.
   A. use standardized measurements in the studies of media violence
   B. initiated the debate over the influence of violent media on reality
   C. assert a direct link between violent media and aggressive behavior
   D. use appropriate methodology in examining aggressive behavior
9. To refute the alarmists, the author advances his argument by first challenging ________.
   A. the source and amount of their data B. the targets of their observation
   C. their system of measurement D. their definition of violence

10. What does the author think of the debate concerning the relationship between the media and violence?

    A. More studies should be conducted before conclusions are drawn.

    B. It should come to an end since the matter has now been settled.

    C. The past studies in this field have proved to be misleading.

    D. He more than agrees with the views held by the alarmists.

Passage 3

Directions: Read the following passage carefully. Then answer the questions or complete the statements in the fewest possible words.

If movie trailers are supposed to cause a reaction, the preview for "United 93" more than succeeds. Featuring no famous actors, it begins with images of a beautiful morning and passengers boarding an airplane. It takes you a minute to realize what the movie's even about. That's when a plane hits the World Trade Center. the effect is visceral. When the trailer played before "Inside Man" last week at a Hollywood theater, audience members began calling out, "Too soon!" In New York City, the response was even more dramatic. The Loews theater in Manhattan took the rare step of pulling the trailer from its screens after several complaints.

"United 93" is the first feature film to deal explicitly with the events of September 11, 2001, and is certain to ignite an emotional debate. Is it too soon? Should the film have been made at all? More to the point, will anyone want to see it? Other 9/11 projects are on the way as the fifth anniversary of the attacks approaches, most notably Oliver Stone's " World Trade Center." but as the forerunner, "United 93"will take most of the heat, whether it deserves it or not.

The real United 93 crashed in a Pennsylvania field after 40 passengers and crew fought back against the terrorists. Writer-director Paul Greengrass has gone to great lengths to be respectful in his depiction of what occurred, proceeding with the film only after securing the approval of every victim's family. "Was I surprised at the agreement? Yes. Very. Usually there're one or two families who're more reluctant," Greengrass writes in an e-mail. "I was surprised at the extraordinary way the United 93 families have welcomed us into their lives and shared their experiences with us." Carole O'Hare, a family member, says, "They were very open and honest with us, and they made us a part of this whole project." Universal, which is releasing the film, plans to donate 10% of its opening weekend gross to the Flight 93 National Memorial Fund. That hasn't stopped criticism that the studio is exploiting a national tragedy. O'Hare thinks that's unfair. "This story has to be told to honor the passengers and crew for what they did," she says. "But more than that, it raises awareness. Our ports aren't secure. Our borders aren't secure. Our airlines still aren't secure, and this is what happens when you're not secure. That's the message I want people to hear."

(417 words)

11. The trailer for "United 93" succeeded in ______________________________ when it played in the theaters in Hollywood and New York City.
12. When the trailer played, it caused ______________________________.
13. What did Paul Greengrass obtain before he proceeded with the movie?

____.

14. What is the most notable feature film to deal with the events of Sep 11, 2001?

____.

15. What is the main purpose of telling the story, according to Carole O'Hare?

____.

Passage 4

Directions: Read the passage and choose the best answer to each question.

What we know of prenatal development makes all this attempt made by a mother to mold the character of her unborn child by studying poetry, art, or mathematics during pregnancy seem utterly impossible. How could such extremely complex influences pass from the mother to the child? There is no connection between their nervous systems. Even the blood vessels of mother and child do not join directly. An emotional shock to the mother will affect her child, because it changes the activity of her glands and so the chemistry her blood. Any chemical change in the mother's blood will affect the child for better or worse. But we can not see how a looking for mathematics or poetic genius can be dissolved in blood and produce a similar liking or genius in the child.

In our discussion of instincts we saw that there was reason to believe that whatever we inherit must be of some very simple sort rather than any complicated or very definite kind of behavior. It is certain that no one inherits a knowledge of mathematics. It may be, however, that children inherit more or less of a rather general ability that we may call intelligence. If very intelligent children become deeply interested in mathematics, they will probably make a success of that study.

As for musical ability, it may be that what is inherited is an especially sensitive ear, a peculiar structure of the hands or the vocal organs connections between nerves and muscles that make it comparatively easy to learn the movements a musician must execute, and particularly vigorous emotions. If these factors are all organized around music, the child may become a musician. The same factors, in other circumstance might be organized about some other center of interest. The rich emotional equipment might find expression in poetry. The capable fingers might develop skill in surgery. It is not the knowledge of music that is inherited, then nor even the love of it, but a certain bodily structure that makes it comparatively easy to acquire musical knowledge and skill. Whether that ability shall be directed toward music or some other undertaking may be decided entirely by forces in the environment in which a child grows up.

16. Which of the following statements is not true?
   A. Some mothers try to influence their unborn children by studying art and other subjects during their pregnancy.
   B. It is utterly impossible for us to learn anything about prenatal development.
   C. The blood vessels of mother and child do not join directly.
   D. There're no connection between mother's nervous systems and her unborn child's.
17. A mother will affect her unborn baby on the condition that ________.
   A. she is emotionally shocked
   B. she has a good knowledge of inheritance
   C. she sticks to studying
   D. she takes part in all kind of activities
18. According to the passage, a child may inherit ________.
   A. everything from his mother
   B. a knowledge of mathematics
   C. a rather general ability that we call intelligence
   D. her mother's musical ability
19. If a child inherits something from his mother, such as an especially sensitive ear, a peculiar structure of the hands or of the vocal organs, he will ________.
   A. surely become a musician
   B. mostly become a poet
   C. possibly become a teacher
   D. become a musician as long as all these factors are organized around music
20. Which of the following is the best title for the passage?
   A. Role of Inheritance
   B. An Unborn Child
   C. Function of instincts
   D. Inherited Talents

Unit 13

Equality and Independence

Part 1 Reading Skills

Section A Skimming

Skimming is a process of speed reading that involves visually searching the sentences of a page for clues to meaning. Skimming is also used to quickly identify the main idea of a text. When you read the newspaper, you're probably not reading it word by word; instead, you're scanning the text.

Skimming is conducted at a higher rate (700 words per minute and above) than normal reading for comprehension (around 200-230 wpm), and results in lower comprehension rates, especially with information-rich reading material.

Skimming has many uses:

1. to gain an overview and see the pattern of the organization of material (previewing)
2. to find specific information (locating)
3. as a substitute for reading when time is short (sampling)
4. as a means of defining purposes in reading (previewing)

5. to assess the level of difficulty of material (sampling)
6. to supplement other techniques (previewing)
7. to decide whether or not to read and to help in the selection of material (sampling)
8. in using dictionaries and handbooks (locating)
9. in reading classified advertisements in newspapers (locating)
10. in assessing the relevance of material to your immediate needs (previewing)

Here are some strategies that can be used when skimming.

1. Read blocks of words.

For example:

Whether we find a joke/funny or not/largely depends on/where we have been brought up. /The sense of humor/is mysteriously bound up/with national characteristics. /A Frenchman /for instance/ might find it hard / to laugh at a Russian joke. /In the same way/a Russian might fail /to see anything amusing / in a joke /which would make an Englishman/laugh to tears.

2. Read the key "signals".

A. title, subtitles, subheading, and illustrations

B. the first and last paragraphs

C. the first sentence of each paragraph

3. Read with key words in mind.

Read the beginning of each sentence, and decide if it is relevant to the key words being searched for. If not, jump to the end of that sentence, or the beginning of next sentence, which is capitalized.

For example, if we want to know how to prepare children for the complex decisions in later life, we should bear the word "decision", or "decide" in mind, and just jump to the last two sentences of the following paragraph.

In some ways, children should be treated as mature people. For one thing, adults should not use baby talk with children; using real words with children helps them develop their language skills more quickly. In most cases, children admire their parents or their elders, and they want to understand and communicate with adults in the way adults do among themselves. Baby talk with children often makes them feel patronized, frustrated, and confused. So, animals should be called "cows" or "dogs", not "mu-mews" and "bow-ows". Second, parents should be consistent when discipline their children. For example, if a parent tells a child "You can not have desert unless you put away your toys", it is important that the parent follow through on the warning. By being consistent, parents will teach children responsibility and give them a stable center around which to grow. Finally and most important, children should be encouraged to join in such off class activities as the boy scouts, the children's band and the teen-court. In doing so, parents will thus be helping their children prepare for the complex decisions that they will have to deal with in later life.

Section B Practice

Directions: Skim the following four paragraphs within 2 minutes, and choose the best title for each paragraph.

A. Gender-Neutral Language B. Create Equal Expectations

C. Promote Integration D. Avoid Assigning Gendered Jobs

Para. 1 Even seemingly innocuous language can promote gender bias. When addressing the class, for example, avoid saying "You guys," which favors boys. Instead, use a gender-neutral term such as "people" or "gang." Encourage your students to use "he or she" when giving examples. If they slip up, don't chastise, but use it as an opportunity to discuss how gender bias invades our language. Similarly, make sure that examples in your lessons alternate between genders. If you are using an old textbook that only uses "he," point it out to students and have them correct the textbook.

Para. 2 No matter what age-group you are teaching, make sure that group work is done without gender separation. Never divide students based on gender. Sometimes, especially in certain age groups, students will tend to divide themselves according to gender. If this is the case, intervene and mix up the groups. Similarly, if you allow students to choose where they sit in the class, don't allow self-selecting gender.

Para. 3 It is every teacher's privilege, especially at the elementary level, to assign jobs to students. Make sure you don't discriminate based on gender. Don't give jobs cleaning up exclusively to girls, and jobs carrying things exclusively to boys. If you need a few students to carry a box of books to another room, make sure you ask both boys and girls to help. If you are doing a unit on cooking or parenting, make sure you get boys involved in volunteering.

Para. 4 Teachers can sometimes unwittingly create different expectations for boys and girls in different disciplines. Be conscious of this and make sure that you hold girls to the same high standard that you expect of boys in conventionally "male" disciplines such as math and science. If you are teaching physical education, make sure not to allow boys to play rougher sports while excluding girls from the competition. Discuss your expectations with the class and make it clear that gender will have no bearing on them.

(From *http://www.ehow.com/info_8637186_ways-stop-gender-bias.html*)

Part 2 Idioms, Proverbs and Sayings

Directions: The following are idioms, proverbs or sayings about equality and independence. Choose what you think is correct and compare with the right ones.

1. Human ________ is all of a color. (Proverb)
   A. skin B. hair C. blood D. heart
2. A ________ may look at a king. (Proverb)
   A. cat B. tiger C. mouse D. dog
3. Everyone is kneaded out of the same dough but not baked in the same ________.
   A. oven B. store C. market D. cooker
4. Better be envied than ________. (Proverb)
   A. hated B. loved C. pitied D. respected
5. Fish and visitors ________ three days. (Benjamin Franklin)
   A. come B. smell C. leave D. worth
6. Before God we are all equally ________ and equally foolish. (Albert Einstein)
   A. tall B. cared C. wise D. strong
7. The first woman was created from the rib of a man. She was not made from his head to top him, nor from his ________ to be trampled on by him, but out of his side to be equal to him. (Confucius)
   A. legs B. feet C. mouth D. arms
8. When you belong to a ________, you have to be better in order to have the right to be equal. (Socrates)
   A. minority B. majority C. group D. nation
9. One of the things about equality is not just that you be treated equally to a man, but that you treat ________ equally to the way you treat a man. (Marlo Thomas)
   A. everybody B. future C. yourself D. history
10. I have a dream that my four little children will one day live in a nation where they will not be judged by the color of their skin but by the content of their ________. (Martin Luther King, Jr.)
    A. character B. life C. education D. mind

Part 3 Reading Passages

Section A Virginia Declaration of Rights

The Virginia Declaration of Rights is a document drafted in 1776 to proclaim the inherent rights of men, including the right to rebel against "inadequate" government. It influenced a number of later documents, including the United States Declaration of Independence (1776), the United States Bill of Rights (1789), and the French Revolution's Declaration of the Rights of Man and of the Citizen (1789).

Full text of Virginia Declaration of Rights

A DECLARATION OF RIGHTS made by the Representatives of the good people of VIRGINIA, assembled in full and free Convention; which rights do pertain to them and their posterity, as the basis and foundation of Government.

I. That all men are by nature equally free and independent, and have certain inherent rights, of which, when they enter into a state of society, they cannot, by any compact, deprive or divest their posterity; namely, the enjoyment of life and liberty, with the means of acquiring and possessing property, and pursuing and obtaining happiness and safety.

II. That all power is vested in, and consequently derived from, the people; that magistrates are their trustees and servants, and at all times amenable to them.

III. That government is, or ought to be, instituted for the common benefit, protection, and security of the people, nation or community; of all the various modes and forms of government that is best, which is capable of producing the greatest degree of happiness and safety and is most effectually secured against the danger of maladministration; and that, whenever any government shall be found inadequate or contrary to these purposes, a majority of the community hath an indubitable, unalienable, and indefeasible right to reform, alter or abolish it, in such manner as shall be judged most conducive to the public weal.

IV. That no man, or set of men, are entitled to exclusive or separate emoluments or privileges from the community, but in consideration of public services; which, not being descendible, neither ought the offices of magistrate, legislator, or judge be hereditary.

V. That the legislative and executive powers of the state should be separate and distinct from the judicative; and, that the members of the two first may be restrained from oppression by feeling and participating the burthens of the people, they should, at fixed periods, be reduced to a private station, return into that body from which they were originally taken, and the vacancies be supplied by frequent, certain, and regular elections in which all, or any part of the former members, to be again eligible, or ineligible, as the laws shall direct.

VI. That elections of members to serve as representatives of the people in assembly ought to be free; and that all men, having sufficient evidence of permanent common interest with, and attachment to, the community have the right of suffrage and cannot be taxed or deprived of their property for public uses without their own consent or that of their representatives so elected, nor bound by any law to which they have not, in like manner, assented, for the public good.

VII. That all power of suspending laws, or the execution of laws, by any authority without consent of the representatives of the people is injurious to their rights and ought not to be exercised.

VIII. That in all capital or criminal prosecutions a man hath a right to demand the cause and nature of his accusation to be confronted with the accusers and witnesses, to call for evidence in his favor, and to a speedy trial by an impartial jury of his vicinage, without whose unanimous consent he cannot be found guilty, nor can he be compelled to give evidence against himself; that no man be deprived of his liberty except by the law of the land or the judgement of his peers.

IX. That excessive bail ought not to be required, nor excessive fines imposed; nor cruel and unusual punishments inflicted.

X. That general warrants, whereby any officer or messenger may be commanded to search suspected places without evidence of a fact committed, or to seize any person or persons not named, or whose offense is not particularly described and supported by evidence, are grievous and oppressive and ought not to be granted.

XI. That in controversies respecting property and in suits between man and man, the ancient trial by jury is preferable to any other and ought to be held sacred.

XII. That the freedom of the press is one of the greatest bulwarks of liberty and can never be restrained but by despotic governments.

XIII. That a well regulated militia, composed of the body of the people, trained to arms, is the proper, natural, and safe defense of a free state; that standing armies, in time of peace, should be avoided as dangerous to liberty; and that, in all cases, the military should be under strict subordination to, and be governed by, the civil power.

XIV. That the people have a right to uniform government; and therefore, that no government separate from, or independent of, the government of Virginia, ought to be erected or established within the limits thereof.

XV. That no free government, or the blessings of liberty, can be preserved to any people but by a firm adherence to justice, moderation, temperance, frugality, and virtue and by frequent recurrence to fundamental principles.

XVI. That religion, or the duty which we owe to our Creator and the manner of discharging it, can be directed by reason and conviction, not by force or violence; and therefore, all men are equally entitled to the free exercise of religion, according to the dictates of conscience; and that it is the mutual duty of all to practice Christian forbearance, love, and charity towards each other.

(952 words, drafted by Mr. George Mason)

I. Reading Comprehension

Directions: Read the following statements and decide if they are True of False, according to the passage.

1. ________ The Virginia Declaration of Rights is the earliest version of "Declaration of Independence".
2. ________ The Virginia Declaration of Rights is made by representatives of people in Virginia.
3. ________ Magistrates are the head of local government, and thus people should at all times amenable to them.
4. ________ When a majority of the community finds the government inadequate, they have the right to separate from the current government and set up a new one within Virginia.
5. ________ Everyone is free to choose their religious belief, without interference from outer force.
6. ________ In time of peace, there is no need to keep standing armies, for that may be dangerous to liberty.
7. ________ In case of controversies respecting property between people, the trial by judge is preferable to make the final decision.
8. ________ The government has the authority to suspend laws, or execute laws.
9. ________ The legislative power, the executive power and the judicative power of the state should be separate.
10. ________ Excessive fines ought not to be imposed; nor cruel and unusual punishments inflicted.

II. Vocabulary

Directions: Fill in each blank with an appropriate word from the box below. Change the form where necessary. Each word can be used only once.

pertain	posterity	dives	magistrates	unalienable	emoluments	eligible
suffrage	impartial	grievous	despotic	subordination	frugality	forbearance

1. The company has rejected suggestions from the Committee on Foreign Investment in the United States that it should __________ the assets.
2. With my monthly __________ just around 7,000 yuan, I just cannot afford to buy a place of my own.
3. Public institutions and companies that carry out energy-saving and emissions-reducing work will be __________ for the funding support.
4. The police tried to make timely releases of information that __________ to case developments and crime tips.

5. The __________ shown by survivors of Japan's earthquake and tsunami has been lauded in the West, but psychologists worry not talking about the hurt could be doing long-term damage.
6. It is universally acknowledged that the individual is the basic unit of human society and is endowed with __________ rights.
7. People are squeezing the last bit out of the shampoo, and financial reports from major companies show __________ with things like razor blades, laundry detergent and toothpaste.
8. Berlusconi has denied doing anything illegal in any of the cases and says he has been unfairly targeted by politically motivated __________ who want to bring him down.
9. La Fontaine's resistance takes the shape of the Fables, a literature of protest against a __________ government in the height of its decline.
10. The government should create an __________ environment for young people to compete freely and build their career.
11. The videographers would record this great moment for __________.
12. At that time, farmers only enjoyed one-quarter of the __________ of their urban counterparts.
13. Migration to cities helps rural woman workers to be free of __________, family conflicts and the major suicide tool: pesticide.
14. Two young men were charged with conspiracy to rob and conspiracy to commit __________ bodily harm.

III. Debate

Directions: Freedom of speech is one of the basic tenets of democracy. A fundamental right enshrined in the US Bill of Rights, the UN Declaration of Human Rights, and the European Convention on Human Rights, freedom of speech is, nevertheless, not an absolute. Most nations have laws against sedition, libel, or speech that threatens public safety. Things have been increasingly complicated with the development of Internet. Debate on the following motion: ***This House would censor the Internet.***

Section B Words in my heart tell me "I am strong"

Directions: Read the following statements, and decide whether they agree with the information provided in the passage. Mark

Y for Yes if the statement agrees with the passage

N for No if the statement does not agree with the passage

NG for NOT GIVEN if it is impossible to know from the passage

Nura Koleji rubs her toe in the ochre dust, hugs her knees to her stomach, and keeps her eyes firmly downcast—until we hit on the one topic she is bubbling to talk about. It is not how she fled her village of Lanya when AK47-wielding soldiers arrived from the north during the Sudanese civil war. Nor how they kidnapped her brother to train him as a child soldier; how she watched as they picked out victims and shot them; or how her two uncles were among those butchered in front of her.

It is not even the topic I am here to speak to her about—why she decided to train as a mechanic. What really riles Nura is men's dominance in the workplace. Last week South Sudan, became an independent country following a 22-year war that ended in 2005. And in this brand new country, women such as Nura are keen to see changes.

"We have a saying that one hand is not enough to clap. It's true," she tells me. "We need both sexes, not just one. There's an hereditary attitude in my village that women are weaker. I ignore those words and despise the people who say them because I have louder words in my heart telling me I am strong."

Nura is not an activist; she has never heard the word "feminist". She is a 20-year-old, softly spoken Sudanese girl, wearing oil-slicked blue mechanic's overalls. When she graduates next year she, along with three other female classmates, will have defied the odds to become the first women mechanics in South Sudan.

By the time we meet at 9am, I've dressed, had breakfast and negotiated the potholed roads of Juba, Southern Sudan's de facto capital, to reach the technical college, a secondary school where the 470 students (85% of whom are boys) train to become electricians, bricklayers, carpenters or mechanics. Nura, meanwhile, has collected water from a borehole, swept her family's compound, poured tea for her six younger siblings, revised, and picked mangoes before her two-hour walk to school. After classes finish at 3 pm, she will sell the fruit at Juba market and put the earnings towards her £41-a-year school fees.

As her 16-year-old classmate Pamela Daniel says: "If you live here, everything is a struggle. But if you don't struggle, you may as well spend your life asleep because nothing will come to you."

Nura chose this profession partly because she loves cars, partly because she would love to drive (but has neither the money nor facilities to learn), and partly because she wanted technical skills and a trade, rather than a traditional academic education. One motive, however, supersedes the rest; Nura believes there are no female role models in Southern Sudan and her ambition is to become the first.

This is quite a task for a girl whose mother is absent (she was separated as they fled Lanya during the war), whose father has no job, and whose income from trading mangoes leaves her with just enough money to pay school fees and buy shoes, but not enough for an exercise book. Even so, Nura has already overcome obstacles that halt the education of the majority of her peers.

Though 87% of Southern Sudanese women are illiterate, Nura and her classmates can read. While they live with their parents, the majority of girls in South Sudan girls are married off at

13. "Parents value the dowry more than their girls' education and freedom," says English teacher Emelda Elizulai Melling. And with the average dowry around 200 cows (vast numbers of the population earn less than £97 a year and the cheapest cow costs £280), it is not hard to understand why.

Even menstruation is a challenge. "When a girl has her period, she does not attend classes because she doesn't have the appropriate facilities," says Angelina Alel Habib, spokeswoman for Plan International in Southern Sudan. Luckily for Nura and her classmates, their teacher spends part of her wage on sanitary towels for the girls.

Then there is the fact that as the only four female mechanics students in a class of 60 boys, they faced relentless teasing and family opposition. "My neighbours laughed [at] my overalls. They said girls should not be mechanics," says 17-year-old Natalina Kiden, who would like to be a chauffeur but "doesn't want to rely on men for anything"—not even fixing a car.

Pamela, who hopes to train as an aeroplane mechanic, spent three days persuading her mother to let her go to technical college. "She thought automechanics was a dangerous and dirty job for men," says Pamela.

Nura, meanwhile, likes her overalls, despite the ridicule they provoke. And she doesn't worry that men might find her independence unattractive, or that when she marries, her husband might ban her from working. "I'll talk to my husband in a polite way and make sure he accepts my work," she tells me. "He will not refuse. I am determined. I will keep talking until he lets me."

This, after all, is a society with stringent gender-based traditions. "When women pour water for their husbands, they must kneel as a sign of respect," says Habib. And while sharia law was not imposed in the south of Sudan as it is in the north, its strict code has still restricted women's behaviour; for instance women are not supposed to speak in public. "One of the exciting changes our independence will bring is that women will finally be able to speak freely," says Habib.

Other equalities, such as increasing numbers of women in the workforce from the current 30%, will inevitably take longer. "It is not easy for men to adjust to the new economic status of women," warns mechanics teacher Francis Osumba. Juba college, which was built in the 1950s, only began accepting female students in 2005 to study bricklaying, and automechanics in 2008.

So far the students have mastered welding and engine cleaning, learned the entire anatomy of a car and even been taught how to make tables and chairs using scrap sheets of zinc—despite a poorly equipped workshop.

Nura dismisses these obstacles with touching optimism. Does she worry that male owners of car repair firms will be reluctant to hire a girl? "No," she says, insisting she will instead be a walking role model when women see her on the street in mechanic's overalls.

Osumba agrees: "The girls want to disprove people who say mechanical work is just for boys. It is not easy for them but they've passed their first and second year exams so why shouldn't they be given the same chance as the males?" Why not, indeed.

(By Laura Powell, from *The Guardian*)

1. Nura Koleji and her classmates were always injured during training. This time, she hurt her toe.
2. Nura suffered a lot during the Civil War.
3. Nura didn't like the topic why she decided to train as a mechanic, because she was worried about others' negative remarks.
4. The most important reason for Nura's decision to be a mechanic is that she wants to show equal ability between men and women.
5. The majority of Northern Sudanese women are illiterate, unable to read.
6. The training school Nura went to is a government-funded one, free of tuition.
7. Nura, on her way of fighting against gender equality, got support from many of her friends and relatives.
8. Like Nura, Pamela Daniel also came from a poor family without her mother.
9. Nura's teacher believed that the number of women in the workforce would soon overtake that of men.
10. Gender discrimination have been exiting in the Southern Sudan for a long time, thus it would be difficult to solve the problem effectively.
11. Nura was so proud that she has become one of the first women mechanics in South Sudan.
12. In spite of the male-dominated society she was living in, Nura was optimistic towards her own future as a successful mechanist.

Part 4 Reading Comprehension Test

Directions: Read the following passages and choose the best answer to each of the following questions.

Passage 1

Last week was the 35th anniversary of the return of the American death penalty. It remains as racist and as random as ever.

Several years after the death penalty was reinstated in 1976, a University of Iowa law professor, David C. Baldus (who died last month), along with two colleagues, published a study examining more than 2,000 homicides that took place in Georgia beginning in 1972. They found that black defendants were 1.7 times more likely to receive the death penalty than white defendants and that murderers of white victims were 4.3 times more likely to be sentenced to death than those who killed blacks.

What became known as the Baldus study was the centerpiece of the Supreme Court's 1987 decision in McCleskey v. Kemp. That case involved a black man, Warren McCleskey, who was sentenced to die for murdering a white Atlanta police officer. Mr. McCleskey argued that the Baldus study established that his death sentence was tainted by racial bias. In a 5-to-4 decision, the Supreme Court ruled that general patterns of discrimination do not prove that racial discrimination operated in particular cases.

Of course, the court had to say that, or America's capital justice system would have screeched to a halt. Georgia is not special. Nationwide, blacks and whites are victims of homicide in roughly equal numbers, yet 80 percent of those executed had murdered white people. Over the past three decades, the Baldus study has been replicated in about a dozen other jurisdictions, and they all reflect the same basic racial bias. By insisting on direct evidence of racial discrimination, the court in McCleskey essentially made the fact of pervasive racism legally irrelevant, because prosecutors rarely write e-mails announcing they are seeking death in a given case because the murderer was black (or because the victim was white).

In Texas, though, they do come close. In 2008, the district attorney of Harris County, Chuck Rosenthal, resigned after news emerged that he had sent and received racist e-mails. His office had sought the death penalty in 25 cases; his successor has sought it in 7. Of the total 32 cases, 29 involve a nonwhite defendant.

Since 1976, Texas has carried out 470 executions (well more than a third of the national total of 1,257). You can count on one hand the number of those executions that involved a white murderer and a black victim and you do not need to use your thumb, ring finger, index finger or pinkie.

Well, you might need the pinkie. On June 16, Texas executed Lee Taylor, who at age 16 beat an elderly couple while robbing their home. The 79-year-old husband died of his injuries. Mr. Taylor was sentenced to life in prison; there he joined the Aryan Brotherhood, a white gang, and, four years into his sentence, murdered a black inmate and was sentenced to death. When Mr. Taylor was executed, it was reported that he was the second white person in Texas executed for killing a black person. Actually, he should be counted as the first. The other inmate, Larry Hayes, executed in 2003, killed two people, one of whom was white.

The facts surrounding Lee Taylor's execution are cause for further shame. John Balentine, a black inmate, was scheduled to die in Texas the day before Lee Taylor's execution. Mr. Balentine's lawyers argued that his court-appointed appellate lawyer had botched his case, and that he should have an opportunity to raise issues the lawyer had neglected. Less than an hour before Mr. Balentine was to die, the Supreme Court issued a stay.

Lee Taylor's lawyers watched the Balentine case closely; their client too had received scandalously bad representation, and, they filed a petition virtually identical to the one in the Balentine case. But by a vote of 5-to-4, the justices permitted the Taylor execution to proceed. If there were differences between the Balentine and Taylor cases, they were far too minor to form the boundary between life and death. But trivial distinctions are commonplace in death penalty cases. Justice Lewis F. Powell Jr., one of the five justices in the McCleskey majority, retired from the court in 1987. Following his retirement he said he had voted the wrong way. If Justice Powell had changed his mind sooner, Warren McCleskey, who was executed in Georgia in 1991, would still be alive.

And because of a vote from a single Supreme Court justice, John Balentine lives while Lee Taylor died. When capital punishment was briefly struck down, in 1972, Justice Potter Stewart said the death penalty was arbitrary, like being struck by lightning.

It still is, and it's the justices themselves who keep throwing the bolts.

(776 words, from *the New York Times* July 8, 2011, by David R. Dow)

1. What is the best title for this passage?
   A. Death Penalty, Still Controversy
   B. Racism, Still a Deep-rooted Problem in US
   C. Death Penalty, Still Racist and Arbitrary
   D. US, On the Way to Abolish Racism
   E. The Complicated American Capital Justice System
2. Which of the following statements is False about Baldus study?
   A. It was carried out several years after 1976, but the result was revealed only last week.
   B. It was published by 3 teachers in University of Iowa.
   C. The study focused on murder cases in the State of Georgia.
   D. People who kill white citizens were 4.3 times more likely to be sentenced to death than those who kill black citizens.
   E. Black people accused of murder were 1.7 times more likely to be sentenced to death than white people who committed the same thing.
3. What can be inferred from the first sentence of the 4th paragraph?
   A. The Supreme Court's decision on McCleskey case is absolutely right and understandable.
   B. The Supreme Court need to reconsider their decision on McCleskey's case.
   C. The Supreme Court should halt the American capital justice system.
   D. The Supreme Court would be in greater trouble if they had made an opposite decision on McCleskey's case.
   E. People will not be angry about racism in judicial system if the Supreme Court had made the opposite decision.
4. Who is actually the first white person in Texas executed for killing a black person?
   A. Larry Hayes B. Balentine C. Lee Taylor D. McCleskey
   E. None of these four
5. How many defendants were actually sentenced to death among these 4 defendants mentioned in Question 4?
   A. 0 B. 1 C. 2 D. 3
   E. 4
6. According to Justice Potter Stewart, whether a murderer would be sentenced to death

depends on ________.

A. race
B. gender
C. state laws
D. the ability of layers
E. luck

7. It can be inferred from the passage that the author's attitude towards American justice system is ________.

A. ambivalent
B. supportive
C. contradictory
D. discontent
E. indifferent

Passage 2 More female grads, but what about pay?

Today, it's no secret that women are more likely to earn college degrees than men. Since 1996, we've been earning more bachelor's degrees. Now, the 2010 Census shows that more women (10.6 million) hold master's degrees than men (10.5 million) do. In the academic year 2008-2009, the Council of Graduate Schools reports that by a bare majority, women also earned more doctoral degrees, 50.4%.

One would be mistaken, though, to assume equality in education has translated to equality in the workforce. Women still earn less than men, roughly 77 cents for every dollar a man working full-time earns. In some sectors, such as financial services, women earn as little as 65 cents to a man's dollar.

Even in higher education, equality in the upper ranks of academia is still lacking. Women are more likely to be found among the untenured than the tenured, and in adjunct instead of full-time teaching. Last year, a study by the National Center for Education Statistics showed that even when men and women hold the same academic rank, pay gaps remain. Female college presidents remain a minority (23%) among academic leaders, just as women are far less likely to head Fortune 500 companies, be elected to public office or hold other positions of power in our society.

This is not to say the headway women are making in education won't one day reshape gender and family dynamics. Women, for example, have had lower jobless rates than men in this recession (in April, the unemployment rate for women was 7.9% vs. 8.8% for men). When women's degrees lead to higher earnings and more jobs, perhaps we'll begin to see more stay-at-home dads, too. In the African-American community, women's higher educational attainment is often associated with lower marriage rates and less childbearing. Will the same become true for other communities?

Indeed, you know the nation has changed when people have even suggested that the continuing gender gap in college admissions—57% women to 43% men, according to the American Council on Education—might necessitate affirmative action for men. But before we declare victory and go there, remember that not all that long ago, the nation was concerned that schoolgirls were lagging far behind boys. So let's cheer our gains in education while understanding that the problem has not been adequately solved until women receive pay equal to their educational attainment.

(393 words, From *USA Today*, by Julianne Malveaux)

8. What is the main idea of the first paragraph?
   A. It should be made known that women earn more college degrees than men.
   B. There are more female doctoral degree holders than male holders since 1996.
   C. Gender equality in education is still a problem in US.
   D. There are more female college degree receivers than male ones during recent years.
   E. Unequal payment for different genders is still popular in US during recent years.
9. Which of the following statements is TRUE according to the passage?
   A. Women in financial services earn even less than women in other fields.
   B. Women are still far less likely to be appointed leaders in many areas.
   C. Women have been making great progress in education, but still it seems impossible to reshape gender and family dynamics.
   D. Women suffered more unemployment cases than men during economic recession.
   E. Most of the women in African American community prefer going to university than marriage.
10. The "affirmative action" in the last paragraph may refer to ________.
   A. policies that take factors including race, color or gender into consideration in order to benefit an underrepresented group
   B. demonstrations against racial and gender discrimination
   C. government bodies in charge of racial and gender equality
   D. educational institutions that recruit mainly women
   E. institutions that make policies about university admission
11. It can be learned from the last paragraph that the author wrote the passage mainly to ________.
   A. appeal to equal admission rate for men and women
   B. appeal to equal graduate rate for men and women
   C. appeal to equal employment rate for men and women
   D. appeal to equal payment for men and women
   E. all of the above

Passage 3

The District government needs to more aggressively test and enforce housing discrimination law because bias still prevents equal access, according to a report released Thursday by the U.S. Commission on Civil Rights.

After years of education and outreach, landlords continue to refuse to rent to African Americans, builders are erecting apartments that are not accessible to the disabled and few subsidized housing units can be found west of Rock Creek Park, said the report compiled by a commission advisory committee.

The report, "Affirmatively Furthering Fair Housing in the District of Columbia," also urged the city to conduct random testing to make sure rentals, sales, mortgage lending and insurance are free from discrimination.

"More testing of housing providers is one critical step needed to identify and then respond to persistent discrimination in the local housing market," said Roberta Achtenberg, a member of the Civil Rights Commission and a former assistant secretary at the Department of Housing and Urban Development.

Although the city has made progress in removing obstacles to fair housing, as the law requires, "we think in the future the District has to focus much more on outcome or results-oriented measures, and less on process," said Gregory D. Squires, another member of the commission. "They've done a lot of education and outreach. We think they need to do more aggressive, investigative type work."

For example, renters who are using federal housing vouchers can use a city Web site, dchousingsearch.org, to find affordable housing. In December, the site listed 544 rental units, but not one was west of Rock Creek Park, an affluent and predominantly white area of the city, the report said. The D.C. Human Rights Act prohibits landlords from refusing to rent to a tenant because he or she wants to pay with government vouchers, although studies over the past five years show it happens often.

"That's almost like a red flag when there are so few [voucher-eligible units] in that big chunk of the city," Squires said.

In addition, the report said the city has failed to assure that new apartment buildings are accessible to the disabled. Forty-eight percent of the housing complaints recorded by the city's Office of Human Rights between 2002 and 2010 were based on disability issues.

The report also said the city insufficiently monitors bank data to be sure the companies are not discriminating in loan origination or foreclosure practices.

That prompted responses from two city agencies. Nicholas A. Majett, director of the Department of Consumer and Regulatory Affairs, said his office was not aware of any building permits issued either by city officials or certified third-party inspectors that did not meet accessibility requirements.

William P. White, the acting commissioner of the Department of Insurance, Securities and Banking, noted that historically the District and all the states are barred from exercising regulatory authority over federally chartered banks, although the city monitors the activities of lenders through third-party reports. The city recently began a program which requires lenders to offer homeowners the option of mediation before foreclosures can begin.

The Equal Rights Center, a national non-profit agency that conducts the kind of undercover investigations of discrimination that the committee encouraged, said in a statement that "more than a dozen ERC surveys conducted in recent years documented multiple accessibility violations at every property."

(547 words, from *Washington Post* 2011/07/15, by Patricia Sullivan)

12. According to the U.S. Commission on Civil Rights, discrimination in housing still exists, against all of the following groups EXCEPT ________.
    A. African Americans
    B. disabled people
    C. residents in Rock Creek Park
    D. government voucher-users
    E. old people
13. Which of the following statement is Not True, according to the passage?
    A. The U.S. Commission on Civil Rights urged the city to conduct random testing.
    B. The U.S. Commission on Civil Rights called for equality in rentals, sales, mortgage lending and insurance.
    C. The Civil Rights Commission considered testing of housing tenants an important step to identify and then respond to persistent discrimination.
    D. The problem of housing discrimination has been less serious after years of education and outreach.
    E. The Civil Rights Commission recommended focusing more on results-oriented measures, rather than process.
14. According to the passage, federal housing voucher holders ________.
    A. can use a city Web site, dchousingsearch.org, to find affordable housing in the west of Rock Creek Park
    B. can establish a city website to campaign against housing discrimination
    C. can resort to the D.C. Human Rights Act if landlords refuse to rent houses to them
    D. seldom face housing discrimination under the protection of the D. C. Human Rights Act in the past five years
    E. are mostly people of ethnic minorities
15. The reports urged the government to ________.
    A. assure accessibility of all apartment buildings to the disabled.
    B. monitor bank data to be sure the companies are not discriminating in loan origination or foreclosure practices
    C. require renters to offer homeowners the option of mediation before foreclosures can begin.
    D. exercise regulatory authority over all the banks and housing companies
    E. close two city agencies

Passage 4 True to Episcopal Church's Past, Bishops Split on Gay Weddings

The Episcopal Church, which has been strained by gay-rights issues since the election of an openly gay bishop in New Hampshire eight years ago, is now divided over how to respond to the legalization of same-sex marriage in New York.

As a result, gay and lesbian Episcopalians will be allowed on Sunday to get married by priests in Brooklyn and Queens, but not in the Bronx or Manhattan or on Staten Island; in Syracuse but not in Albany.

That is because the church has not taken a firm position nationally on same-sex marriage, leaving local bishops with wide latitude to decide what priests may do when the law takes effect in New York State. In the state, with six Episcopal dioceses, the bishops arc split: two have given the green light for priests to officiate at same-sex marriages, one has said absolutely not, two are undecided and one has staked out a middle ground, allowing priests to bless, but not officiate at, weddings of gay men and lesbians.

The Episcopal Church, known as one of the most welcoming to gay men and lesbians among mainline Protestant denominations, finds itself in an uneasy position on the issue—embracing neither the clear stance against same-sex marriage taken by Roman Catholic, evangelical Protestant, Muslim, Mormon and Orthodox Jewish leaders, nor the supportive position of Reform Jewish, Unitarian Universalist and many liberal Protestant leaders. The Episcopal Church is a small denomination—the church claims 172,623 members in New York State—but is also prestigious and influential.

Now, gay and lesbian Episcopalians are finding their joy at the legalization of same-sex marriage tempered by the ambiguity over where they stand in their church.

"The Episcopal Church should really communicate that God loves everybody," said Roy Kim, 40, who is engaged to an Episcopal priest, the Rev. Clayton Crawley. "The Episcopal Church does do that better than most churches, but it's a great opportunity now to really, unequivocally say that."

He and Father Crawley worship at St. Paul's Chapel, which is part of Trinity Wall Street in Lower Manhattan. In keeping with the local bishop's directive, Trinity's priests will not officiate at same-sex marriages, and the parish has not decided whether to allow them to bless such unions.

The Episcopal Church's rules define marriage as a "union of a man and a woman" but also say the clergy must "conform to the laws of the state" governing marriage. In 2009, the denomination approved a resolution saying that "bishops, particularly those in dioceses within civil jurisdictions where same-gender marriage, civil unions or domestic partnerships are legal, may provide generous pastoral response to meet the needs of members of this church."

But New York State's bishops differ over just what a "generous pastoral response" means, and even the bishops most supportive of gay rights are struggling to balance their desire to sanctify the relationships of all of their parishioners with their reluctance to further alienate conservative Anglicans in Africa and even the United States.

The bishops of the Long Island and Central New York Dioceses have authorized priests to preside at same-sex weddings; the bishop of the New York Diocese (which includes three of the city's five boroughs) is allowing them to bless but not officiate at such rites; the bishop of the Albany Diocese is barring any involvement by priests; and the bishops of the Rochester and Western New York Dioceses remain undeclared.

"It could appear to someone looking from outside the church that this is all we're talking about, and it isn't," said Bishop Lawrence C. Provenzano of the Long Island Diocese. "It finds its place in the larger question of how you minister to the wider world."

Bishop Provenzano, whose diocese includes Brooklyn and Queens, concluded that a "generous response" allowed presiding over the marriage rite. But Bishop Mark S. Sisk of the New York Diocese found that the "generous response" resolution did not supersede the canon law defining marriage.

"The landscape regarding marriage is still changing across the country, within the church and for gay or lesbian couples themselves," Bishop Sisk, who supported the legalization of same-sex marriage, said in an interview conducted by e-mail. "The church is still in the process of creating liturgies for these rites and incorporating them into church law."

A number of gay Episcopalians professed sympathy for what they viewed as Bishop Sisk's effort to balance competing views.

"That's a fair middle-of-the road-position," said Mary O'Shaughnessy, coordinator of the New York metropolitan area chapter of Integrity USA, which advocates equal treatment for gay men and lesbians in the Episcopal Church. "There is nothing that I will call homophobic about that."

Derek Baker, 46, also expressed understanding for Bishop Sisk's predicament.

"He's between a very pointy rock and a very firm hard place," said Mr. Baker, who plans to have his marriage blessed at the Church of the Ascension in Greenwich Village, where he has been a parishioner for two decades.

The situation is particularly awkward for gay priests like Father Crawley. Bishop Sisk has said that gay and lesbian priests "living in committed relationships" should marry—even though they cannot do so in church.

"That's called hypocrisy," said the Rev. Michael W. Hopkins, rector of the Church of St. Luke & St. Simon Cyrene in Rochester. Father Hopkins is a past president of Integrity USA.

But Bishop Sisk responded, "The expectation that clergy in relationships will marry is not a demand, nor does it come with a specific timeline." He also said clergy members could be creative in fashioning liturgies that might include a civil marriage conducted in the church but solemnized by a secular official, followed by a pastoral blessing offered by a priest.

Some gay and lesbian Episcopalians said they were content to allow the church to proceed slowly because they believed it was moving in what they viewed as the right direction. The issue of same-sex marriage will most likely be raised again at the church's next national conference, next summer.

"The bishop might be completely behind gay marriage, but he also understands that unless we have the conversation, and unless we are patient, the church will break," said Javier Galitó-Cava, a gay Episcopalian and actor who worships at St. Paul's. "I want to kick and scream and say 'How dare you, I'm not a second class citizen'—but if I want this to happen, for myself and for my children, we have to take it one step at a time."

(1,075 words, from *The New York Times*, July, 19, 2011)

16. The decision that Gay and lesbian Episcopalians will be allowed on Sunday to get married by priests in Brooklyn, Queens and Syracuse was actually made by ________.

A. local bishops there B. New York State laws there

C. national regulation D. the majority of citizens there

E. the majority of religious groups there

17. In New York State, where are six Episcopal dioceses, ________ bishops have made their stands clear about same-sex marriage.

A. 2 B. 3 C. 4 D. 5

E. 6

18. According to the passage, which of the following statement is true?

A. Roman Catholic supports same-sex marriage.

B. Muslim supports same-sex marriage.

C. Reform Jewish supports same-sex marriage.

D. the Episcopal Church supports same-sex marriage.

E. Mormon is still hesitating about their position about same-sex marriage

19. Among Roy Kim, Bishop Provenzano, Bishop Sisk, Mary O'Shaughnessy, and Javier Galitó-Cava, ________ of them would probably take a supportive position about same-sex marriage in Church

A. 1 B. 2 C. 3 D. 4

E. 5

20. It can be inferred from the passage that ________.

A. conservative Anglicans in Africa is supportive towards same-sex marriage

B. Bishop Mark S. Sisk of the New York Diocese allowed presiding over the marriage rite

C. An overwhelming majority of gay and lesbian Episcopalians expressed their satisfaction on the current situation

D. after the church's next national conference, a clear result about the church's stand may come out

E. Javier Galitó-Cava were quite angry about the Church's hesitation and lack of progress in this issue

Unit 14

Crime and Punishment

Part 1 Reading Skills

Section A Scanning

Now look at the following table and try to find the answer to each question on the right as quickly as you can.

TRENTON BUS COMPANY

MONDAY TO FRIDAY									
Murrayfield Drive	07.41	08.42	09.42	10.42		15.42	16.42	17.45	19.01
Trenton Parade	07.48	08.49	09.49	10.49		15.49	16.50	17.51	19.08
St. Clement's Church	07.54	08.55	09.55	10.55	and every hour until	15.55	16.56	17.58	19.16
Tilfield Park	07.59	08.59	09.59	10.59		15.59	17.00	18.03	19.21
Trenton Hospital	08.02	09.02		11.02		16.02	17.03	18.07	19.28
Gately Road	08.10			11.10		16.10	17.12	18.16	19.38
The Broadwalk	08.15	09.15		11.15		16.15	17.18	18.25	19.47
Town Centre	08.22	09.22	10.17	11.22		16.22	17.26	18.34	19.56
SATURDAY TO SUNDAY									
Murrayfield Drive	07.40	09.42	11.42	13.41	15.43		17.48		
Trenton Parade	07.47	09.49	11.49	13.49	15.51		17.54		
St. Clement's Church	07.53	09.55	11.55	13.55	15.57		18.00		
Tilfield Park	07.58	10.00	11.59	13.59	16.01	17.02	18.06		
Trenton Hospital	08.02	10.04	12.03	14.02	16.04	17.07	18.11		
Gately Road	08.11	10.12	12.10	14.12	16.05	17.16	18.21		
The Broadwalk	08.16	10.17	12.15	14.19	16.20	17.23	18.29		
Town Centre	08.23	10.25	12.22	14.27	16.27	17.32	18.40		

1. At what time does the 10:49 bus from Trenton Parade arrive at Gately Road on a Monday?

   A. 11:10　　B. 12:10

   C. 12:15　　D. 11:55

2. If you need to be in the town centre by 11a.m. on a Saturday morning, which bus do you need to catch from Tilfield Park?

   A. 07:58　　B. 10:04

   C. 10:00　　D. 11:59

3. If you want to arrive at The Broadwalk by 15:30 on a Tuesday, which bus do you need to catch from St. Clement's Church?

   A. 14:55　　B. 13:55

   C. 13:59　　D. 14:59

(Quoted from BBC)

When you do the above exercise, you are actually scanning. Scanning is a useful reading skill both in your daily life and in your study. For example, when you look up a name in the telephone book or a word in a dictionary, you use scanning.

Like skimming, scanning is also a way of speed reading. However, different from it, scanning involves looking for specific words or particular details rather than the overall idea. When you read a text, for example, you may only want to find a percentage figure or the dates of particular historical events instead of the main idea. In this case you only need to scan the text, that is, to move your eyes quickly down the page until you find the relevant figure or dates.

Scanning is used when you first find a resource to determine whether it will answer your questions. In most cases when you use scanning, you know what you're looking for, so you just concentrate on finding a particular answer. Scanning is especially useful when you take a linguistic test. Here are some tips to help you find information more efficiently when you take a reading comprehension test.

1. Read the questions first instead of the passage and underline the key words or proper names, numbers etc. in each question.

2. Before scanning, use clues on the page, such as headings and subtitles, to help you.

3. Remember never to try to read every word of the passage.

4. Just move on quickly until you find what you are looking for. While scanning, you should look for the author's use of organizers such as numbers, letters, steps, or the words like first, second, or next etc. You also should pay attention to words that are bold faced, italics, or in a different font size, style, or color.

5. Read the sentence more carefully where the key words are located and sometimes the sentences before or after it and then you will find the correct answer.

Follow the above steps and you will improve both your speed and accuracy.

Section B Practice

Directions: Scan the following passage quickly and finish the exercises. For questions 1-3, write down "T" for true or "F" for false for each statement. For questions 4-5, complete the sentences with the information given in the passage.

Computer Crime

A computer crime is generally defined as one that involves the use of computers and software for illegal purposes. This doesn't mean that all the crimes are new types of crime. On the contrary, many of these crimes, such as embezzlement of funds, the alteration of records, theft, vandalism, sabotage, and terrorism, can be committed without a computer. But with a computer, these offenses can be carried out more quickly and with less chance that the person responsible for the crime will be discovered.

Computer crimes are on the rise and have been for the last twelve years. Just how much these computer crimes cost the American public is in dispute, but estimates range from $3 billion to $5 billion annually. Even the FBI, which attempts to keep track of the growth or decline of all kinds of crimes, is unable to say precisely how large a loss is involved; however, it estimates that the average take from a company hit by computer crime is $600,000. A number of reasons are given for the increase in computer crime: (a) more computers in use and, thus, more people who are familiar with basic computer operation; (b) more computers tied together in satellite and other data—transmission networks; and (c) the easy access of microcomputers to huge mainframe data bases.

The Criminal

Movies and newspaper stories might lead us to believe that most computer crimes are committed by teenage "hackers"—brilliant and basically good children who let their imagination and technical genius get them into trouble. But a realistic look at the crimes reveals that the offender is likely to be an employee of the firm against which the crime has been committed, i.e., an "insider".

Difficulty of Detection and Prevention

Given the kind of person who commits a computer crime and the environment in which the crime occurs, it is often difficult to detect who the criminal is. First of all, the crime may be so complex that months or years go by before anyone discovers it.

Second, once the crime has been revealed, it is not easy to find a clear trail of evidence that leads back to the guilty party. After all, looking for "weapons" or fingerprints does not occur as it might in the investigation of more conventional crimes.

Third, there are usually no witnesses to the computer crime, even though it may be taking place in a room filled with people. Who is to say if the person at the next terminal, calmly keying in data, is doing the company's work or committing a criminal act?

Fourth, not enough people in management and law enforcement know enough about computer technology to prevent the crimes. Authorities have to be familiar with the computer's capabilities within a given situation to guard against its misuses. In some large cities, such as Los Angeles, police departments have set up specially trained computer crime units.

But even when an offender is caught, the investigators, attorneys, judges, or juries may find the alleged crime too complicated and perplexing to handle. More attorneys are specializing in computer law and studying the computer's potential for misuse.

After a computer crime has been discovered, many companies do not report it or prosecute the person responsible. A company may not announce the crime out of fear that the pubic will find out the weaknesses of its computer system and lose confidence in its organization. Banks, credit card companies, and investment firms are especially sensitive about revealing their vulnerabilities because they rely heavily on customer trust.

To avoid public attention, cautious companies will often settle cases of computer tampering out of court. And if cases do go to trial and the offenders are convicted, they may be punished only by a fine or light sentence because the judge or jury isn't fully trained to understand the nature and seriousness of the crime. Not all companies are timid in apprehending computer criminals. For example, Connecticut General Life Insurance Company decided it had to get tough on violators. So when the company discovered that one of its computer technicians had embezzled $200,000 by entering false benefit claims, it presented its findings to the state's attorney and aided in the prosecution of the technician. The technician was found guilty and sentenced to prison, not just for the computer misuse, but also for grand theft and insurance fraud. Connecticut General now has a policy of reporting all incidents of theft or fraud, no matter how small.

(742 words)

1. ________ The FBI knows exactly how large a loss is involved in computer crimes.
2. ________ It is implied in Paragraph 3 that most computer criminals are the employees of the concerned companies.
3. ________ When computer crime takes place in a room filled with people, there are usually many witnesses to the crime.
4. Banks, credit card companies, and investment firms are especially sensitive about revealing their vulnerabilities because they place too much reliance on ________________________.
5. Connecticut General Life Insurance Company is cited as ________________________ of companies that took serious measures to fight against computer crimes.

Part 2 Idioms, Proverbs and Sayings

Directions: The following are idioms, proverbs or sayings by famous people about law. Choose what you think is correct and compare with the right ones.

1. I disapprove of what you say, but I will defend to the death your ________ to say it. (Voltaire)

   A. power B. right C. freedom D. responsibility

2. O ________, how many crimes have been committed in thy name. (Madame Roland)

   A. honesty B. justice C. liberty D. power

3. If there were no bad people, there would be no good ________. (Charles Dickens)

   A. governments B. judges C. courts D. lawyers

4. An upright judge has more ________ to justice than to men.
   A. regard B. respect C. adoration D. criticism
5. Where might is ________, justice is servant.
   A. boss B. owner C. lord D. master
6. Justice has long ________.
   A. hands B. legs C. arms D. teeth
7. Though ________ may darken truth, it cannot put it out.
   A. malice B. lies C. cheat D. evil
8. There is ________ among thieves.
   A. honesty B. honour C. justice D. disagreement
9. ________ is not a crime.
   A. Poverty B. Injustice C. Dishonesty D. Misdeed
10. One of the following statements that sounds logic is made by the British jurist Frederick Pollck. Which do you think is logic?
   A. The law can make all men equal, but they are not all equal before the law.
   B. The law cannot make all men equal, nor are they all equal before the law.
   C. The law cannot make all men equal, but they are all equal before the law.
   D. The law can make all men equal, and they are all equal before the law.

Part 3 Reading Passages

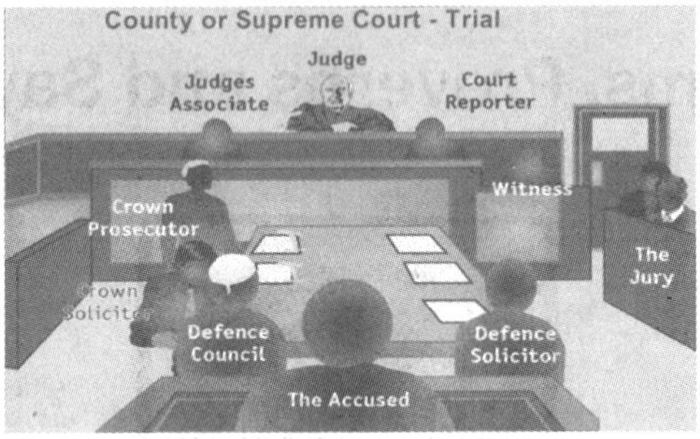

Section A Grad Student's Arrest Makes International News

by Matt Neuteboom

Zhai Tiantian, or TJ as he was called by his friends, was a regular graduate student here at Stevens Institute of Technology before he was arrested on charges of making terroristic threats to the school. Now he sits in the Hudson County Correctional Facility, awaiting his trial and possible deportation, and his case has unexpectedly caught the eye of international press outlets, whose coverage, according to Institute officials, has blown the case out of proportion.

On April 15, Zhai called into the Howe Center Desk and made a verbal threat to burn down one of the campus buildings. The dispatcher reported this threat to the police, who found the threat to be credible and arrested Zhai later that day, said Michael Schinelli, Assistant Vice President of Graduate Marketing and Communications. Since Zhai is a foreign national, a Chinese citizen, the police also informed the Department of Homeland Security (DHS) that they would be making an arrest. The DHS then independently made a decision as to their involvement, and aided campus police with the arrest. There will be a grand jury hearing for Zhai on June 1, when some members of the administration will be testifying. Campus police would not confirm which campus building was threatened in Zhai's call.

Zhai matriculated at Stevens in 2003 and received his Bachelor of Engineering in Civil Engineering and his Master of Engineering in Systems. He was pursuing a Ph.D. in Enterprise Systems at the time of his suspension. Schinelli described Zhai as "well-Americanized and integrated into the Stevens community." The first complaints about Zhai began in February of this year, when members of the Stevens community raised concerns about Zhai's behavior in academics and the workplace. Around early March, Zhai began showing alarming behavior. Stevens officials had an official meeting with Zhai on March 9 to discuss his behavior. An investigation concluded that Zhai's behavior violated the Stevens student code of conduct, though Schinelli could not comment upon the specific infractions because of student privacy laws. Stevens determined that Zhai's behavior was putting other students in jeopardy, and on March 11 he was indefinitely suspended from the school. Zhai appealed the suspension, but the appeal was turned down.

Days earlier on March 5, Zhai was visiting Manhattan to see someone affiliated with NYU. On March 10, he was arrested by the NYPD for aggravated harassment in the second degree connected to events that transpired on March 5. Joseph Stahley, Assistant Vice President of Student Life, clarified that Zhai's suspension was unrelated to this arrest by the NYPD and was a result of a series of events that transpired here on campus alone.

According to media outlets, Zhai denies the charges against him and says he never mentioned destroying campus buildings to anyone. He sees the arrest as an attempt by the Institute to deal with his questioning of the school's authority. Before his suspension, Zhai claims that he had argued with a professor over his academics. In addition, he also previously spoke out against the Institute in a TV interview, threatening to sue the school for discrimination. Hai Ming, Zhai's government-appointed lawyer, said "this is probably the real reason why the school is dealing with him this way."

Zhai's story is notable because it has been taken up by international media who, according to Schinelli, are misreporting the details. China Daily, for example, has reported that Zhai was arrested for charges of terrorism. According to their website, "Zhai has been accused of trying to set fire to a campus building and of making threats to one of his professors with whom he had a disagreement."

However, Schinelli says that these are not the facts of the case. Schinelli said Zhai is charged with making terroristic threats, not with being a terrorist. "Making a terroristic threat is not the same as being accused of being a terrorist. It covers a broad range of offenses and threats...We're not sure what was pushed out there that generated what's probably a hard-to-believe story in this country. Over [in China], it certainly seems plausible that someone might be thrown in jail because they disagreed with a professor. [It's]...not anything that would happen over here in real life. That's obviously not how things work in an American university."

Schinelli does not know where the source of this misinformation came from. Since the story broke, several Chinese press outlets have contacted Schinelli for Stevens' side of the story, and Schinelli has corrected several of their reports. One press outlet thanked him for the corrections and reprinted their story. They even stated that Chinese readers were interested in Stevens side of the story. Other sources such as NJ.com and the Associated Press have contacted Schinelli as well.

Schinelli said that they chose not to publicize the arrest in order to avoid embarrassment for both Zhai and the school. It was not until foreign press became recently involved that the school began receiving phone calls and emails on the matter. Schinelli said, "We do not want to have Mr. Zhai vilified by the media nor do we want Stevens' reputation to be affected."

Schinelli said, "We have an incredible international student community here that we value tremendously." He added, "We were hoping that Mr. Zhai can obviously be returned to his family, that he can receive any help that he needs, and we wish him well. But we certainly want to dispel the stories that we've seen in the foreign press."

(944 words)

I. Reading comprehension

Directions: Choose the best answer to each question according to the passage.

1. Zhai Tiantian, a 27-year-old Chinese citizen was pursuing a ________ at Stevens Institute of Technology in New Jersey.
   A. master degree　B. bachelor degree　C. PhD　D. MBA
2. On April 15, he was arrested found himself charged with ________.
   A. making terroristic threats to the school　B. terrorism
   C. disagreement with the professors　D. racial discrimination
3. The reason for his indefinite suspension from the school is that ________.
   A. Zhai intended to burn down the campus building
   B. Zhai had poor performance in academics and the workplace
   C. Zhai's action was putting other students in danger
   D. Zhai showed his alarming behavior to the public
4. Which of the following statement is not true according to the passage?
   A. Schinelli says that Chinese readers tended to believe that if someone disagreed with a professor, he might be put into prison.

B. According to Schinelli, some international media, such as China Daily, are misreporting the details about Zhai's story.

C. Chinese press outlets contacted Schinelli, and he corrected several misunderstandings in their reports.

D. Making a terroristic threat is just the same as being a terrorist.

5. We may infer from the passage that ________.

A. the reputation of Stevens Institute of Technology has been ruined by this event

B. there is misunderstanding about this event

C. Zhai Tiantian has been criticized by the media

D. Stevens Institute of Technology chooses to hide the truth of this event

II. Vocabulary

Directions: Fill in each blank with an appropriate word from the box below. Each word can be used only once.

dispel	accused	affiliated	suspend
sue	testify	transpired	credible

1. At least 70 witnesses summoned to __________ in Hong Kong will not attend the public inquest on Feb 14, Philippine Justice Minister Leila De Lima announced Friday.
2. China's telecom giant Huawei issued an open letter on Friday saying it welcomes investigations from the US government, if that could __________ misperceptions about the company.
3. US President Barack Obama said on Thursday night that the Egyptian government must put forward "a __________, concrete and unequivocal path toward genuine democracy."
4. It should be provided if you open a bank account, apply for reduction, refund and delay of tax payment, purchase invoices or __________ your business.
5. Google's Street View software has not only pictured almost everyone's residence on the Internet, but it __________ that they also collected individual's wifi data in the process.
6. Pop singer Lady Gaga has threatened to __________ a specialist ice cream parlor in London for naming its breast milk ice cream "Baby Gaga," the shop's owner said on Wednesday.
7. Some US politicians have __________ China of manipulating its currency and claimed the manipulation harms the US economy by thwarting its exports to China.
8. In the US, there are many different sports national organizations, including sports teams like the NBA and NFL, two national collegiate athletic associations, the US Olympic Committee with 45 __________ national sports governing bodies and 35 multi-sports organizations, and a multitude of other organizations.

III. Discussion

Directions: Read the following news and discuss what your interpretation of "bribery" is.

PhD sent to jail for attempted bribery

by Wen Wei Po

A mainland doctorate student at the City University of Hong Kong was sentenced to six months' jail by the district magistrate in Kowloon Town after she admitted to attempted bribery.

The case was the first of its type in Hong Kong. The 25-year-old woman came to Hong Kong from Wuhan, Central China's Hubei Province, in September to do a Ph D in mathematics.

She was accused of offering HK$10,000 to an associate professor in exchange for the details of an examination to be held on December 6.

The academic did not accept the cash and reported her to the Independent Commission Against Corruption (ICAC).

The woman told the court she had sent an anonymous email to her lecturer asking for exam-related confidential information and had left an envelope containing HK$10,000 in his mailbox.

(From *China Daily*, 2006-12-19)

Section B Helicopter Moms vs. Free-Range Kids

Directions: Skim or scan the passage quickly and choose the best answer from the four choices marked A, B, C and D.

Would you let your fourth-grader ride public transportation without an adult? Probably not. Still, when Lenore Skenazy, a columnist for the New York Sun, wrote about letting her son take the subway alone to get back to "Long story short: my son got home from a department store on the Upper East Side, she didn't expect to get hit with a wave of criticism from readers.

"Long story short: My son got home, overjoyed with independence," Skenazy wrote on April 4 in the New York Sun. "Long story longer: Half the people I've told this episode to now want to turn on in for child abuse. As if keeping kids under lock and key and cell phone and careful watch is the right way to rear kids. It's not. It's debilitating—for us and for them."

Online message boards were soon full of people both applauding and condemning Skenazy's decision to let her son go it alone. She wound up defending herself on CNN (accompanied by her son) and on popular blogs like the buffing ton post, where her follow-up piece was ironically headlined "More From America's Worst Mom."

The episode has ignited another one of those debates that divides parents into vocal opposing camps. Are Modern parents needlessly overprotective, or is the world a more complicated and dangerous place than it was when previous generations were allowed to wander about unsupervised?

From the "she's an irresponsible mother" camp came: "Shame on you for being so careless about his safety," in Comments on the buffing ton post. And there was this from a mother of four: "How would you have felt if he didn't come home?" But Skenazy got a lot of support, too, with women and men writing in with stories about how they were allowed to take trips all by themselves at seven or eight. She also got heaps of praise for bucking the "helicopter parent" trend: "Good for this Mom," one commenter wrote on the buffing ton post. "This is a much-needed reality check."

Last week, encouraged by all the attention, Skenazy started her own blog—Free Range, kids—promoting the idea that modern children need some of the same independence that her generation had. In the good old days nine-year-old baby boomers rode their bikes to school, walked to the store, took buses—and even subways—all by themselves. Her blog, she says, is dedicated to sensible parenting. "At Free Range Kids, we believe in safe kids. We believe in car seats and safety belts. We do NOT believe that every time school-age children go outside, they need a security guard."

So why are some parents so nervous about letting their children out of their sight? Are cities and towns less safe and kids more vulnerable to crimes like child kidnap and sexual abuse than they were in previous generations?

Not exactly. New York City, for instance, is safer than it's ever been; it's ranked 36th in crime among all American cities. Nationwide, stringer kidnaps are extremely rare; there's a one-in-a-million chance a child will be taken by a stranger, according to the Justice Department. And 90 percent of sexual abuse cases are committed by someone the child knows. Mortality rates from all causes, including disease and accidents, for American children are lower now than they were 25 years' ago. According to Child Trends, a nonprofit research group, between 1980 and 2003 death rates dropped by 44 percent for children aged 5 to 14 and 32 percent for teens aged 15 to 19.

Then there's the whole question of whether modern parents are more watchful and nervous about safety than previous generations. Yes, some are. Part of the problem is that with wall to wall Internet and cable news, every missing child case gets so much airtime that it's not surprising even normal parental anxiety can be amplified. And many middle-class parents have gotten used to managing their children's time and shuttling them to various enriching activities, so the idea of letting them out on their own can seem like a risk. Back in 1972, when many of today's parents were kids, 87 percent of children who lived within a mile of school walked or biked every day. But today, the Centers for Disease Control report that only 13 percent of children bike, walk or otherwise t themselves to school.

The extra supervision is both a city and a suburb phenomenon. Parents are worried about crime, and they are worried about kids getting caught in traffic in a city that's not used to pedestrians. On the other hand, there are still plenty of kids whose parents give them a lot of independence, by choice or by necessity. The After School Alliance finds that more than 14 million kids aged 5 to 17 are responsible for taking care of themselves after school. Only 6.5

million kids participate in organized programs. "Many children who have working parents have to take the subway or bus to get to school. Many do this by themselves because they have no other way to get to the schools," says Dr. Richard Gallagher, director of the Parenting Institute at the New York University Child Study Center.

For those parents who wonder how and when they should start allowing their kids more freedom, there's no clear-cut answer. Child experts discourage a one-size-fits-all approach to parenting. What's right for Skenazy's nine-year-old could be inappropriate for another one. It all depends on developmental issue, maturity, and the psychological and emotional makeup of that child. Several factors must be taken into account, says Gallagher. "The ability to follow parent guidelines, the child's level of comfort in handling such situations, and a child's general judgment should be weighed."

Gallagher agrees with Skenazy that many nine-year-olds are ready for independence like taking public transportation alone. "At certain times of the day, on certain routes, the subways are generally safe for these children, especially if they have grown up in the city and have been taught how to be safe, how to obtain help if they are concerned for their safety, and how to avoid unsafe situations by being watchful and on their toes."

But even with more traffic and fewer sidewalks, modern parents do have one advantage their parents didn't: the cell phone. Being able to check in with a child anytime goes a long way toward relieving parental anxiety and may help parents loosen their control a little sooner. Skenazy got a lot of criticism because she didn't give her kid her cell phone because she thought he'd lose it and wanted him to learn to go it alone without depending on mom—a major principle of free-range parenting. But most parents are more than happy to use cell phones to keep track of their kids.

And for those who like the idea of free-range kids but still struggle with their inner helicopter parent, there may be a middle way. A new generation of GPS cell phones with tracking software make it easier than ever to follow a child's every movement via the Internet—without seeming to interfere or hover. Of course, when they go to college, they might start objecting to being monitored as they're on parole.

(1,209 words)

1. When Lenore Skenazy's son was allowed to take the subway alone, he ________.
   A. was afraid that he might get lost　　B. enjoyed having the independence
   C. was only too pleased to take the risk　　D. thought he was an exceptional child
2. Lenore Skenazy believes that keeping kids under careful watch ________.
   A. hinders their healthy growth　　B. adds too much to parents' expenses
   C. shows traditional parental caution　　D. bucks the latest parenting trend
3. Skenazy's decision to let her son take the Subway alone has met with ________.
   A. opposition from her own family　　B. share parenting experience
   C. fight against child abuse　　D. protect children's rights
4. According to the author, New York City ________.

A. ranks high in road accidents
B. is much safe than before
C. ranks low in child mortality rates
D. is less dangerous than small cities

5. According to child experts, how and when kids may be allowed more freedom depends on ________.

A. the traditions and customs of the community
B. the safety conditions of their neighborhood
C. their parents' psychological makeup
D. their maturity and personal qualities

Part 4 Reading Comprehension Test

Passage 1

Directions: Skim the following passage as quickly as possible and choose the best answer to the question.

First read the question.

1. The main purpose of the passage is to ________.

A. demonstrate how to prevent crime
B. show the seriousness of crime
C. look into the causes of crime
D. call for more government efforts

Now scan the TEXT quickly to answer the question.

For three weeks, every night at 11 p.m., correspondents, officers and judges from justice courts, police departments and prisons, psychiatrists, criminologists, victims and even criminals in prisons made their appearance on TV to debate on a topic "Crime in the United States".

Indeed, crime has been disturbing the American people and has become a serious social problem just next to the unemployment problem. Some figures are terrifying: 1 of 4 Americans has been a victim of some kind of crimes; nearly 22 million crime cases occurred last year throughout the country. A simple arithmetic calculation indicates that on average, a crime is being committed in every 2 seconds. Now the Americans are living in a horrible environment. Their safety and property are threatened by various crimes: robbery, theft, rape, kidnapping, murder, arson, vandalism and violence.

The most worrisome problem comes from the fact that about one third of crime cases were committed by the juvenile and 53% of criminals in jails are youngsters below 25. A poll indicates that about 73% of citizens said they avoided teenagers in streets, especially at night.

To protect themselves from crime, according to a released figure, 52% of Americans keep guns at home. But some gun owners turn out to be potential criminals. Some people demand that strict law for gun control be enforced; but others oppose the ban of gun. No decision is in sight.

Some experts said poverty, unemployment and racial discrimination are the cause of crime. They cited figures to show that 47% of crime cases were committed by the black, though they account for only about 12% of the population of the nation.

Others argued that about 54% of convicted criminals came from families associated with these evils. The American state government and federal government spend billions of dollars each year in maintaining the police departments and jails. But police authorities complain that they have not sufficient well-trained hands and advanced equipment to detect and stop crimes. Several cases of criminal insurgence were reported as a result of resentment at overcrowded prisons. Taxpayers complain that they pay more and more tax but receive less and less protection from crime for their lives and property.

Though the host of the live TV programme made great efforts to search for a solution, so far no participant could put forward a measure that was approved by most of the attendants.

(397 words)

Passage 2

Directions: Scan the following three pieces of news and write down "T" for true or "F" for false for each statement based on the passages.

Woman's injury now an international issue

by GENE WARNER

The alleged beating of a Chinese businesswoman by a Customs and Border Protection officer at the Rainbow Bridge last week has turned into an international issue.

The attack against Zhao Yan, a 37-year-old woman visiting the Falls on a business trip to the United States, left her with both eyes nearly swollen shut and the officer, Robert Rhodes, 43, of Niagara Falls, facing a serious criminal charge.

But the incident, which occurred at about 11:15 p.m. last Wednesday night, also has led to these developments: Secretary of State Colin L. Powell and Chinese Foreign Minister Li Zhaoxing have discussed the incident, with the Chinese official demanding an investigation and the State Department later vowing to conduct a thorough probe.

Zhao's attorney has vowed to file a lawsuit seeking at least $5 million in the incident, which the attorney called an assault on an innocent civilian. The incident at the Rainbow Bridge also has led to headlines in at least several newspapers in China, with the victim calling the United States a "barbarous" and "brutal" place. "I felt deeply humiliated," Zhao told the *South China Morning Post*. "I have been to many countries, but the U.S. is the most brutal place."

The China Daily showed a photo of Zhao's bruise-covered face. And *the People's Daily* quoted her as saying that she's been to many nations for business reasons, "and the United

States is the most barbarous." Rhodes was accused of using excessive physical force and pepper spray to subdue Zhao. The officer apparently thought—mistakenly—that she was one of three women accompanying a drug suspect at the pedestrian checkpoint on the bridge. Law-enforcement officials said Rhodes was suspended from his job, before being charged with a federal civil-rights violation involving bodily harm. The charge is punishable by up to 10 years in prison and a $250,000 fine. Rhodes was released on a $50,000 signature bond and ordered to appear again before U.S. Magistrate Judge Hugh B. Scott on Sept. 20.

"We take this matter very seriously," U.S. Attorney Michael A. Battle said Tuesday. "It's the responsibility of our office to investigate cases of alleged civil-rights violations." The incident started when a male pedestrian had cleared customs at the bridge, before he was found carrying several pounds of marijuana. According to an affidavit filed in U.S. District Court by the Department of Homeland Security, Rhodes hit the "duress" button and called for assistance. He later told superiors he asked the three women to come inside the inspection station, but instead they started to run. He then grabbed the nearest woman, Zhao. Rhodes told officials that the woman tried to pull away from him and swung her arms at him, before he sprayed her with pepper spray. Other officers, however, have claimed that Rhodes also threw Zhao into a wall, grabbed her hair, kneed her in the head and struck her head on the ground, according to the affidavit. In his affidavit, Senior Special Agent Steven MacMartin of the Department of Homeland Security stated that the Chinese woman suffered swollen eyes, bruises around the eyes and a contusion on her forehead.

Zhao has claimed that her two friends fled immediately when officers first approached them, but she felt she had done nothing wrong, so she stayed put. "Whenever I hear a man speaking English or see one wearing a U.S. police uniform, it makes me cringe," Zhao told the South China Morning Post. "The assault not only physically harmed me, but also left me with mental trauma."

(587 words, from *News Staff Reporter* 7/28/2004)

US regrets for beating of Chinese woman

In a telephone call to Lan Lijun, charge d'affaires of the Chinese embassy, Ridge described the beating of the Chinese businesswoman as "a horrible incident" which was "totally unacceptable" and expressed "great regret" to the Chinese government and people.

Ridge said that Robert Rhodes, the first officer of the US Customs and Border Protection to attack Zhao Yan, had been charged with felony assault, Chinese embassy officials said.

Ridge said he had asked the US Customs and Border Protection officers to take measures to prevent such incidents from happening again, Chinese embassy officials said.

Lan Lijun urged the US side to make thorough investigations into the case, punish persons responsible and keep the Chinese side informed of the investigation and handling process.

Zhao Yan, a businesswoman from China's northern coastal city of Tianjin, was on her first US business trip when she was attacked at the Niagara Falls near the US-Canadian border on

July 21 by Rhodes and other officers of the US Customs and Border Protection. Zhao Yan said on Wednesday that six days after she was brutally attacked, she was still suffering from a bad headache, swollen eyes and mental trauma. She also had a broken tooth and severe back pains which forced her to ride a wheelchair. Because of the sharp physical pain and mental trauma caused by the beating, she could "barely sleep two to three hours a day."

Chinese Foreign Minister Li Zhaoxing, during a telephone conversation with US Secretary of State Colin Powell on Monday, urged the US government to carry out a thorough investigation into the attack and bring those responsible for the incident to justice.

"We regret the apparent mistreatment of a Chinese national by a US customs officer in Niagara Falls," the US State Department said in a statement Thursday.

"We have communicated to the Chinese Government that the US customs officer was arrested by Customs and Border Patrol Police and his case referred for criminal prosecution," it said.

Powell also wrote to his Chinese counterpart Li Zhaoxing after their phone conversation that the United States government would thoroughly investigate the beating case of a Chinese citizen Zhao Yan according to US laws.

In a letter that Chinese Foreign Minister Li Zhaoxing received in Beijing on Thursday, Powell said he felt deeply disturbed when he learned of the mistreatment that Chinese citizen Zhao Yan underwent at the hands of US Customs and Border Protection officers.

Powell said that the accused officer has been suspended from his post and detained on charges of felony assault, pledging that the US government would continue its thorough investigation. "Secretary Powell has been very clear that America is an open society; we welcome visitors from around the world, and our goal is to ensure that they have a safe and enjoyable stay in the United States," the State Department statement said. It said the United States would ensure that such incidents did not recur.

The department had pledged earlier this week that the US authorities would get to the bottom of the case.

(507 words, from *http://newyork.china-consulate.org*)

American pleads not guilty in Zhao Yan case

NEW YORK, Aug. 13 (Xinhuanet)—US Homeland Security Customs Inspector Robert Rhodes entered a not-guilty plea Friday to federal charges of violating the civil rights of Chinese businesswoman Zhao Yan.

Speaking to reporters after he appeared at federal court in Buffalo, Rhodes claimed he did his job the way he had been trained and used the proper level of force.

Zhao said Rhodes grabbed her, kneed her in the head and slammed her head into the ground in the mistaken belief that she was involved in a drug case.

Rhodes was indicted by a federal grand jury for beating up Zhao Wednesday. According to the indictment, Rhodes "while acting undercolor of law, did strike and hit Yan Zhao with his knee and did forcibly drive her head into contact with the pavement, resulting in bodily injury to Yan Zhao, and thereby did willfully deprive her of the right secured and protected by the Constitution and laws of the United States to be free from the use of unreasonable force by one acting under color of law."

Rhodes said she kicked and scratched him and his reaction was appropriate.

Assistant US Attorney Martin Littlefield said the prosecutors were ready to present evidence and "could start trial Monday."

He denied charges by Rhodes' attorney Steve Cohen that there was political pressure to prosecute Rhodes quickly and firmly.

Rhodes' attorney has until Oct. 1 to conduct any fact finding and report back to Federal Court.

(243 words, from *http://www.people.com.cn*)

2. Many Chinese news media called the United States a "barbarous" and "brutal" place. ________
3. The Customs and Border Protection officer thought Zhao Yan was one of the three women accompanying a drug suspect at the pedestrian checkpoint on the Rainbow Bridge. ________
4. The assault not only left her physical pain, but also mental trauma. ________
5. At federal court in Buffalo, Rhodes claimed he was told to use force to do his job. ________
6. Rhodes did strike and hit Yan Zhao, resulting in bodily injury, but he did not deprive her of the right secured and protected by American laws. ________
7. Rhodes' attorney Steve Cohen claimed that there was political pressure to prosecute Rhodes quickly and firmly. ________
8. Ridge expressed "great regret" to the Chinese government and people, describing the beating of the Chincsc businesswoman as "a horrible incident." ________
9. The accused officer has been suspended from his post and sentenced to 10 years in prison and a $250,000 fine. ________
10. Rhodes' attorney has to conduct any fact finding and report back to Federal Court after Oct. 1. ________

Passage 3

Directions: Read the passage carefully and choose the best answer from the four choices marked A, B, C and D.

A court is a form of tribunal, often a governmental institution, with the authority to adjudicate legal disputes between parties and carry out the administration of justice in civil, criminal, and administrative matters in accordance with the rule of law. In both common law and civil law legal systems, courts are the central means for dispute resolution, and it is generally understood that all persons have an ability to bring their claims before a court.

Similarly, the rights of those accused of a crime include the right to present a defense before a court.

The system of courts that interpret and apply the law are collectively known as the judiciary. The place where a court sits is known as a venue. The room where court proceedings occur is known as a courtroom, and the building as a courthouse; court facilities range from simple and very small facilities in rural communities to large buildings in cities.

The practical authority given to the court is known as its jurisdiction—the court's power to decide certain kinds of questions or petitions put to it. According to William Blackstone's *Commentaries on the Laws of England,* a court is constituted by a minimum of three parties: the *actor* or plaintiff, who complains of an injury done; the *reus* or defendant, who is called upon to make satisfaction for it, and the *judex* or judicial power, which is to examine the truth of the fact, to determine the law arising upon that fact, and, if any injury appears to have been done, to ascertain and by its officers to apply a legal remedy. It is also usual in the superior courts to have attorneys, and advocates or counsel, as assistants, though, often, courts consist of additional attorneys, bailiffs, reporters, and perhaps a jury.

The term "the court" is also used to refer to the presiding officer or officials, usually one or more judges. The judge or panel of judges may also be collectively referred to as "the bench" (in contrast to attorneys and barristers, collectively referred to as "the bar"). In the United States, and other common law jurisdictions, the term "court" (in the case of U.S. federal courts) by law is used to describe the judge himself or herself.

In the United States, the legal authority of a court to take action is based on personal jurisdiction, subject-matter jurisdiction, and venue over the parties to the litigation.

11. A court implements the administration of justice in ________ in accordance with the rule of law.

    A. national, criminal and administrative matters

    B. civil, criminal, and administrative affairs

    C. national, criminal and management matters

    D. civil, criminal and management affairs

12. In the system of courts, the room where court proceedings occur is known as a ________, and the building as a ________.

    A. courtroom, courtbuilding   B. courthouse, courtplace

    C. courthouse, courtbuilding   D. courtroom, courthouse

13. The practical authority given to the court is known as ________.

    A. judiciary   B. venue   C. jurisdiction   D. juries

14. According to William Blackstone's *Commentaries on the Laws of England,* the *judex* is to ________.

    A. present a defendant and a plaintiff before the court.

    B. examine the truth of the fact

    C. determine the law arising upon that fact

D. both B and C

15. "The bar" has been used to refer to ________.

A. bailiffs and reporters B. the judge or panel of judges

C. attorneys and barristers D. the presiding officer or officials

Passage 4

Directions: Read the passage carefully and choose the best answer from the four choices marked A, B, C and D.

Should anyone much care whether an American boy living overseas gets six cruel thwacks on his backside? So much has been argued about the case of Michael Fay, an 18-year-old convicted of vandalism and sentenced to a caning in Singapore. The affair has outraged Americans even as it has aroused a general debate about morality East and West and the proper functioning of U.S. law and order, which, to all appearances, is what Singapore wanted.

The question of whether anyone should care about Michael Fay is idle: though Singapore officials declare shock at the attention his case has drawn, they know Americans care deeply about the many sides of this issue. Does a teenager convicted of spraying cars with easily removed paint deserve half a dozen powerful strokes on the buttocks with a sopping-wet bamboo staff? At what moral authority can America, with its rates of lawlessness and license, preach to a safe society about human rights? Isn't the shipshape and abundant little city-state molded by Lee Kuan Yew a model of civic virtues?

The caning sentence has fascinated many Americans who had never heard of Singapore. It has concentrated minds wondrously on an already lively domestic debate over what constitutes a due balance between individual and majority rights. Too bad Michael Fay has become the focus for this discussion. Not only does he seem destined to be beaten by an instrument of ordeal, but the use of Singapore as a standard for judging any other society, let alone the discordant U.S. is fairly worthless.

To begin with, Singapore is an offshore republic that tightly limits immigration. Beyond that, Singapore began its life as a British colony designed to serve as a shipping, administrative and financial center. Today it is a highly skilled society without the urban sprawl and rural poverty that afflict larger nations.

Even without its government's disciplinary measures, Singapore would be much the same as it is now. An academic commonplace today is that the major factor determining social peace and prosperity is culture—a sense of common identity, tradition and values. The house that Lee built is 76% ethnic Chinese, a people with one of the most self-disciplined cultures in the world. Prizing family, learning and hard work, overseas Chinese have proposed wherever they have settled. Heavily Chinese Hong Kong is a somewhat more disordered place than Singapore. But without social engineering or the whipping of vandals, Hong Kong is still very safe and quite rich. Its crime rate: 1,522 reported offenses for every 100,000 people in 1992.

Singapore's was 1507.

Singaporeans have every right to be proud of their achievements. Does that mean Michael Fay must be caned?

16. Why did the case of Michael Fay draw Americans' wide attention?
    A. Because Michael Fay is an 18 year old American boy.
    B. Because many Americans have never heard of Singapore and they think the caning sentence is fascinating.
    C. Because Americans think Michael Fay only committed a minor crime and shouldn't be punished so severely.
    D. Because in the eyes of Americans, Singapore is a model of civic virtues.
17. According to the passage, the use of Singapore as a standard for judging US is worthless because of the following causes EXCEPT that ________.
    A. Singapore is an offshore republic that strongly objects to immigration
    B. Singapore's caning is too cruel and has aroused a debate over the morality of the East
    C. Singapore, unlike USA, is a highly skilled society without urban sprawl and rural poverty.
    D. Singapore consists of a people with one of the most self-disciplined cultures in the world.
18. The authors' attitude towards Chinese is ________.
    A. affirmative B. negative C. critical D. neutral
19. The author compared Chinese Hong Kong with Singapore to show that ________.
    A. they consist of the same people with one of the most self-disciplined cultures in the world
    B. Chinese Hong Kong's crime rate was a little higher than Singapore in 1992.
    C. Chinese Hong Kong is a somewhat more disordered place than Singapore.
    D. Chinese Hong Kong's crime rate was almost as low as Singapore although it didn't carry out cruel vandals.
20. What's the attitude of the author towards Michael Fay's caning sentence?
    A. He thought he deserved it.
    B. He took a neutral attitude toward it.
    C. He objected to it.
    D. He thought Americans should respect Singapore's decision.

Unit 15

Beliefs and Religions

Part 1 Reading Skills

Section A Detailed Reading

Detailed reading focuses on the secondary ideas and details which support, explain and develop the main ideas. It is usually described as a more comprehensive reading. It involves a slower and more careful reading process, and even requires a second or third reading.

Here are some tips that can be used in detailed reading, when you take a reading comprehension test.

1. Locate the key words that you are scanning for, before the actual detailed reading. In other words, to save time, detailed reading is only used when necessary.
2. The right answers are usually not exactly the same sentences mentioned in the text, but probably paraphrased, thus requiring a careful comparison.
3. Pay special attention to the transitional words like *however, but, otherwise, instead, yet, though, furthermore, what is worse*, etc.

4. The full understanding of one sentence may require the detailed reading of two or more sentences preceding or following that sentence.

Once you persist in practicing these skills in your reading, you are sure to improve both your reading speed and efficiency.

Section B Practice

Directions: Read the following passage, and decide whether the following sentences carry the same meaning as the sentences mentioned in the text. Put YES if they are true, and NO if they mean differently.

Every year about two million people visit Mount Rushmore, where the faces of four U.S. presidents were carved in granite by sculptor Gutzon Borglum and his son, the late Lincoln Borglum. The creation of the Mount Rushmore monument took 14 years—from 1927 to 1941—and nearly a million dollars. These were times when money was difficult to come by and many people were jobless. To move the more than 400,000 tons of rock, Borglum hired laid-off workers from the closed-down mines in the Black Hills area. He taught these men to dynamite, drill, carve, and finish the granite as they were hanging in midair in his specially devised chairs, which had many safety features. Borglum was proud of the fact that no workers were killed or severely injured during the years of blasting and carving.

During the carving, many changes in the original design had to be made to keep the carved heads free of large fissures that were uncovered. However, not all the cracks could be avoided, so Borglum concocted a mixture of granite dust, white lead, and linseed oil to fill them.

1. There are approximately two million visitors to Mount Rushmore, where the faces of four U.S. presidents were carved in granite, every year. ________
2. The two sculptors contributed to the carving of Mount Rushmore is the dead Lincoln Borglum, and his father. ________
3. It took 14 years and over a million dollars to finish the carving of Mount Rushmore. ________
4. 1927 to 1941 is a time of economic recession, compared with other periods of time in the United States. ________
5. Borglum persuaded many mine workers to quit and work for him. ________
6. Borglum trained the workers before actual carving. ________
7. Blasting caused some serious injuries at that time, but fortunately, no one was killed. ________
8. The heads are not as originally planned. ________
9. During carving, all the large fissures had to be covered. ________
10. Borglum invented a mixture of different materials to fill in many of the cracks. ________

Part 2 Idioms, Proverbs and Sayings

Directions: The following are idioms, proverbs or sayings about beliefs and religions. Choose what you think is correct and compare with the right ones.

1. Man proposes, God ________. (Proverb)
   A. loses B. disposes C. supposes D. studies
2. God gives nothing to those who keep their arms ________. (West African Proverb)
   A. opened B. high C. crossed D. backward
3. If God were not forgiving, ________ would be empty. (Berber Proverb)
   A. heaven B. hearts C. family D. human minds
4. I tell you the truth, if you have ________ as small as a mustard seed, you can say to this mountain, "Move from here to there" and it will move. (Bible)
   A. bravery B. fear C. faith D. imagination
5. He deserves paradise who makes his companions ________. (Quran)
   A. laugh B. ill C. strong D. win
6. God help those who help ________. (Proverb)
   A. others B. everybody C. themselves D. children
7. The danger past and God ________. (Proverb)
   A. left B. forgotten C. came D. dismissed
8. God sends fortune to ________. (Proverb)
   A. everybody B. church-goers C. fools D. himself
9. When there is a ________, there is a god. (Proverb)
   A. family B. friend C. trouble D. success
10. God never shuts one door ________ he opens another. (Proverb)
    A. but B. and C. without D. then

Part 3 Reading Passages

Section A Early History of Christianity

Early Church and Christological Councils

Christianity began as a Jewish sect in the eastern Mediterranean in the mid-1st century. Its earliest development took place under the leadership of the Twelve Apostles, particularly Saint Peter and Paul the Apostle, followed by the early bishops, whom Christians considered the successors of the Apostles.

According to the scriptures, Christians were from the beginning subject to persecution by some Jewish religious authorities, who disagreed with the apostles' teachings. This involved punishments, including death, for Christians such as Stephen and James, son of Zebedee. Larger-scale persecutions followed at the hands of the authorities of the Roman Empire, first in the year 64, when Emperor Nero blamed them for the Great Fire of Rome. According to Church tradition, it was under Nero's persecution that early Church leaders Peter and Paul of Tarsus were each martyred in Rome. Further widespread persecutions of the Church occurred under nine subsequent Roman emperors, most intensely under Decius and Diocletian. From the year 150, Christian teachers began to produce theological and apologetic works aimed at defending the faith. These authors are known as the Church Fathers, and study of them is called Patristics. Notable early Fathers include Ignatius of Antioch, Polycarp, Justin Martyr, Irenaeus, Tertullian, Clement of Alexandria, and Origen.

State persecution ceased in the 4th century, when Constantine I issued an edict of toleration in 313. On 27 February 380, Emperor Theodosius I enacted a law establishing Christianity as the official religion of the Roman Empire. From at least the 4th century, Christianity has played a prominent role in the shaping of Western civilization.

Constantine was also instrumental in the convocation of the First Council of Nicaea in 325, which sought to address the Arian heresy and formulated the Nicene Creed, which is still used by the Roman Catholic Church, Eastern Orthodoxy, Anglican Communion, and many Protestant churches. Nicaea was the first of a series of Ecumenical (worldwide) Councils which formally defined critical elements of the theology of the Church, notably concerning Christology. The Assyrian Church of the East did not accept the third and following Ecumenical Councils, and are still separate today. In 395, the most Christianized regions of the world were Crete, Cyprus, Anatolia, Armenia, the Nile delta, and Numidia (present-day Tunisia and Algeria).

The presence of Christianity in Africa began in the middle of the 1st century in Egypt, and by the end of the 2nd century in the region around Carthage. Important Africans who influenced the early development of Christianity includes Tertullian, Clement of Alexandria, Origen of Alexandria, Cyprian, Athanasius and Augustine of Hippo. The later rise of Islam in North Africa reduced the size and numbers of Christian congregations, leaving only the Coptic Church in Egypt and the Ethiopian Orthodox Tewahedo Church in the Horn of Africa. The History of Christianity in Africa began in the 1st century when Mark the Evangelist started the Orthodox Church of Alexandria in about 43 AD.

With the decline and fall of the Roman Empire in the west, the papacy became a political player, first visible in Pope Leo's diplomatic dealings with Huns and Vandals. The church also entered into a long period of missionary activity and expansion among the various tribes. Whilst arianists instituted the death penalty for practicing pagans, Catholicism also spread among the Germanic peoples, the Celtic and Slavic peoples, the Hungarians, and the Baltic peoples.

Around 500, St. Benedict set out his Monastic Rule, establishing a system of regulations for the foundation and running of monasteries. Monasticism became a powerful force throughout Europe, and gave rise to many early centers of learning, most famously in Ireland, Scotland and Gaul, contributing to the Carolingian Renaissance of the 9th century.

From the 7th century onwards, Islam conquered the Christian lands of the Middle East, North Africa and much of Spain, resulting in oppression of Christianity and numerous military struggles, including the Crusades, the Spanish Reconquista and wars against the Turks.

The Middle Ages brought about major changes within the church. Pope Gregory the Great dramatically reformed ecclesiastical structure and administration. In the early 8th century, iconoclasm became a divisive issue, when it was sponsored by the Byzantine emperors. The Second Ecumenical Council of Nicaea (787) finally pronounced in favor of icons. In the early 10th century, western monasticism was further rejuvenated through the leadership of the great Benedictine monastery of Cluny.

In the west, from the 11th century onward, older cathedral schools developed into universities. Originally teaching only theology, these steadily added subjects including medicine, philosophy and law, becoming the direct ancestors of modern western institutions of learning.

Accompanying the rise of the "new towns" throughout Western Europe, mendicant orders were founded, bringing the consecrated religious life out of the monastery and into the new urban setting. The two principal mendicant movements were the Franciscans and the Dominicans founded by St. Francis and St. Dominic respectively. Both orders made significant contributions to the development of the great universities of Europe. Another new order were the Cistercians, whose large isolated monasteries spearheaded the settlement of former wilderness areas. In this period church building and ecclesiastical architecture reached new heights, culminating in the orders of Romanesque and Gothic architecture and the building of the great European cathedrals.

From 1095 under the pontificate of Urban II, the Crusades were launched. These were a series of military campaigns in the Holy Land and elsewhere, initiated in response to pleas from the Byzantine Emperor Alexios I for aid against Turkish expansion. The Crusades ultimately failed to stifle Islamic aggression and even contributed to Christian enmity with the sacking of Constantinople during the Fourth Crusade.

Over a period stretching from the 7th to the 13th century, the Christian Church underwent gradual alienation, resulting in a schism dividing it into a so-called Latin or Western branch, the Roman Catholic Church, and an Eastern, largely Greek, branch, the Orthodox Church. These two churches disagree on a number of administrative, liturgical, and doctrinal issues, most notably papal primacy of jurisdiction. The Second Council of Lyon (1274) and the Council of Florence (1439) attempted to reunite the churches, but in both cases the Eastern Orthodox refused to implement the decisions and the two principal churches remain in schism to the present day. However, the Roman Catholic Church has achieved union with various smaller eastern churches.

Beginning around 1184, following the crusade against the Cathar heresy, various institutions, broadly referred to as the Inquisition, were established with the aim of suppressing heresy and securing religious and doctrinal unity within Christianity through conversion and prosecution.

(1,081 words, based on *http://en.wikipedia.org/wiki/Christianity*)

I. Reading Comprehension

Directions: Put the following sentences in chronological order according to the text.

A. Thanks to Constantine I, State persecution of early Christianity ceased.

B. Persecutions of the Church became common, under many Roman emperors, mainly for disagreements with the apostles' teachings.

C. Christianity was established as the official religion of the Roman Empire.

D. The Church Fathers began to produce theological and apologetic works aimed at defending the faith.

E. Inquisition were established, to suppress heresy and securing religious and doctrinal unity within Christianity.

F. A series of military campaigns, the Crusades, were launched.

G. Islam conquered the Christian lands of the Middle East, North Africa and much of Spain, resulting in oppression of Christianity.

H. St. Benedict established a system of regulations for the foundation and running of monasteries.

I. Older cathedral schools developed into universities.

____

II. Vocabulary

Directions: Fill in each blank with an appropriate word from the box below. Change the form where necessary. Each word can be used only once.

sect	scripture	persecution	martyr	subsequent
edict	theological	congregation	monastery	rejuvenate
ancestor	culminate	stifle	alienation	implement

1. Mass migration gave millions of Europeans an escape route from poverty and __________, and fed the dynamism and development of countries like the United States, the United Kingdom, and various colonies.
2. "The Dark Knight" held up better in __________ weekends than most of Hollywood's biggest debuts.
3. Terrorism in its essence is a religious phenomenon, which can best be handled by a __________ language.
4. Scientists have found that the female __________ of all polar bears was a brown bear, which lived in present-day Britain and Ireland during the last ice age 20,000 to 50,000 years ago.
5. The Japanese Buddhist __________ Shinnyo-en organizes the annual Memorial Day ceremony, which is expected to draw about 40,000 people.
6. The consumer price index (CPI) hit a 34-month high of 5.5 percent in May, despite the country's efforts to __________ inflation.
7. In the service, Middleton will not promise to "obey" William as part of her wedding vows in front of a __________ gathering royals, politicians, celebrities and friends.
8. Many protesters carried banners and placards inscribed with anti-US slogans and describing bin Laden as a "__________ of Islam."
9. This will not only make brand awareness measurement awkward, it may actually create confusion or even __________ in the minds of the most brand loyal consumers.
10. The country will continue to eliminate out-of-date capacity, develop public transportation, __________ energy-saving projects and promote the use of energy-saving products
11. Obama's remarks were tailored for a religious service, with quotes from __________, references to the love that binds people to each other, and comments on the essential goodness of humanity.
12. Good Friday, of course, would be the start of the Easter weekend, which would __________ on Easter Sunday.
13. Some youths from the village ride their motorcycles to a crossroad section and wait for tourists who have come to visit a famous Lama __________ near the village.
14. Besides uncertainties lying with ever-changing market conditions, the gap between government __________ and the business community's interpretation of policy has always been a concern.

15. The government needs to make new breakthroughs in key technologies in order to __________ the nation's old industrial bases and build an innovative country.

III. Debate

Directions: Religion has always been one of the most influential forces in the world. It has been a force for peace, but it also has served as a cause, if not a genuine reason, for some of the greatest wars. It is a stronger force than any material incentives. It is far better at directing behavior toward social betterment than either laws or physical force, but it can also be used to justify brutal actions.

Please debate on one of the following two topics:

1. This House believes that religion is a positive influence on people.
2. This House believes that church and state must be kept separate.

Section B Hindu-Muslim Family's Choice of Cremation Arouses Anger

I. Directions: Read the following passage and the statements after it, and decide whether they agree with the information provided in the passage. Mark

Y for YES	if the statement agrees with the passage
N for NO	if the statement does not agree with the passage
NG for NOT GIVEN	if it is impossible to know from the passage

Friends and family remember Shafayet Reja as an affectionate young man who stayed up late to write poetry, danced exuberantly at weddings and explored the faiths of his father and mother with an openheartedness that led him to declare on his Facebook page, "I never get tired of learning the new things that life has to offer."

But within hours of his death on Sept. 10 after a car accident, his memory—in fact, his very body—had become the object of a tug-of-war over religious freedom and obligation. It began when his mother, who was raised Hindu, and his father, who is Muslim, decided to have his body cremated in the Hindu tradition, rather than burying him in a shroud, as Islam prescribes.

His parents, Mina and Farhad Reja, say a small group of Muslims who do not understand their approach to religion are trying to intimidate them over the most private of family choices. "This is America," Mrs. Reja said. "This is a family decision."

The couple say that people accosted them at their son's funeral, that an angry crowd threatened to boycott a shopping center they own in Jackson Heights, Queens, and that on Sept. 13, two men they know threatened to bomb and burn down the building.

The men they accused in a complaint filed with the police—one is a doctor and the father of a close friend of Shafayet Reja, the other a Bangladeshi business leader—say that they made no threats and deny that they have called for a boycott. They say they and others simply expressed their concern about what they see as a deep violation of their religion and of the wishes of the son, who, according to some of his college friends, had recently chosen Islam as his sole religion.

The Police Department's hate crimes unit is investigating whether the threats took place, whether they would constitute aggravated harassment, and whether they qualify as bias crimes, which carry tougher penalties, a spokesman for the department said. No charges have been filed.

What is not in doubt is that the episode is a source of consternation, from the Queens neighborhoods where Mr. Reja's parents live and work to their native Bangladesh, one of the world's most populous Muslim countries, where it has been national news.

The dispute has especially swept up several bustling blocks in Jackson Heights, where dozens of businesses are Bengali. It had business owners on edge during the busy shopping season before this week's Id al-Fitr festival. The festival marks the end of the Muslim holy month of Ramadan and brings throngs of shoppers to dine and to buy jewelry and sparkling traditional dresses.

The neighborhood is a place where business rivalries and family arguments often intersect with disputes over Bangladesh politics, especially in the case of Mrs. Reja, a prominent property owner and outspoken advocate of the rights of Bangladesh's religious minorities. Her 1999 self-published book, "God on Trial," angered some Muslims in the neighborhood with its critique of Islamic fundamentalism.

The cremation dispute goes to the heart of a debate among Muslims in America about what makes someone a Muslim—to some of the critics, the fact that Shafayet Reja listed Islam as his religion on Facebook is enough—and how to reconcile this country's freedom of religion with what some Muslims see as a communal obligation to uphold religious observance.

But to the family, the dispute is a frightening imposition that they say violates their civil rights.

"We have freedom of religion, and we have the Constitution," said the Rejas' son Mishal, 19, who studies at Washington University in St. Louis. "Why would they bother us? It's none of their business. Even if he was the most hard-core Muslim."

To some Muslims, the fact that Shafayet Reja prayed and attended mosques trumps his family's wishes.

"It was the community's business because the community knew he was a Muslim," said Junnun Choudhury, secretary of the Jamaica Muslim Center, one of several mosques around the city whose worshipers came to the funeral to plead with the family. "It is our job to bury him in the Muslim way."

Neither he nor any other mosque leader has been accused of making threats, and there have been no further protests.

Abu Zafar Mahmood, an adviser to the Jackson Heights Bangladeshi Business Association, said he was disturbed by the cremation but was urging people not to confront Mrs. Reja. "It would be harmful," he said. "We have a multicultural community."

Mrs. Reja said she brought up her children by attending both Hindu temples and Muslim mosques. "Humanism is what I taught my children," she said. "I want to see my son as a perfect human being, and not as a perfect religious person."

Whether or not her son was beginning to move closer to Islam is another thread in the tangle of hurt feelings and disagreements.

Shafayet Reja, 22, graduated from the State University of New York at Stony Brook in 2007. He was living with his parents in Richmond Hill, studying to be a licensed insurance broker.

He was also spending a lot of time at the Long Island home of Dr. Khondeker Masud Rahman—who was eventually accused of threatening his parents—and Dr. Rahman's daughter, Farah, a friend from Stony Brook.

Farah Rahman said that he had begun praying more often and talking to Dr. Rahman about Islam, and that he had quarreled with his mother, saying she blamed the religion unfairly for the mistakes of some of its followers. He had even, she said in an interview, mentioned that he wanted a Muslim burial. His family members and childhood friends say he would have wanted his mother to choose.

On Sept. 2, Shafayet Reja broke the daily Ramadan fast with friends at Stony Brook's Muslim Students Association. Afterward, Farah Rahman was in the car behind his when he lost control on a wet road. He was hospitalized, and died on Sept. 10 without regaining consciousness.

When word spread that the family would hold both Muslim and Hindu rites for their son and then have him cremated, the Rahmans and others were upset. Father and daughter both asked the family to give him a Muslim burial. They said the conversations were polite; the Rejas said they were hostile.

Several dozen people, including the imams of the Jamaica Muslim Center and other mosques, came to the funeral home in Richmond Hill on Sept. 12, to attend the Muslim rite and express objections to the cremation. The Rejas say people crowded around them to press their case as they wept beside their son's body. "I was having my last moment with my son," Mrs. Reja said. "What gave them the guts to do that?"

The funeral staff called the police in part because the Rejas feared the crowd would try to block the hearse going to the crematorium. Mishal Reja stood in the door of the funeral home, asked the group to leave the family in peace, and promised he would try to get the cremation canceled—just to get them to leave, he said. The crowd dispersed peacefully.

Later that day, Dr. Rahman, an anesthesiologist at Elmhurst Hospital Center in Jackson Heights, spoke to a group of people breaking the daily Ramadan fast at a restaurant across the street from the family's Bangladesh Plaza mall.

According to the Rejas, and a report in a local Bengali-language newspaper, he called for a boycott of the mall and for shop owners there to stop paying rent, though he denied that in an interview.

Afterward, some of the people from the restaurant gathered outside the mall, waving their sandals in an insulting gesture and threatening to boycott the mall, according to two men who run shops there, who did not want to be quoted by name for fear of damaging business relationships. One said that at least one person in the crowd threatened to burn the building.

In the crowd, according to the merchants, was the secretary of the Jackson Heights Bangladeshi Business Association, Zakaria Masud. Mr. Masud, too, denied calling for a boycott, but said that protesting the cremation was "a social obligation and a religious obligation."

The next day, Mina Reja held a press conference at the mall, at which she denounced the critics and asked for privacy.

Afterward, according to complaints the Rejas made to the police, Dr. Rahman told Mishal Reja, "We will bomb your building," and Giash Ahmed, a real estate broker and former Republican candidate for state senator, told Farhad Reja it would be burned.

Dr. Rahman and Mr. Ahmed said in interviews that they never threatened anyone and were not even at the mall that day. Mr. Ahmed said Mrs. Reja's decision was her business.

Dr. Rahman said expressions of anger at Mrs. Reja should wait: "She should have a time of healing." He accused her of orchestrating the scandal and fabricating the threat.

Meanwhile, under the neon signs and rainbow lights of Bangladesh Plaza, shopkeepers worry that a boycott even by part of the community will hurt their holiday business.

"Why should they involve people who are not involved? How will we survive?" one of the shop owners said. Another said of the cremation: "It's a family matter. The parents, they decide."

(1,549 words, from *The New York Times* by Anne Barnard)

1. ________ In the eyes of relatives and friends, Shafayet Reja is an open-hearted young man who loves poems and dances.
2. ________ The real reason for Shafayet Reja's death is religious reason.
3. ________ Shafayet Reja's mother decided to have his body cremated in the Hindu tradition, while his father, who is Muslim, wanted to bury him in a shroud, as Islam prescribes.
4. ________ A small group of Muslims who do not understand the decision to cremate Shafayet Reja bombed and burned down the building they live in.
5. ________ Shafayet Reja recently chose Islam as his sole religion.
6. ________ After investigation, the Police dismissed the case as bias crimes.
7. ________ Shafayet Reja's parents came from Bangladesh, one of the world's most populous Muslim countries.
8. ________ Id al-Fitr festival marks the end of the Muslim holy month of Ramadan and brings throngs of shoppers to dine and to buy jewelry and sparkling traditional dresses.
9. ________ ,Shafayet Reja's mother is a prominent property owner and outspoken advocate

of the rights of Bangladesh's religious minorities.

10. ________ Shafayet Reja, 22, was a scholarship winner in the State University of New York at Stony Brook before 2007.

II. *Directions: Choose the right answers according to the passage.*

A. Mishal   B. Abu Zafar Mahmood   C. Junnun Choudhury
D. Khondeker Masud Rahman   E Zakaria Masud   F. Giash Ahmed

1. ________ studies in Washington University in St. Louis.
2. ________ was eventually accused of threatening Shafayet Reja's parents.
3. ________ was the secretary of the Jackson Heights Bangladeshi Business Association.
4. ________ is the secretary of the Jamaica Muslim Center.
5. ________ was disturbed by the cremation but was urging people not to confront Mrs. Reja.

Part 4 Reading Comprehension Test

Directions: Read the following passages and choose the best answer to each question.

Passage 1 How many Catholics are there in Britain?

Pope Benedict XVI is the head of the biggest Christian denomination in the world, some one billion Roman Catholics, or one in six people. In Britain there are about five million Catholics, or about one in 12 people.

As he arrives in the UK for the first visit by a pontiff since 1982, what do statistics tell us about the state of the Roman Catholic Church in this country?

According to the 2001 census, there were 41 million Christians in Great Britain, making up almost three quarters of the population (72%). This group included the Church of England, Church of Scotland, Church in Wales, Catholic, Protestant and all other Christian denominations.

How this 41 million breaks down is harder to work out. The Church of England says about 26 million people have been baptised, the Catholic Church claims just over four million members in England and Wales - and another 695,000 in Scotland. Out of a total population of about 60 million, that means about one in 12 people in Great Britain is Catholic.

Figures for church attendance suggest both the Catholic and Anglican churches suffered a gradual fall in numbers up to around the turn of the century, but since then numbers appear to have more or less stabilized.

Numbers from the Catholic Directory suggest that currently about one million Catholics in England and Wales regularly attend mass. But according to the Catholic National Library, figures for mass attendance were not kept before 1989 and therefore no comparison is possible with the 1982 papal visit.

The Bishops' Conference of Scotland says an estimated 184,283 attended mass regularly in 2008. There's no equivalent figure for All Ireland—but the Catholic directory says there were an estimated 4.3 million Catholics living in Northern Ireland and the Republic of Ireland in 2008.

Figures for the number of men entering the priesthood show that after a fairly steep decline in the late 1980s and 1990s, the numbers have begun to pick up again.

The Christian Research group which looks at trends in Christian faiths in Britain says numbers have stabilized in recent years—contrary to its claim in 2007 that congregations would continue to decline.

It seems numbers for the Catholic Church may have been boosted by an influx of immigrants—from Eastern Europe and Africa. While rural congregations have been dwindling, inner city churches have seen numbers rise.

The National Secular Society feels any boost in numbers will be shortlived. It estimates there will only be 101,700 Catholics attending church annually by 2050, compared to the current total of about one million.

Figures gathered by the National Centre for Social Research show that membership of most religions is lower now than it was 30 years ago, with a marked decline appearing among people who say they belong to the Church of England from 40% to 20%.

By comparison, the numbers of those claiming to be Catholic has remained fairly stable, dropping only 1% from 10% to 9% since 1983.

The number of people of all faiths attending church services appears to be at a low ebb, with 58% of those polled saying they never attend services.

But attendance does peak at Christmas. According to Church of England statistics, 35% of the population attends a Christmas service of some sort, rising to 42% in London.

(555 words, from *http://www.bbc.co.uk/news*)

1. Which of the following statements is False about Roman Catholics, according to the passage?
   A. It is the biggest Christian denomination in the world.
   B. There are about one billion Roman Catholics, accounting for approximately 16% of the total population in the world.
   C. The proportion of Roman Catholics is relatively high in Britain, compared with most of the other European countries.
   D. Pope Benedict XVI is the head of Roman Catholics.
   E. Church of England has a lot more followers than Roman Catholics in Britain.
2. Anglican Churches in Paragraph 5 probably refers to ________.
   A. Roman Catholics B. Church of England C. Christianity D. Baptist
   E. Protestant

3. Which of the following statements about the number of Roman Catholic Church goers is True about church attendance in UK?
   A. It has been decreased, especially after 2000.
   B. It has been stabilized until after 2000.
   C. It has been increased until after 2000.
   D. It has been stabilized, especially after 2000.
   E. It was decreased before 2000, but has been stabilized after then.
4. It can be inferred from the passage that in recent years ________.
   A. there are more Catholics in England and Wales who regularly attend mass than those in 1982
   B. the number of Christians have been stabilized, as claimed by the Christian Research group in 2007
   C. the development of Catholic Church may partly due to the increasing number of immigrants from Eastern Europe and Africa
   D. there are more Catholics in rural areas than those in inner cities
   E. there are more Catholics in Britain than other denominations since 1983
5. According to ________, the number of Catholics in Britain will be decreasing in the following decades.
   A. the National Secular Society
   B. National Centre for Social Research
   C. the Christian Research group
   D. Bishops' Conference of Scotland
   E. the Catholic Directory

Passage 2 Is Scientology a Religion?

Since 1993, Scientology, which many people have long considered to be a "cult," has been a religion in the eyes of the United States government, with the tax exemption that goes along with that. But whether it is actually a "religion" in the way that most of us think about religion is a wholly different matter.

To address the basics: there is no God in Scientology. There is also no prayer, no concept of Heaven or Hell, no turn-the-other-cheek forgiveness or love, nor any of the other things we typically associate with religion, at least in the Judeo-Christian context. There is also no "faith"—no concept of belief. Instead, there is knowledge, a certainty beyond a shadow of a doubt that Scientology's doctrine, all of which was authored by the church's founder, L. Ron Hubbard, is the absolute truth.

I like to describe Scientology as a global spiritual enterprise—a religious corporation with a far greater emphasis on the "corporate," profit-making side of the ledger. Since its founding in 1954, Scientology has appealed to people initially as self-help, something Americans, and many others, have been more than willing to pay for. And as self-help, Scientology essentially promises that there are techniques one can learn—through the rigorous study and exact application of L. Ron Hubbard's ideas—that can, for instance, help a person overcome their shyness, or empower them to end a bad marriage, or help them sell themselves more effectively in the workplace. But there is also a spiritual component to Scientology, which has to do with people realizing, through the counseling known as "auditing," that they have lived many past lives. That's where the religion comes in.

When I was reporting on Scientology, I was amazed by the number of ordinary people I met who truly knew—not just believed, but claimed to know—that they had lived before and would live again. That meant death was no longer scary! It also meant that we might even remember our prior lives so saying goodbye to friends and family would not really be a "goodbye." Even to me, a person who is agnostic about most religion, it was attractive.

That is what draws people deeply "in" to Scientology. And once in, Scientology becomes different things to different people. One woman I know compares Scientology to an onion. The outer layer, where the celebrities tend to be, is a place where people experience the church as self-help and community. For stars like Tom Cruise or John Travolta, it is the safest of communities because celebrities are catered to in Scientology in both a material way, with added perks and private counseling sessions, but also in a way that shields them from critics or intrusion into their private lives. Wealthy Scientologists are also considered "celebrities" because they tend to donate the most money and involve themselves most in Scientology causes, all of which raises their status.

Much is made of the celebrities in Scientology, though their numbers are very few—there are maybe a dozen actual "celebrities" who belong to the church. But these people serve a promotional function, and because of it are treated like rare birds, put on pedestals by all members, including church staff who endeavor to keep their experience in Scientology positive. This leads to profound isolation from some of Scientology's harsher truths. Celebrities certainly would not be aware of any abuse or harsh treatment of Scientology staff, which, though Scientology officials deny it, has been alleged numerous times by ex-officials over the years. While they would be obliged to obey the policy of "disconnection," by which church members shun anyone, including their closest friends or family members, who leave Scientology on bad terms, they would also tend to believe the word of church officials far more than "apostates," as those who have left Scientology and spoken out are called.

Screenwriter/director Paul Haggis, for instance, believed a senior Scientology official when he pledged that the Church of Scientology did not back the California anti-gay marriage bill, something the church—along with many other religious organizations—did in fact support. When Haggis discovered the truth, it propelled him to leave the church altogether. But Haggis is, so far, somewhat unique in that he did discover the truth. No Scientologist—be they celebrities or ordinary members—is supposed to read general media reports about the church. These pieces—anything critical—is considered off-limits or "entheta" in the lexicon of the Church of Scientology, and thus harmful to a member's spiritual progress. The truth is what they know via L Ron Hubbard; media criticisms of Scientology, on the other hand, are to

Scientologists, lies or "religious bigotry." Thus they remain very much in the dark; they will not, assuredly, be reading my new book "Inside Scientology: The Story of America's Most Secretive Religion."

Beyond celebrities, the average middle class person, who for most of its history has formed the bulk of Scientology's membership, has a different far different experience in Scientology. For them, the deeper they are drawn into Scientology, the more indebted to it they become. In some cases, members have been driven into bankruptcy, forcing them to work for the church to continue to afford Scientology counseling. Once they sign up to work for Scientology, their experience turns more punitive: they work extremely long hours, at very low pay, and are expected to adhere to a paramilitary-style discipline that is absent in any workplace I've ever heard of outside of the United States military. At the innermost level of this management, within the Sea Organization, which is the senior management body of the church, there is far more, if not total, ideological control over members, strict adherence to the demands of a leader who has cast himself as a sort of pope, and many other things that would define Scientology, in that context as a more traditional "cult."

But it is only a cult to some. To others it is a community. To others it is self-help. And to others, it is absolutely religion—and in the case of young people who've grown up in the church it is the only religion they've ever known. I think the future of Scientology, if it has one, lies in its ability to retain its identity as religion and community, and even self-help, while losing the ideological totalism that makes it cultic for many. It is a significant challenge, and one that the church in its current incarnation may not be able to shoulder, but it is also the only way, in my opinion, that Scientology will become an enduring, and evolving, religion.

(1,102 words, by Janet Reitman from *http://www.washingtonpost.com*)

6. What can be inferred from the passage?

A. US government considered Scientology to be a "cult" since 1993.

B. Many people have long considered Scientology to be a "cult," but the majority of American people considered it to be a religion since 1993.

C. In the United States, religious groups don't have to pay taxes, but Scientology is an exception.

D. In the United States, religious groups also need to pay taxes, but Scientology is lucky to be an exception.

E. American government has long considered Scientology as a religion after 1993, and thus allows it to stay out of the tax system.

7. Which of the following statements is true according to Scientology?

A. There is no God, nor concept of belief in Scientology.

B. The main difference between Scientology and other religions is that the doctrine is about absolute truth.

C. The church was founded by L. Ron Hubbard, and the doctrine was written in the Judeo-Christian context.

D. Even within Scientology, people hold a shadow of a doubt towards its doctrine.

E. The prayers of Scientology consider everything L. Ron Hubbard said to be absolute truth.

8. The author described Scientology as a global spiritual enterprise mainly because ________.

A. it provides people with the concept of "self-help"

B. it pays special attention to making profits

C. Americans, and many others, have been more than willing to pay for the doctrine

D. it promises that there are techniques one can learn

E. there is a spiritual component to Scientology, which has to do with people realizing, through the counseling known as "auditing," that they have lived many past lives.

9. The last sentence of Paragraph 4 indicates that ________.

A. although the author is an expert on religions, still he likes the idea that people have lived many past lives

B. because the author is an expert on religions, he likes the idea that people have lived many past lives

C. although the author knows little about religions, still he likes the idea that people have lived many past lives

D. because the author knows little about religions, he likes the idea that people have lived many past lives

E. because the author knows little about religions, he couldn't understand the idea that people have lived many past lives

10. Which of the following statements is Not True about celebrities in Scientology?

A. The celebrities tend to experience the church as self-help and community.

B. Celebrities are catered to in Scientology in both a material way and in a way that shields them from critics or intrusion into their private lives.

C. Wealthy Scientologists tend to donate the most money and involve themselves most in Scientology causes.

D. Celebrities were actually experiencing abuse or harsh treatment of Scientology staff over the years, but they chose to remain silent about the truth.

E. Celebrities are put on pedestals by all members, including church staff.

11. By publishing the new book "Inside Scientology: The Story of America's Most Secretive Religion," the author probably wants to ________.

A. advocate for the development and popularity of Scientology

B. inform the public about the unknown truth within Scientology

C. tell stories about celebrities in Scientology

D. put an end to the spread and development of Scientology

E. give an example of studying a religious cult

12. It can be inferred from the last paragraph that ________.

A. the author is one member of Scientology

B. the author sees great potential for the development of Scientology

C. the author would advocate for freedom of religious belief, to those who wants to end Scientology

D. the author doubt the bright future of Scientology

E. the author is actually in favor of ideological totalism

Passage 3

His parents had been immigrants from Italy, setting up home in Ireland before the island was partitioned.

He was a cafe owner. An ice-cream man. He was Catholic. And he was innocent.

But being Catholic was enough.

Alfredo Fusco was gunned down in front of his wife for being a Catholic. The gunman reportedly told Mrs. Fusco to stop screaming or she'd be shot too.

It was a Saturday evening in early February 1973. Around 7pm two men walked into Fusco's cafe on the York Road. One was armed with a sub-machine gun, the other with a revolver.

The man who shot Alfredo Fusco was Robert Clarke, now 59 years old, with an address at Dundrod Road, Nutt's Corner.

Thirty-eight years ago, Clarke had been the man with the sub-machine gun. He planned to use it to kill Mr. Fusco.

As soon as Mr. Fusco saw the men he knew what was about to happen. He ran.

Clarke's gun jammed. But instead of abandoning the murder bid, Clarke walked back to his colleague with the revolver, who was standing guard at the door of the cafe.

Clarke took the revolver and went back for Alfredo Fusco. By this stage the cafe owner had managed to make it in to his store, using his body to keep the door shut.

According to a police officer who was at the crime scene, Clarke shot twice through the door. At least one of the bullets hit Mr. Fusco in the head, killing him instantly.

But Clarke wasn't finished. According to the same police officer he used his hand to push the door open as far as he could, and shot the already dead Alfredo Fusco again. In the back.

By putting his hand on the door, Clarke left a vital trace. A clue which would eventually lead to his arrest. But not for another 35 years.

In the interim the Troubles continued.

Clarke killed again. In 15 June 1973, he indiscriminately murdered a Catholic woman called Margaret O'Neill.

It was a drive-by shooting, Clarke firing on a group on the pavement in the New Lodge area of Belfast.

Clarke was caught for that murder. He pleaded guilty and was given a life sentence in 1976. He was released in 1990.

Twenty years later, the killing he carried out in Fusco's Cafe on that February evening in 1973, caught up with Robert Clarke.

The Historical Enquiries Team looked at the case. A re-examination of the handprint and fingerprints found at the scene matched Clarke.

He was arrested and charged last year. He denied the murder, but Mr. Justice McLaughlin—sitting without a jury—found Clarke guilty. He was given the mandatory life sentence.

At that time, Mr. Justice McLaughlin told Clarke: "Mr. Fusco's killer acted in a brutal and cruel manner showing a chilling determination to kill an entirely innocent and defenceless man.

"All indications are that it was a sectarian killing carried out by loyalist paramilitaries as part of the blood-letting in this community," he said.

"Few people in relative numbers are capable of that kind of act."

On Friday he set a minimum tariff of 25 years, the judge told Clarke he had assassinated Alfredo Fusco in a brutal and terrifying manner.

"Inhumanity of this scale to any fellow human being demands that the courts impose a sentence to mark the rejection by civilised society of such acts," Mr Justice McLaughlin said.

But Clarke will not serve anything close to 25 years. He will be freed under the law governing historical Troubles-related crimes in just under two years.

(598 words, by Eunan MConville from *http://www.bbc.co.uk/news/*)

13. What is the best title for this passage?
    A. The Cold-blooded Killers
    B. Innocent Man Killed over His Religion
    C. Religious Conflicts in Northern Ireland
    D. A Mysterious Murder Case
    E. A Case Study on Irish Judicial System
14. It can be inferred that this article is written in the year ________.
    A. 1998
    B. 2001
    C. 2005
    D. 2008
    E. 2011
15. Robert Clarke killed ________.
    A. Alfredo Fusco
    B. Alfredo Fusco and his wife
    C. Margaret O'Neill
    D. both Margaret O'Neill and Alfredo Fusco
    E. Alfredo Fusco, his wife and Margaret O'Neill
16. Robert Clarke was arrested for the murder case in the café about ________ after the actual happening.
    A. less than 1 year
    B. 15 years
    C. 20 years
    D. 25 years
    E. 37 years
17. The underlined word "indiscriminately" is closest in meaning to ________.
    A. randomly
    B. angrily
    C. purposely
    D. cruelly
    E. unconsciously

Passage 4 Campaign for the future of RE in schools

Cornwall Council's religious education adviser says he hopes the government will listen to calls to include RE in the new English Baccalaureate.

David Hampshire was speaking in a week which saw a petition containing more than 100,000 signatures handed into Downing Street, calling for Religious Education to be included.

Mr Hampshire said: "I think it's part of a broad and balanced education. Unless you have had exploration about the rule, purpose and nature of religion within society at large, I think that you are a less educated person."

The controversy surrounding its exclusion has been heavily criticized by leaders of all faiths.

They fear it will mean a generation of children will have no knowledge of the role Faith plays in society.

Now the campaign says Prime Minister, David Cameron, must honor his election promise to debate any issue which has more than 100,000 signatures on a petition.

Sue Green, the Diocese of Truro's head of education says, it is important to recognize RE as a significant subject:

"Religious Education is an incredibly important subject for our young people in so many ways. We're hoping that a re-think will give RE the status it deserves."

In a statement Downing Street said:

"In line with the commitments in the Programme for Government published in May 2010, e-petitions that receive 100,000 signatures or more will be eligible for debate in Parliament.

"Cabinet Office, Directgov and the Office of the Leader of the House of Commons are working together on the implementation of this system and further announcements will be made soon."

(259 words, from *http://www.bbc.co.uk/news*)

18. Cornwall Council's religious education adviser believes that ________.
   A. the education system in UK would not be completed without Religious Education
   B. children will be fond of exploring the nation of religion
   C. the petition will probably e supported by people from different religions
   D. the government has the responsibility to provide religious education to all school goers
   E. Christianity will decline in the next decades without Religious Education.
19. According to the passage, ________ are/is advocating the inclusion of Religious Education in the new English Baccalaureate.
   A. David Hampshire B. Sue Green C. David Cameron D. All of the above
   E. Both A and B
20. It can be inferred from the passage that ________.
   A. David Cameron has to support this campaign, because of his promise during the election.

B. David Cameron has to support this campaign, because it represents the will of the majority.

C. David Cameron will probably oppose the campaign, because it is criticized by leaders of all faiths.

D. The Parliament will not debate on this issue, although the petition has received 100,000 signatures.

E. The Parliament will debate on this issue, but the result remains unknown.